CALIFORNIA MISSIONS
AND THEIR ROMANCES

CALIFORNIA MISSIONS
and Their Romances

By Mrs. FREMONT OLDER

Foreword by HERBERT E. BOLTON
Preface by R. L. DUFFUS

ILLUSTRATED

TUDOR PUBLISHING CO.

NEW YORK

1945

TUDOR EDITION 1945

F
864
.O52

28545

TO
FATHER JOHN A. LEAL
MISSION SAN JOSÉ, CALIFORNIA
IN APPRECIATION OF HIS
PATIENT CRITICISM

Foreword

MRS. OLDER is no novice in the writers' craft. A seasoned journalist, she has written history, biography, and fiction. Her wide experience is everywhere reflected in the present work. Aiming at a general audience, she knows what her readers want and how to present it. This volume is just what its title indicates—a story of the California missions and their romances. It will be a cherished companion for visitors to the missions, and a well of information for all who delight in their lore.

There are many kinds of books about early California, but this one is different from all others. In it each of the twenty-one missions is treated in a single short and lively chapter, complete in itself. Regarding each mission the author gives factual data adequate for her purpose, but her special interest, and that which gives the book its outstanding quality, is in their legends and their romances. In her book the general phases of history common to all the California establishments is illustrated by each mission with varying detail: the founding days, temporary buildings, permanent structures, native customs, religious and industrial discipline, achievements in agriculture and stock raising, and a multitude of other activities.

But the author's emphasis is on mission life, the comedy and tragedy, joy and sorrow, toil and merrymaking, religious fervor and worldliness, which filled the days at the missions and their neighbor establishments; for mission life was intimately associated with that of the towns, presidios, and ranches. In Mrs. Older's story the actors in the drama of early California become human. Serra crosses her pages as a saintly figure, whose stature is no less impressive when we are told that he made a dress for an Indian child. We learn of Monterey's starving time, which was relieved by hunting bears at San Luis Obispo; of Lasuén's ragged clothes; of Palóu's famous garden at Carmel; of the martyrdom of Father Jayme at San Diego; of the quarrel there over the right of sanctuary; of the first public execution in California; of wine making, schools, water problems, and the echoes of the American Revolution in the distant Spanish province. We read of a colorful fiesta at Santa Isabel, and of how Señorita Josefa Carrillo, one of that continuous line of California beauties, "danced the new American waltz, and caused greater scandal by losing her heart to an American," and eloping with him, and how as a penance the bold Yankee gave a bell to the Plaza church of Los Angeles, where it hangs today.

These are but a few examples of matters treated in the book, chosen at random out of thousands. And thus the author, in serious and in lighter vein, with swift strokes tells of mission founding, social life, ranching, foreign intruders, the secularization of the missions, their neglect and ruin thereafter, the passing of the rule of Spain and of Mexico, and the raising of the American flag over the remote but colorful province. Mrs. Older has written an interesting and a useful book, and one with a character all its own.

HERBERT E. BOLTON.

Preface

I HAVE especially happy memories of two of the Missions of which Mrs. Older writes: San Carlos Borromeo (better known as Carmel Mission) and San Juan Bautista. I am somehow glad to remember that I came upon the first unsuspectingly, many years ago, as I walked along the beach from Carmel. The brown walls, the tiled roof of the beautiful old church caught my eye, across the still pool where the waters of the Carmel River were collecting behind the sand bar. No modern structure spoiled the illusion. On that coast time seems to stand still, for all the roads and their traffic, for all the glaring new houses; and even these were invisible, or not then in existence. I knew then how Carmel Mission had looked in the days of its glory, to men coming up from the sea. For an instant I would not have been surprised to see the gray figure of good Father Junípero limping around the corner on that leg whose lameness he took to be a manifestation of the favor of the Almighty. Well, perhaps he was a man sent from God. I, not of his faith, shall not say he was not.

San Juan Bautista, too, I first approached on foot, on a walking tour with a companion; that night we slept in an alfalfa field, looking up at a heaven full of stars as bright as angels. I think it is a good thing to approach the Missions on foot, and to sleep in the open afterwards, though such practices become increasingly difficult in California. A blister or two, the smell of dust, and good, honest sweat may help us to come nearer, from our vast distance, the frame of mind in which Father Serra and his companions walked the Camino Real. For them it was no royal road after the manner of this earth, but they walked royally, disdaining even mules or ox-carts unless their legs would no longer carry them. I think of Father Serra coming to Mission Dolores a day and a night after leaving Santa Clara. I think, and have long thought at intervals in a busy life, of the way the days must have gone by in those old outposts of Christianity, close to the sea where so few sails were spread, as remote as the moon from close touch with what we call civilization.

No doubt it is easy to over-romanticize the mission period in California. One cannot read Mrs. Older's careful and detailed account of what went on without realizing that the life was anything but easy and serene. It only seems so in retrospect because we think in terms of bells ringing the Angelus, of voices that the other day had been heathen singing Christian chants in Latin, of the warm sun shining in flowered gardens on the bent backs of holy men who had, after all, earned a little peace. We must think, too, of young love, sweet and bitter as death, of sin and forgiveness, of plaintive music under the moon, of the greed and savagery of men, of all the ebb and flow of human life that the Missions saw. And now, even in our hard twentieth-century light, there is a mist about them. How can we even understand the motives of the missionaries who built the Missions, who suffered so much, gave up so much, risked so much, to save the souls and care for the bodies of savages they had neven seen?

I think Mrs. Older's book rescues the true from the false romance. We shall not have many illusions about the golden age of the Missions when we have finished it. We shall know that they were built in sweat and weariness, in danger and continued disappointment. It is all too clear that the military forces which were thought necessary for the protection of the enterprise were frequently a cause of failure. They carried disease, they corrupted the native women, they were often cruel. Perhaps the Padres would have done as well without them—it is evidently not from lack of courage that they did not dispense with them. In a sense the Mission system was a kind of serfdom, yet Mrs. Older makes plain, without argument, that so far as most of the Padres were concerned, it was a kindly and loving servitude. How often they intervened to save even murderers from punishments too severe! And they mourned when their "sons" fell under the musket balls of the soldiery. Had they been left a little longer free from interference they might have civilized the sad remnants of the aboriginal

Californians. It remained for the white adventurers from the other side of the Mississippi to "civilize" the Indians in worse ways—by dispossession, starvation, butchery. The Padres shine like the saints of old compared with those who came after them. They did their work without a single motive that we can now recognize as self-interested.

It is not for me to pass a scholar's judgment on what Mrs. Older has written. For me her book bears the evidence of loving and painstaking study. Many of its scenes, I know, are associated with pilgrimages she made with her husband, Fremont Older—a man who thought himself a pagan, yet had a heart as warm as Father Serra himself, and who would have understood, and been understood by, that holy man. I wish that I might have made a pilgrimage of my own through the Missions of California, with the Olders for company and guidance. That did not come to pass, but when next I do go I shall carry this book with me. With its aid, I think, I shall be able to hear the bells ringing and see the neophytes trooping in; I shall watch men trampling the straw and adobe to make bricks; I shall catch sight of the Indians struggling down from the hills with redwood beams on their shoulders; I shall see the wheat fields, the olive trees, the vines, in bearing as in the days of old; I shall hear the murmur of prayers, chanted by priests broken by rheumatism, hardship and fasting, but rarely broken in spirit.

What I shall see and hear will be as romantic to me as my first sight of Carmel Mission. It will be romantic in a different, truer way. For that I shall thank Mrs. Older, who has so carefully separated the trash from the sacred relics, and who has achieved the miracle of writing a book about the California Missions with no claptrap or Hollywood nonsense in it.

R. L. DUFFUS.

Contents

Contents

Illustrations

Illustrations

Introduction

THE story of California's Missions begins with Isabella, Queen of Spain. Her courage, faith, and fortune sent Christopher Columbus on his way in 1492.

Juan Pérez, at one time her confessor, was guardian of the monastery of Santa Maria at La Rabida. Within its walls the friar sheltered Columbus, a wandering sailor, who had journeyed even to far Iceland. Into the royal presence Friar Juan brought the adventurer with the mad dream of finding the Indies. Would not Her Majesty aid him to carry the banners of Castile and Aragon to the land of Marco Polo, and there to plant the Holy Cross?

Ferdinand opposed the wild project, but Isabella seven years later pledged her jewels to aid Columbus. To him she gave her most precious Madonna, painted on wood.

And so, one portentous August morning, he set sail from Palos for the Indies with seven and eighty followers, carrying a letter of introduction from Her Majesty to the Grand Khan of Cathay. Upon an unknown world he was bestowing the soul of Spain, Rome, and Greece. On October 12, 1492, he kneeled down and kissed the ground of America.

When Columbus returned to America on his second voyage, his friend, Fray Juan Pérez, also came. In a little chapel built of green boughs at Port Concepción on the island of Hispaniola (Haiti), was celebrated the first American Mass.

At Santo Domingo the Franciscans erected the first monastery on the continent, with Father Juan Pérez as guardian. Ten years after the discovery of America they brought from Spain the first church bells.

The Roman Pontiff bestowed the entire Northern Hemisphere upon Spain. In 1519 Cortés came to Mexico with the *padres*. To

Cortés each missionary was worth a thousand soldiers in subduing natives. Flemish Franciscans arrived in Mexico in 1523. Spanish Franciscans followed in May, 1524. At the heels of the Franciscans were the Dominicans and the Augustinians. Jesuits followed.

Even before Cortés came, the lilting word California, land of Queen Califía, was heard from Biscay to Cadiz. In Montalvo's romance, *Las Sergas de Esplandian,* it was said to be an island on the right hand of the Indies, peopled with strong black Amazons bedecked and armed with gold.

Cortés half believed in the fabled Golden Isle of California. He spent 200,000 of his own ducats discovering islands in an uncharted sea. Charles V ordered: "Explore. Find gold. Find the island of Queen Califía."

The islands of Santo Tomás and Cedros were discovered, and the Gulf of California and Baja California. Don Bernál Diaz del Castillo gave the land its singing name. For the first time it was known that California was a peninsula, not an island. In 1535 Cortés made the first settlement, Santa Cruz on the Bay of La Paz; but he found no gold.

Royal favor failed Cortés. Cast off by Charles V, he died near Seville in 1547.

Spain went on. There came another adventurer to seek royal favor, Juan Rodríguez, a Portuguese—Cabrillo. In what is now the Bay of San Diego he appeared with two small ships, the *San Salvador* and *La Vitoria,* on September 28, 1542.

Viceroy Antonio Mendoza of Mexico had sent Cabrillo to find the fabled northern Strait of Anian leading into the Atlantic. He named the bay San Miguel, and so it was called for more than sixty years.

At Point Loma, Cabrillo took possession in the name of Charles V of Castile and Aragon. He christened it *La Punta de California.*

All Indians fled but two. Cabrillo gave them gifts. Other Indians shot arrows at the Spaniards from behind trees. Cabrillo gave shirts to some venturesome children. The gifts brought peace.

On his return journey from Point Mendocino, Cabrillo fell and broke his shoulder. Dying January 3, 1543, as a result of the accident, he commanded his pilot: "Sail north. Find the Strait of Anian."

Somewhere in the sand of the wind-swept island, San Miguel, off Santa Barbara, sleeps Cabrillo. His followers reported to the Viceroy of Mexico that they had discovered a vast new territory, California.

For sixty years Spain made little effort to follow Cabrillo. But Queen Elizabeth of England, true daughter of Henry VIII, sent her favorite freebooter, Francis Drake, to prey upon Spain. She filled his ship, the *Golden Hinde,* with provisions, perfumed water, and silver plate for dazzling the natives. Nor did she forget four violins to enchant them and a chaplain to pray for their souls.

Swearing to Elizabeth that he would bring back all the golden treasure of Queen Califía's land, Drake secretly fared forth on December 13, 1577. Robbing every galleon that he met, he passed along the coast, and with millions in loot, he set foot, probably on June 17, 1579, in northern California. New Albion he named the land, and took possession in the name of Elizabeth.

Her Majesty's chaplain, the Reverend Francis Fletcher, held a service of the new Church of England, using for the first time the Book of Common Prayer on the American continent. The Indians placed a crown upon Drake's head, calling him *Hióh,* Chief.

Once more in England with only 50 of the crew of 164, Drake laid the Indian chieftain's feather headdress at the feet of his sovereign—the crown of California. In return Elizabeth dined with the freebooter on his ship and knighted him.

Fifteen years later, Viceroy Luis de Velasco of Mexico directed Sebastian Rodríguez Cermeñon, a Portuguese navigator, to survey all harbors to and from the Philippines. In 1595 Cermeñon, on the *San Agustín* on his way back from the Philippines with a cargo of silk and beeswax, coasted down from Cape Mendocino and landed in a large bay north of the Farallones. A Franciscan friar, Francisco de la Concepción, held the second church service in California when he said Mass.

Cermeñon rowed along the coast in a small boat to make observations, and returned to find that a sudden storm had sunk the *San Agustín.* He and the seventy survivors built an open boat from a giant tree, the *San Buenaventura,* and set out for Mexico. Only a few reached Navidad.

Although the court of Spain was weary of tales of islands on which pearls were swept with a broom and of Queen Califía's golden mountains, it decided to chart California's coast. During the reign of Philip III, a rich merchant navigator, Sebastian Vizcaíno, was sent by Viceroy Conde de Monterey northward with the *San Diego, Santo Tomás,* and *Tres Reyes,* carrying two hundred men.

Sunday, November 10, 1602, Vizcaíno arrived at Cabrillo's *Puerto de San Miguel.* It was the feast day of San Diego de Alcalá, and Vizcaíno named Cabrillo's Port of San Miguel, San Diego. And so it has remained.

Vizcanío's men built a hut in which three Carmelite friars, Fray Antonio de la Ascensión, Fray Tomás de Aquino, and Fray Andrés de la Asunción, were saying Mass, when suddenly they heard fearful yells. A hundred Indians with feathered headdresses and bodies painted blue, red, and black appeared, threatening with bows and arrows. The explorer requested Fray Antonio to approach them and make peace. Attended by soldiers, the friar embraced the Indians and gave necklaces to the weeping Indian women. The Indians accepted the gifts, and brought pelts of wildcats and sable, and fish with nets for catching them.

Six days later the Spaniards went northward. Vizcaíno christened Catalina Island, where the friars planted the Cross and celebrated Mass. Tall handsome Indians clad in sealskin showed the visitors their own circular temple ornamented with birds' feathers, over which presided a strange headless god with a dog at his feet. Later they visited and named the head of Santa Barbara Channel.

Monte-Rey was the name given by the explorer to a new bay he found shaped like the letter "o." In the name of Spain he took possession of the port, forested with rose trees, poplars, and pines. Under a great oak the Carmelite friars said Mass here for the first time. A rushing river was discovered near by and called Carmelo for Mount Carmel.

Mexico felt the need not only of swords but of prayers to subdue the pagan land. In 1525 the Franciscans added an Indian school for boys to their central house in Mexico City. The Poor Clares there founded in 1531 the first woman's school on the continent. In

1590 the Franciscans established several Missions in Durango and Chihuahua.

The Jesuits under the Tyrolean Father Francisco Kino and the Italian Father Juan Maria Salvatierra founded many Missions in Baja California. In 1697 they obtained from the Spanish King permission to collect funds for founding Missions there. This was the beginning of the Pious Fund.

Don Juan Cavallero y Ozio gave $20,000. The Marqués de Villa Puente and his wife, the Marquésa de las Torres de Rada, donated over $200,000. Doña María Rosa de la Peña gave spacious haciendas. María Borgia, Duchess of Gandia, descended from St. Francis Borgia of the good-bad Italian family, offered $70,000. These men and women, greatly aided by the King of Spain, financed the California Missions, which were policed by soldiers.

In the cactus-tangled dust of Baja California the Jesuits established thirty-two stations and sixteen Missions. They planned to enter Alta California. They grew rich and powerful. In France a Jesuit refused absolution to Madame de Pompadour unless she severed relations with Louis XV. She declared the Jesuits must leave France. In Spain Jesuits questioned the legitimacy of Carlos III. He banished them from his territory. On February 27, 1767, the Council passed the edict. Execution of the order in Mexico was placed in the hands of Don Gaspar de Portolá, captain of dragoons, and later Governor of California.

On the evening of June 24, 1767, the Viceroy, Marqués de Croix, read the King's decree to the Archbishop of Mexico and the other Church officials assembled in his palace:

Repair with an armed force to the houses of the Jesuits. . . . Seize the persons of all of them and within twenty-four hours transport them as prisoners to the port of Vera Cruz. . . . Cause to be sealed the records of said houses and records of such persons, without allowing them to remove anything but their breviaries and such garments as are absolutely necessary for their journey. If after the embarkation there should be found one Jesuit in that district, even if ill or dying, you shall suffer the penalty of death.

Signed

Yo, El Rey (I, the King).

Hundreds of Jesuits, some ill and dying, departed from Mexico. Records of their expulsion were destroyed. Their belongings were confiscated. The Pious Fund was seized by the government. The Jesuit Missions of Baja California were placed under the control of the Franciscan College of San Fernando at Mexico City. Father Junípero Serra was summoned from the Sierra Gorda Mission and was told that he was President of the Missions in Baja California.

Even as a small sickly boy the desire to serve possessed Serra. Of peasant parents, he was born November 24, 1713, at Petra on the island of Majorca. Baptized Miguel José, when he finished his profession at the Lullian University, Palma, the blue-eyed friar took the name Junípero because of his devotion to Junípero, the companion of Saint Francis. For fifteen years he taught philosophy at Palma, praying that he might go to New Spain.

Life beyond the sea summoned Serra. He preached his farewell sermon. Without disclosing to his parents that it was forever, he took leave of them and sailed with Father Francisco Palóu from Cadiz for Vera Cruz.

With Franciscan austerity Serra walked a hundred leagues to the College of San Fernando at Mexico City. He arrived limping. On the journey a snake had given him a wound that refused to heal. It was the beginning of his prolonged, rapturous martyrdom. For the remainder of his life he was lame.

Serra was little pleased with the self-indulgent City of Mexico. He welcomed being sent to the savage Pame Indians. He learned their language. Although he was made President of the Sierra Gorda Missions, he resigned the office.

Like Saint Francis, Serra thought the body an enemy of the soul. He wore haircloth, he slept on boards. Even in the pulpit, with one hand he held high a crucifix and with the other he beat his breast with a stone until blood ran. At times he scorched his flesh with a burning taper, and the congregation sobbed. In six years he walked 2,000 miles—a new-world Saint Francis.

Serra led the Franciscans to Baja California, and he and his associates served more than a year in its rocky, thorny wastes. Suddenly a great fear stirred Spain. Russia threatened; the Bear rumbled slowly down the Pacific coast from the strait discovered by Bering. England also claimed the territory. Serra was summoned from Loreto for conference at Santa Ana with Galvez.

Don José Galvez, Visitador-General of Mexico, explained to Serra the King's three-fold purpose: to establish the Catholic religion among the heathen people, to protect California from encroachments, to extend the dominion of Spain.

This first California pioneer, Galvez, was a man of might, a tireless soldier for Spain. Day and night he drove himself, and he enjoyed driving others. Serra was fifty-five years old, but Galvez relied upon him to subdue the pagans of Alta California. For Serra it was a joyous task. He limped from Mission to Mission gathering vestments, sacred vessels, and even church bells purchased by wealthy followers of the Jesuits.

Galvez collected food and building material; gathered grain and flower seeds; corralled cattle, mules, and sheep; urged forward friars, soldiers, sailors, laborers—always with a smile.

Three missionaries were to go north by two land expeditions, and three on the *San Carlos.* The vessel set sail January 9, 1769, from La Paz, commanded by Captain Vicente Vila. On February 15 of the same year, the *San Antonio* departed from Cape San Lucas. The *San José* sailed June 16, 1770, from the same place, but was lost at sea.

Don Fernando Rivera y Moncada, captain of the first land expedition, was instructed to lead his forces through all the Missions, taking what was needed of flour and meat. He was to leave a receipt so that supplies might be paid for. From one Mission he drove off two hundred head of cattle. Rivera marched north from Velicatá March 24, 1769.

Serra remained with the second and more important land expedition commanded by Don Gaspar de Portolá. On the way he visited each Mission, but finally he could not walk. Portolá would have had him carried back to the frontier Mission.

"Please do not speak to me about the matter, *Señor Comandante,*" replied Serra. He turned to a muleteer when he saw a litter being prepared for him and said, "My son, do you not know how to make a remedy for my foot and leg?"

"*Padre,* I cure only galls on the backs of pack animals."

"Very well," replied Serra, "consider me like one of your beasts of burden. Please make me a remedy and apply it as if I were one of your animals."

The muleteer poulticed the friar's leg. In the morning Father Junípero said Mass as if he were not suffering. Serra was prepared for the great unknown north.

After many delays came the historic morning, May 15, 1769. Carrying the royal standard of Spain, impaled with the arms of Castile and Leon in red and gold, Portolá with his entire company left Velicatá to found the Mission and Presidio of San Diego.

Acknowledgment

THIS BOOK represents so many years of research and reading, largely for pleasure rather than with a definite objective, that it is impossible to compile an adequate bibliography. Most valuable sources of information have been: the Bancroft Library at the University of California; Hubert Howe Bancroft, *History of California*; Fr. Zephyrin Engelhardt's histories of the California Missions; Fr. Francisco Palóu, *Vida de Junípero Serra*; Fr. Juan Crespi, *Diary*; Governor Pedro Fages' journals; Fr. Gerónimo Boscana's treatise, *Chinigchinich*; Fr. Felipe Arroyo de la Cuesta, *Grammar of the Mutsun Language*, and the *Vocabulary or Phrase-Book*; *Font's Complete Diary*, translated by Dr. Herbert E. Bolton; Richard Henry Dana, *Two Years Before the Mast*; Zoeth S. Eldredge, *The Beginnings of San Francisco*, and *History of California*; Honoria Tuomey, *History of Sonoma County*; George H. Tinkham, *California Men and Events*; H. A. van Coenen Torchiana, *History of Mission Santa Cruz*; Irving B. Richman, *California Under Mexico and Spain*; Father St. John O'Sullivan's pamphlets on Mission San Juan Capistrano; Marie T. Walsh, *The Mission Bells of California*, and *The Mission of the Passes*; Mrs. A. S. C. Forbes, *California Missions and Landmarks*; Alberta Johnston Denis, *Spanish Alta California*; Nellie Van de Grift Sanchez, *Spanish Arcadia*; *California Historical Society Quarterly*; California County histories.

Thanks are due to Evelyn Wells Podesta; A. Salome Holliday; Mary d'Antonio; the late Fremont Older; Father John A. Leal of Mission San José; Father Fermin Chanal, S.J., of the Institute of Sciences at Guadalajara, Mexico; Dr. Herbert E. Bolton of the University of California; Robert Ray, librarian of the San Francisco Public Library, and also to Miss Byrne of the Reference Room; Edith Daley and assistants of the San José Public Library; Fr. Maynard Geiger, O.F.M., of the Santa Barbara Mission; Fr. Tiburcio Wand, O.F.M., of the San Miguel Mission; Harry Downie of Carmel Mission; all assistants of the Bancroft Library, University of California.

Nor should there be forgotten the many unmentioned American and Spanish-Californian pioneers, friends and acquaintances, as well as the clergy at the Missions who have always been willing to give information and aid.

CALIFORNIA MISSIONS
AND THEIR ROMANCES

I

San Diego de Alcalá

BRAVELY THEY CAME FORWARD, MEN OF THE SWORD IN blue and red, and men of prayer in gray—founders of California. Some were on horses, some on mules. Ignoring pain, Father Junípero Serra, President of the Missions to be founded, rejoiced.

Troubles were many. Indians were deserting. Serra did not reproach them, poor alarmed creatures, going one hundred leagues northward through a thorny desert with alien white conquerors.

Some Indians had died. Others had tried to rob Serra of even his habit. *Comandante* Portolá's leather jacket and boots had barely escaped. Serra overlooked the Indians' misdemeanors. He had lost his heart to the pagans. They were better than he had expected. The women were "modestly covered."

Spaniards and Mexicans were nearly as restive as the Indians. Portolá goaded them forward. The Hercules of the expedition was Sergeant José Francisco Ortega, future discoverer of San Francisco Bay. Three times daily over the rock-strewn trail he went, cutting with *machetes* through thickets to find camping sites and water holes. The frail friar and the rough-driving soldier formed an imperishable friendship.

Hunger caused the colonists to clamor. "Food will be plentiful at San Diego," promised Portolá. Serra tightened the white knotted cord of Saint Francis over his tattered habit and rejoiced in the half-ripe wild grapes, the belated poppies, but above all in the roses of Castile. With rose petals Serra cooled his face, burnt by the summer sun. He wished he might distill their fragrance. In his diary he wrote, "Blessed be He who created them."

3

On July 1, 1769, California's natal day, these pilgrims of the Pacific, forty-six days from Velicatá, from a slight eminence saw San Diego Bay. Triumphant red and gold Spanish flags floated from the *San Carlos* and the *San Antonio* riding at anchor. The travelers shouted, ran forward, embraced each other, fired rejoicing guns. The salvos were returned by the *San Carlos* and the *San Antonio*.

For a short time the pioneers forgot to ask questions. But things had gone badly indeed. A floating pesthouse, the *San Carlos* had come into harbor; the *San José* had not arrived. Of 226 colonists only 126 survived. Three-quarters of the camp were scurvy-stricken. Surgeon Pedro Prat was concocting herbal remedies for the sick in the brushwood hospital close to the beach, mounted with two cannon.

Serra would not allow himself to think of his weakened condition and his ulcered leg. His goal was unshaken: to spread the faith in California and to establish the white man's civilization in this blue and gold Paradise.

Portolá, abandoning hope of the coming of the *San José,* sent the *San Antonio* to San Blas for supplies. Father Juan Crespi wrote from the "heart of heathenism, San Diego," begging the Father Guardian of the San Fernando College at Mexico City to send him another habit, cowl, and tunic. He also asked for a strong Cross for the rosary on his girdle; his own was broken. Serra, too, requested clothing; but in writing his friend Palóu in Lower California he called the port of San Diego "truly magnificent."

Serra and the other Fathers visited the sick, administering the last sacraments. Surgeon Prat had scurvy; he could not heal even himself. Greedily he ate wild onions, his favorite remedy.

By giving Indians ribbons and glass beads, Lieutenant Fages, who had arrived on the *San Carlos,* found drinking water in the river to the southeast. Near by in pyramid-shaped huts made of branches covered with earth, lived a friendly village of Indians, one of the eleven *rancherías* at San Diego. The men wore nothing on their painted bodies. Their noses were pierced with a sliver of shell. The women also painted, but they modestly wore a fiber girdle of net made from a plant, *lechuguila*. In cold weather they appeared in mantles of rabbit skin.

Portolá left the founding of the first Mission in California to Serra. Taking with him Father Juan Crespi, Sergeant José Francisco Ortega, Lieutenant Pedro Fages, and the strongest men, with an excellent food supply, Portolá set out July 14, 1769, to find Monterey and establish the projected Mission.

At Cosoy, near Ramona's Marriage Place, Old Town of today, were left Fathers Serra, Vizcaíno and Parrón, Captain Vila, Surgeon Prat, eight leather-jacket soldiers, five seamen, a carpenter, a blacksmith, three servants, and eight Lower California Indians. Nearly all were ill.

Serra determined to establish the Mission without delay on a site selected by Fages on a high bluff within two gunshots of the beach looking toward the north of the port. On Sunday, July 16, 1769, Father Junípero Serra founded the first Mission in Alta California. He was aided by all not attending the sick. A small brushwood structure was erected and roofed with *tule* to be used as a chapel. Serra in rich vestments blessed the large Cross planted in front of the chapel. Assisted by Fathers Vizcaíno and Parrón, he sang High Mass. He delivered a moving address. The Indians were dazzled by the priests' robes, but they remained at a distance from the chapel.

San Diego (St. Didacus), for whom Mission San Diego de Alcalá was named, was born of lowly parents near Seville. He died at Alcalá on November 12, 1463, revered for miracles he was supposed to have performed. But he could not move the hearts of the Indians. Natives brought from Baja California tried to entice Diegueños to take part in the services. Although they greedily accepted gifts, they distrusted the ceremonies. Clothing presented by the Fathers moved the Indians to mirth. Spanish food they also declined. Indian children spat out gifts of *dulces*.

One native lad, however, visited the Spaniards. The *padres* taught him Spanish and tried to learn the Indian language from him. Even fireworks did not beguile the other Indians. Soldiers discharged muskets into the air to frighten them. Indians laughed and mimicked the sounds. Boldly they crept into tents and tried to steal sheets from the pallets. Before the *San Carlos* set out for San Blas, they were discovered cutting off the sails.

Serra had regarded the Indians as spoiled children, but after Mass on August 15, he had his first alarm. Natives shot arrows at the guards, and soldiers killed three Indians, wounding others.

The natives returned three days later. Serra and Vizcaíno remained on their knees in a brushwood hut praying that none of the Indians might be killed and die without baptism. Vizcaíno himself was wounded. Joseph Maria, the muleteer, rushed to Serra, an arrow in his throat, crying, "Padre, absolve me. The Indians have killed me!" Several Indians were shot. Wailing natives carried away their dead and buried them. In a few days the humbled Indians returned with their wounded and Surgeon Prat gave aid.

After this encounter a stockade was thrown up around the Mission, and two cannon were mounted thereon. In the stockade the Fathers displayed a painting of the Virgin and Child, the first picture to come to San Diego. Women especially were curious to see the Mother and Child. They thrust their breasts between the stockade poles, signifying their desire to nurse the Infant, but they refused to enter the chapel. Serra prayed and scourged himself, but death was the only visitor to the poor little Mission.

Finally Serra prevailed on an Indian to bring his infant son to the chapel for baptism. He offered the child clothing.

Hesitatingly the Indian entrusted his son to Serra. The Mission founder was delighted. During his missionary experience he had learned to cut out clothing and sew. He made a dress for the child. Soldiers and colonists assembled to watch the baptism. Serra was about to pour the water.

Fearing that some evil spell lay in the strange ceremony, the father seized the infant and fled to the *rancheria*. Soldiers followed trying to take the child by force. Serra forbade violence, but he was disheartened. Woefully he had failed.

Death and rain shut in the winter camp. Dead Men's Point (*La Punta de los Muertos*) today marks where the dead were buried. When Portolá and his men returned in January, only twenty of the forty remained at San Diego.

Portolá, back from his six months' journey in the north, had lost no men. On July 22, at a *rancheria* a hundred miles distant, the first two Indian children had been baptized in California—by Father Francisco Gómez. Magnificent trees had been discovered—redwoods. Ortega had found a great bay in the far north. It had been named for Saint Francis. The Bay of Monterey that Vizcaíno saw two centuries previously, they reported, had been filled with sand.

Serra believed that Vizcaíno's Monterey Bay still existed. "I will go north myself, and if possible find it."

Portolá was impatient. The *San Antonio* had not arrived with supplies. He said to Serra, "If the ship does not come by tomorrow, March 19, we will march back to Lower California. My men did not come here to perish from hunger."

"*Señor Comandante*, men carrying God's banner cannot retreat," replied Serra. "Even if you retire from California I will live on a *tortilla* a day and some herbs. So will Captain Vila of the *San Carlos*. The Captain, Father Juan Crespi, and I will wait for the *San Antonio*. Let us make a novena to San José, the patron of our expedition."

Captain of dragoons that he was, Portolá was touched by Serra's faith. "*Bueno, Padre* Junípero, nine days' prayer and no more."

The Fathers were subsisting on half a pint of corn, twenty ounces of flour, and a little milk each day. They prayed. But no ship appeared. The soldiers rejoiced. Back to Mexico!

On the last day, a sail! The *San Antonio!* California was saved!

Portolá set out by land on another journey to find Monterey Bay. With the same objective Serra and Crespi sailed on the *San Antonio*. Fathers Parrón and Gómez were left in charge of San Diego. With them were Sergeant Ortega, Captain Vila, a mate and five sailors from the *San Carlos*, and eight soldiers of the guard. The first Mission grapes in California were planted. Grain was sown; the rising stream destroyed the entire crop.

Baptisms were made, but in a revolt of later time the baptismal book disappeared. Afterwards Serra recalled that the first baptism was made in April, 1770. The child, three years of age, was baptized Francisco Antonio. His parents were Carlos and Praxedis of the Ranchería of San Diego.

Fathers Parrón and Gómez, stricken with scurvy, returned to

Mexico. They were replaced by Father Francisco Dumetz and Father Luis Jayme, who was afterwards killed by the Indians.

In May, 1772, all were on the verge of starvation. Two years later they harvested 50 bushels of wheat and corn and had 306 cattle, but there was little food to offer Indians. Besides, natives preferred their own airy brush houses; they burned them when overrun with fleas.

Building progressed rapidly. Adobe bricks were made by soldiers, seamen, and a few Indians attached to the Mission. A house for the friars and barracks rose. Discontent sprang up. Nine soldiers deserted to Mexico, driving off Mission cattle. The ever-conquering Ortega brought back the fugitives.

By November, 1773, twelve couples had been married. Indians suddenly ceased coming to the Mission. They were jealous of Spanish soldiers who attracted the maidens.

Father Jayme wished to move the buildings far from the soldiers. Soil must be found without alkali and saltpeter so that there would be more grain. Nipaguay, a new site two leagues northeast from the Presidio through a tangle of cacti, was chosen. Its Spanish name was *Nuestra Señora del Pilár*. There thirteen houses were built for neophytes.

The first *ranchería*, the one that attacked the Fathers, was now nearly Christianized. At the beginning of 1775, 116 adults and children had been baptized.

More land was prepared for sowing; a well was dug. Thousands of adobe bricks were made ready. The temporary church was completed in December, 1774. Although it was made of poles and roofed with *tules*, and measured only 53 feet by 17, to the Fathers it seemed magnificent.

Indian women liked the new Spanish clothes: chemises, gowns, ribbons. Neophytes from Lower California taught them to spin and weave. The men strutted proudly in overalls and sashes. They liked the new food and ways of fishing. Men and women were busy treading clay and straw to make adobe bricks. Sixty natives were baptized.

These rapid conversions aroused Chiefs Carlos and Francisco.

Suddenly they turned apostate. Speeding from *ranchería* to *ranchería* they went east as far as the Colorado River shouting, "Death to Christians! Burn the Mission and the Presidio!"

At midnight on November 4, 1775, eight hundred Indians from mountain and valley, armed with war clubs, fell yelling upon the Mission.

Sacred vessels were destroyed. Books and manuscripts were burned. The sacristy was looted. The barracks were fired. Father Vicente Fuster hastened to put out the blaze. A carpenter shot one of the Indians. Another carpenter received a mortal wound. Father Jayme ventured into a group of Indians and said, *"Amad a Dios, hijos!"* (Love God, my children).

The Indians dragged the missionary to the river bed, tore off his garments, and clubbed him to a bleeding mass.

The soldiers took refuge in an adobe building and shot through the cracks in the walls. Father Vicente shielded a bag of gunpowder and prayed for deliverance. Outnumbered a hundred to one, the Spaniards fought till dawn; then their powder gave out.

The Indians withdrew with their dead and wounded. Spaniards carried their dead six miles to the Presidio. Sadly Father Fuster buried Father Jayme and the blacksmith, José Romero.

"Thanks be to God," said Serra at San Carlos when he heard of the tragedy, "that the land is irrigated with the blood of martyrs!' He envied Father Jayme's martyrdom, and he asked the Viceroy "to have mercy upon the murderers...."

Comandante Rivera at Monterey hastened to San Diego to make reprisals, rejoicing that no soldier was killed. He found the missionaries huddled together in the Presidio warehouse now used as a chapel.

Indian Carlos, leader of the revolt, took refuge in the chapel demanding right of sanctuary claimed by criminals for centuries. Rivera surrounded the chapel with troops, commanding, "Surrender!"

"This is a chapel, *Comandante*," said Father Fuster. "Carlos has right of sanctuary."

"Seize the culprit!" ordered Rivera. Carlos was taken.

On Sunday when Father Fuster was about to celebrate Mass he said, "*Señores,* all those who took part in removing the Indian from the church now held as prisoner in the guardhouse are excommunicated.... If any of them should be in church, he will leave."

Rivera left. His defense was that the warehouse was not a church. Serra, who arrived from Monterey on the *San Antonio,* maintained that the building had been blessed and was used as a church. He ordered Rivera to return the Indian. This was done.

Serra went on with the work, assisted by sea captain Choquet. Guarded by a corporal and five soldiers, the captain directed a mate, sailors, and Indians in making adobe bricks.

Captain Guillermo Carrillo came from Mexico with soldiers as guard. In two weeks 7,000 adobe bricks were made, and the quadrangle wall was completed. Fathers Lasuén and Figuér were in charge at San Diego, and on October 17, 1776, the new building was ready for occupancy.

During the following year an adobe church with thatched roof was erected. Eighty feet long by fourteen wide, it had only two windows and a door. To celebrate its opening, the prisoners who had taken part in the massacre were released while soldiers and Indians cheered and cannon boomed.

The French-Spanish aristocrat, Father Fermin Francisco de Lasuén, who presided over San Diego de Alcalá after Father Jayme's death, had a Gallic sense of humor. In requesting clothing of his Superior, he said that he "came to California denuded of underwear and without sandals.... Perhaps the deep love of the Indians for me resulted in this want of clothing.... I indeed resemble them in having so little."

Contributions poured in upon the Mother Mission, vestments, clothing for the Indians, cooking utensils, and Guadalajara pottery from Mexico. San Gabriel gave grain and tools. From San Carlos, Serra sent a red chasuble, a silver ciborium, silver cruets, and books. Three *fanégas* of grain he gave, but he warned Lasuén, "Use it sparingly, only three grains to a hole."

Lack of provisions so greatly discouraged Fathers Lasuén and Figuér that in 1779 they applied for permission to retire to their college in Mexico. Serra wrote from Carmel the story of a community that had entered the choir for Matins. "One of the friars asked permission to retire to his cell because he was not in the proper mood. The Superior replied, 'Brother, stay in your place, for God's sake. Were we all to leave the choir because of being in an unfit mood, there would be no Matins, because we should all walk out, and I should be the first one.'" Serra wrote a thousand congratulations. The missionaries remained at San Diego.

Again in 1778 conflict rose, resulting in the first public execution in California. Chief Aaran of the Pamó Indians dared the soldiers to come to be slain. Corporal Carrillo killed two Indians, burned several in a hut, seized four chiefs, and brought them into San Diego. Aaran, Aachil, Aalcuirin, and Taguagui were sentenced to be shot April 11, 1778.

Fathers Lasuén and Figuér were asked to prepare the condemned chieftains for their end, but Lasuén saved one or more of the rebels. The others were shot in the presence of Indians and troops.

By the end of 1780 the Mission had 818 converts. A larger church was built, eighty-four feet long and fifteen wide, with pine beams, poplar rafters, and walls three feet thick. Soon was erected a house for the missionaries with a corridor, soldiers' quarters, guest rooms, an infirmary for women, storerooms, a tanning tank, and a harness and saddle room.

At this Mission, as at other establishments, Indians morning and evening were given a dipper of gruel or *atole;* at noon, stew or *pozole*. Sometimes they were permitted to gather wild fruit in the mountains.

Every six months the males received a new shirt and a pair of breeches, but often they burned or gambled away clothing and went without. Playing the guitar and violin they enjoyed. They worked seven hours a day, fifty adobe bricks being a fair task. Men became masons, bricklayers, carpenters, blacksmiths, saddlers, tailors, hatters, butchers, tanners, cooks, and makers of tile, harness, shoes, tallow, candles, and soap.

Twice a year females received a new chemise and skirt. Girls slept at the Mission under lock and key guarded by a woman. During the day they visited parents and families at their *rancheria*. They not only ground corn on *metates,* stone mills, but they helped carry sand and straw to make tile and adobe bricks. A capable artisan, Antonio Henriquez, with his Indian wife made spinning wheels, warping frames, combs, and looms for the women, and taught them to card, spin, and weave. Pregnant women washed wool or pulled weeds. Children helped in lighter tasks.

At San Diego livestock increased rapidly. The Mission was soon able to lend San Juan Capistrano colts, plows, and Indians expert in cultivating flax. In 1784 vegetables and fruits flourished. Wine making began in 1797 as an industry in California. Its fame spread to Mexico. The Viceroy wrote to the Fathers that he would like "wine of New California and Mission San Diego for our august monarch, Don Fernando VII." He also asked for a barrel for himself.

In September, 1783, San Diego saw Serra for the fourth and last time. He came from Monterey by sea, remained a few days, and confirmed 233 neophytes. At this Mission there had been 1,000 baptisms. Seven hundred and forty converts were living under missionary care in wood and grass cabins. When, a few months later, death summoned Serra, Father Fermin Lasuén of San Diego took his place as President of the California Missions.

Foreigners were not permitted to enter California; but Captain George Vancouver, the English navigator, ignored the law, and on November 27, 1793, came to San Diego on the *Discovery.* He gave President Lasuén a barrel organ, the first in California, and it was taken to San Carlos. Vancouver reported that the San Diego Presidio had only three brass cannon.

Five years later some Americans came—William Katt, Barnaby Jan, and John Stephens, Boston sailors left by an American ship in Lower California. The first American vessel arrived in 1800— the *Betsy,* commanded by Captain Charles Winship, who left in ten days. Two years later William Shaler, the American smuggler, came on the *Lelia Byrd,* and was nearly sunk by cannon fired from Point Guijarros.

Slowly schools were established. In 1795 the retired Sergeant

Manuel de Vargas, who had already taught school at the Pueblo of San José, was the first teacher. He had twenty-two pupils. The Presidio school in 1825 was presided over by a Dominican, Father Antonio Menéndez, who had a salary of $15 a month.

Drouth brought to Mission San Diego a water problem in 1801. Nine miles above the Mission the Fathers built a dam two hundred feet long with a gateway twelve feet high. Its brick-lined walls were thirteen feet thick. An aqueduct was laid through gulches often impassable on horseback. The dam stood until 1874.

The most ambitious church was built at San Diego de Alcalá in 1808. Vast numbers of Indians hewed timbers on the mountain now called Smith's, sixty miles distant. Stationed in relays, they brought the timbers on their shoulders to the Mission.

Father Pedro Panto had eagerly looked forward to building the church, but Indian Nazario, his cook, placed an herb in the friar's soup, powdered *cuchasquelaai,* a deadly poison. The Father died on June 30, 1812, but he declined to testify against the culprit. Nazario said he had received violent floggings, and so he had poisoned the missionary.

Father José Bernardo Sanchez went on with Father Panto's work. San Diego's own day, November 12, 1813, saw the new building blessed. Ceremonies were conducted by Father José Barona of Mission San Juan Capistrano. The first sermon was preached by Father Gerónimo Boscana of Mission San Luis Rey.

On the day of dedication the body of martyred Father Jayme was exhumed, and his remains were placed near the statue of the Virgin. A Cross stands on the spot where he fell. The first Mission guidepost on El Camino Real, the Royal Road, joining all Franciscan Missions in California, four Presidios, and three Pueblos, commemorates his memory.

At the time of its greatest development, the Mother Mission San Diego had a rectangle of buildings 165 feet square enclosing the central court. Behind was a series of five corrals. Orchard and garden were on low ground west and south of the buildings.

Mission San Diego de Alcalá withstood the shock of a great earthquake in 1812. The church, with its Oriental appearance, its austere, satisfying façade, later was the model for the one at San Luis Rey.

As the first decade of the nineteenth century turned, revolution blazed in New Spain. Transports ceased to visit California. The Mission was asked to support the Presidio. Activity increased.

In 1821 a spectacular crop of wheat, barley, and corn was garnered—23,000 bushels, the largest ever raised, with a single exception, at any Mission. San Diego was still dominant in 1830. The Mission owned 16,120 sheep, 8,422 head of cattle, 1,192 horses and mules. There were 1,544 Indians registered.

Zeal for making converts grew. Even in the mountains near the line of the Colorado Desert, seventy-one miles from San Diego at a place the Indians called *Elcuanam,* an *asistencia* was founded September 20, 1818. Four hundred neophytes worshiped at this mountain chapel, Santa Isabel, often spoken of as the Church of the Desert. There were several houses and a granary filled with wheat, maize, pumpkins, and beans. Six thousand vines furnished grapes for wine making.

In the 'fifties Santa Isabel was a ruin. A tall Cross of saplings marked the heap of dust. Bells of Santa Isabel swung from the crossbeam. On Sundays the important man of the tribe read the service. One bell bore the lettering: N. S. DE LORETO 1729. The second bell was inscribed: SAN PEDRO 1767.

Annually when Santa Isabel's *fiesta* came, its ruins were transformed into a flower-bedecked altar; and the offspring of Mission converts attended service held by visiting priests. In recent time the bells of Santa Isabel were stolen. The late Father Eugene Le Pointe erected a church at Santa Isabel.

In 1825 San Diego had the distinction of becoming the temporary capital of California. Governor José Maria Echeandia said he liked the climate. In reality, he was interested in Señorita Josefa Carrillo, daughter of Don Joaquin. She danced the new American waltz, and caused greater scandal by losing her heart to an American, Captain Henry Delano Fitch. Señorita Josefa and the blue-eyed captain were betrothed. Josefa should not marry a foreigner, a Protestant, said the Carrillos. The Captain had himself baptized, and Father Menéndez was about to perform the ceremony.

A messenger arrived from the Governor forbidding the marriage. "Why don't you carry me off?" weepingly asked Señorita Josefa of the captain.

That night Don Pio Pico, afterwards Governor of California, took his cousin, Señorita Josefa, upon his horse and rode swiftly to the boat at the water's edge. Captain Fitch sailed with his betrothed four thousand miles to Valparaiso, where they were married.

When, the next year, Captain Fitch returned with his bride and son, Governor Echeandia had the pair dragged before an ecclesiastical court at San Gabriel and tried. The Vicar-General, Father José Sanchez, decided that "considering the great scandal which Don Enrique has caused in this Province, I condemn him to give as penance and reparation a bell of at least fifty pounds in weight for the church at Los Angeles." The penance bell given by Captain Fitch hangs in the *campanario* of the Plaza Church at Los Angeles.

Governor Echeandia throve on melodrama. In 1828 he discovered "Spanish spies." They proved to be two Americans, Sylvester Pattie— Kentuckian, ranger, trapper—and his fifteen-year-old son, James Ohio Pattie. The Governor imprisoned them. The father died without being able to see his son. The boy seemed doomed.

Young Pattie learned that the Governor feared smallpox raging in the north. He had some vaccine. If given liberty he promised to vaccinate the Governor and the inhabitants of the northern Missions. The Governor modified his decision and paroled Pattie and his companions. It is said that Pattie treated more than 20,000 persons in California. For a week's service at the Russian Fort Ross he received $100. Back in the United States he wrote a book about his experiences.

At the time of Governor Echeandia the house now known as Ramona's Marriage Place, at San Diego, was the center of social life. It was the dwelling of Don José Antonio Estudillo, son of *Comandante* Don José Maria Estudillo. During the American occupation in 1846 Casa Estudillo was a refuge for women and children. Helen Hunt Jackson's Ramona was supposed to have been married in the Estudillo chapel. Historians, however, declare that Ramona became a bride in the adobe Church of the Immaculate Conception.

The Estudillo house renewed its youth about 1910. The late Mr. John D. and Mr. Adolph Spreckels bought the dwelling, as a terminus to their streetcar line, and employed Mrs. Hazel W. Waterman to renovate it. Castilian roses festoon the walls, a grapevine clambers over an arbor, a fountain plashes. Near Ramona's well, where lovers make a wish, is a transplanted palm that for more than a century guarded Presidio Hill.

When California was no longer Spain but Mexico, the Governor asked the Fathers to swear allegiance; but Father Vicente Oliva and Father Fernando Martín as Spaniards refused. In 1831 the Governor sent soldiers to seize 21,000 bushels of grain harvested on Mission ranches. The Fathers demanded a fair price. They were obliged to support 1622 Indians and 70 officers and soldiers. Without authority from Mexico City, Governor Echeandia, on June 6, 1831, secularized the Missions.

On his arrival the new Governor, Manuel Victoria, thwarted secularization. Echeandia remained at San Diego stirring up revolt. Victoria himself was obliged to depart. With him left many Fathers.

José Figueroa, whose mistress and illegitimate children were the scandal of California, was nonetheless an able Mexican governor. At his order ten Mexican Franciscans replaced the Spanish Franciscans, on August 9, 1834, and the Mexican Government seized the Missions. After secularization of the Missions, San Diego became a parish of the second class. Mission records ceased. At this time Mission San Diego owned 52,208 acres of land. It extended south thirteen leagues to El Rosario, east seventeen leagues to Santa Isabel, and north seven leagues to the Cañada de San Bernardo.

When Richard Henry Dana visited the Mission in 1836 he found silent, deserted white buildings. The Indians used brutish language.

Eugene de Mofras, French diplomat from Mexico City, wrote of the decaying buildings in 1841. There were few olive trees, vineyards were unpruned, and the soil was untilled. The wine was still famous, however, and the cotton superior. Father Vicente Pasqual Oliva, a white family, and a few Indians occupied the Mission. There were still 800 neophytes nominally under control of the ex-Mission authorities.

De Mofras wrote of the recent Ibarra tragedy. Mountain Indians brooded over the barbarities of Lieutenant Juan Ibarra. After a battle at Santa Isabel in 1826 he had cut off twenty pairs of Indian ears. Ten years later the Indians had not forgotten. They surrounded the Ibarra dwelling at Rancho San Isidro, murdered Ibarra and two *vaqueros*, burned the ranch houses, stripped off Doña Juana Ibarra's clothing with the order "Leave for San Diego!" Near the Mission she was liberated, but her daughters were captured. Their brothers, attempting to rescue them, were wounded. De Mofras says that one of the Ibarra girls became the wife of an Indian chief. While the men of the tribe were absent hunting, the women, out of jealousy, hung her to a tree and stoned her to death.

An inventory made in 1846 by Andrés Pico and Juan Manso showed that aside from the church and the Fathers' dwelling, the Mission and its possessions were valued at $1,654. In that year Governor Pio Pico ordered Father Oliva to surrender the Mission to Santiago Argüello for services to the Mexican Government.

Adiós-hour came to Spanish-California when the United States warship *Cyane*, commanded by Captain Samuel Dupont, cast anchor at Old Town on July 29, 1846, and took possession twenty-two days after the United States flag was raised at Monterey. The colors of Mexico drooped to the ground. Weeping Doña Antonia Machado carried away the faded colors. An American, Alfred B. Smith, climbed the flagpole carrying the Stars and Stripes while some Mexicans shot at him.

Farsighted Spanish-Californians like Don Juan Bandini and his family opened their doors to the new rulers. Don Juan gave Colonel John C. Frémont his favorite horse. His daughters, Josefa, Isidora and Arcadia, made an American flag from white muslin sheets striped with red and blue silk from their gowns—the seventh flag to float over California—and presented it to the conquerors.

There had been the flag of Spain in 1542. Drake in 1579 flaunted England's banner. In 1811 came the Russian Bear. Emperor Agustín I of Mexico had his moment in 1822. The Mexican Republic raised its colors in 1823. For a few days in 1846 the Bear flag fluttered at

Sonoma. Since July of that year California has been under the Stars and Stripes.

Father Oliva, who had passed thirty-six years at San Diego, departed when he saw the Mission, the church in which 7,126 Indians had been baptized, turned into a barracks. Most of the time between 1852 and 1862 United States troops occupied the buildings. The church roof was removed, the doors were taken away. Soldiers felled the orchards for fuel, sparing only a few olive, pear, and fig trees. Soon the tower plunged downward carrying the bells.

Vestments and sacred vessels, found buried in an arroyo, were rescued by an aged woman, Doña Apolinaria Lorenzana, who devoted her life to the Mission. Father J. Chrisostom Holbein in 1853 removed the remains of Fathers Lazaro, Panto, and Martín, buried in the presbytery of the church of Mission San Diego, and placed them in a near-by cemetery. Already Fathers Jayme, Figuér, and Mariner had been interred between the main and side altars.

Governor R. B. Mason ordered the property placed at the disposition of Father José Maria González, Governor of the Bishopric of Santa Barbara. On December 18, 1855, the United States Land Commission granted the Mission property of 22.21 acres to Archbishop Joseph Sadoc Alemany for the Roman Catholic Church.

During its occupation by American forces, a second story was built into a portion of the Mission. In the 'eighties these rooms were the scene of frequent *bailes*. After the troops left, the Mission was used as a stable. In 1883 little was left of the Mission buildings save a portion of the church and adjacent dormitories, which were occupied by bees and owls.

For decades the crumbling Mission stood on the hill, a broken Mother of Sorrows. In 1891 Father Antonio Ubach, many years priest in Old Town and at St. Joseph's Church, San Diego, began a campaign to have the Mission restored.

Two of the bells were at his church. A pair dated 1802 hung in the decaying chapel at Ramona's Marriage Place. One of the cracked 1802 bells was replaced by another of the sextet then at the Indian school. Colonel Brayton, on request, returned a fourth bell serving as dinner bell at the United States Military Barracks. Father Ubach had the four bells recast at San Diego. The *campana, Mater Dolorosa,* contains the bells of 1790, 1791, 1796, and 1802. When the old Mission was restored in 1931, the other bell inscribed 1802 was suspended therein. The oldest bell at the Mission, probably of Spanish manufacture, has the inscription: SANTA MARIA AMADALENA. 1738. (SAINT MARY MAGDALEN. 1738.)

Death interrupted Father Ubach's work in 1907. When the plans for the Panama-California Exposition took shape, a nonsectarian group headed by Mayor Albert Mayrhofer carried it forward. They collected and spent about $100,000 in restoring the building, which was re-dedicated on September 13, 1931.

The Sisters of Nazareth, whose society gave $25,000 toward the restoration, built Nazareth House adjoining the Mission and have charge of it as a museum. They exhibit vestments worn by the founder, Father Junípero Serra. Baptismal, confirmation, marriage, and death registers bear his clear, determined signature.

On Presidio Hill in front of the Marston Museum, Serra's material work may still be found: a low, broken adobe wall looking out over the sea paths of Cabrillo, Drake, and Vizcaíno. It is all that remains of the chapel of the first Mission San Diego de Alcalá. Close by are two date palms, seeds of those sent by Galvez and sown in 1769, which a hundred years later had their first crop of dates. These palms are California's most distinguished garden pioneers.

Directly behind them is a massive Cross fortified with steel and concrete, fashioned of fragments of tile from the building erected by Serra. This Cross welds present and past. At its base is a bronze tablet inscribed:

In this ancient Indian village of Cosoy discovered and named San Miguel by Cabrillo in 1542, visited and christened San Diego de Alcalá by Vizcaíno in 1602, here the first citizen Fray Junípero Serra planted civilization in California. Here he first raised the Cross, here began the first Mission, here founded the first town, San Diego, July 16, 1769.

II

San Carlos Borromeo (Carmelo)

IT WAS at Mission Carmel and Monterey, the old Spanish capital of California, that this book germinated. Soon after our marriage in the 'nineties, Fremont Older and I strolled from the Hotel Del Monte to the near-by town of Monterey.

In a walled-in garden in Alvarado Street stood a two-story adobe house smothered with an aged rosebush weighed down with yellow roses, the Chromatella. A small bright-eyed, brown-skinned woman no longer young, dressed in black, stood in the doorway, Doña María Ignacia Bonifacio, the heroine of the Sherman Rose Romance.

For the first time I heard the story. Young Lieutenant William Tecumseh Sherman was stationed here in the 'fifties. Doña María Ignacia and he fell in love. They planted this bush. He promised, it was said, to come back with its first blooming, and make her his bride.

Sherman did not return. His wedding at Washington was attended by President Taylor and his cabinet. The young officer went marching through Georgia. Doña María Ignacia's gowns and her dainty fan are now in the Custom House Museum.

In the early 'eighties again the Sherman rose garden became the shrine of lovers. Robert Louis Stevenson came to this very garden to woo Fanny Osbourne, who occupied a wing of the Bonifacio adobe with her children, Lloyd and Isobel. He lived a few doors from here, and he was writing *Prince Otto*. Much of it he read aloud to Fanny Osbourne. From Monterey she went to San Francisco to become Stevenson's bride.

Doña María Ignacia's house has been razed to make way for a bank building. An artist, Mr. Percy Gray, reconstructed her dwelling on the mesa and installed therein the woodwork of the old house. His garden wall is roofed from the tiles of Doña María Ignacia's wall. Mr. Gray also transplanted the Sherman rosebush, and the Castilian root survives after ninety years.

From Monterey, Fremont Older and I went in a horse and buggy over Serra's *Via Crucis* to the ruin of Carmel Mission. At that time a few artists had painted the abandoned buildings. An occasional tourist visited the place where Father Junípero Serra spent most of his California life. In the period of our visit the Mission was the habitation of coyotes, deer, and owls. The ruin has been half unroofed, and Serra with his companions lay under the vault of California's blue sky.

As we toiled over the sandy, flower-starred fields surrounding the Mission ruin, we were unaware that on this very spot in 1769 Portolá had planted the Cross while seeking Vizcaíno's long-discovered Bay of Monterey. On their return journey from San Francisco, Portolá, Fages, and their men placed in a bottle at the foot of the Cross a paper recording their failure to find Vizcaíno's bay. On the Cross they carved the words, "Dig at the base and you will find writing." Then they went south to San Diego.

Coppery-skinned natives with rabbit mantles slung over their shoulders soon gathered round the fresh-hewn Cross overlooking Carmel Valley. They caught the largest fish in the bay. From the arms of the Cross they dangled salmon and strings of clams. Plumes and arrows were offered. The Indians fled to the mountains.

Soon the white men returned to the Bay of Monterey: Don Gaspar Portolá, Lieutenant Pedro Fages, Father Juan Crespi, and a force of sixty soldiers. Amazed, they found the Cross planted by them the preceding December now bedecked with Indian plumes and arrows. But the paper left by them was untouched.

Even on his return journey, however, Portolá could not find Vizcaíno's bay. He recalled the first letter ever sent from Monterey. Vizcaíno had written to someone near the King of Spain:

Harbor of Monterey,
28 December, 1602.

There is a great extent of pine forest from which to obtain masts and yards, even though the vessel be of one thousand tons burthen, live oaks ind white oaks for shipbuilding, and this close to the seaside in great number. And the harbor is very secure against all winds. . . .

The Indians have given me to understand concerning the people of the interior. . . . They will receive readily the holy gospel. . . . And since His Majesty is lord and master of all, let him provide as may seem best to him, as to what behooves me best to do. On my part I will serve him till death.

Portolá remembered that the Carmelite friars, Andrés de la Asunción, Antonio de la Ascensión, and Tomás Aquino, had pitched the tent in the shadow of an oak with branches touching the water at tide. Here they said Mass. Three leagues distant they had found a river; Carmelo they christened it for their own Order. Elk grazed, their wool dangling on the ground. There were rosemary, nuts, game, and "climate like our own Castile." Indians said the land was rich in silver and gold.

Portolá and his men were beset by bewilderments; they stumbled in circles. They camped that night on what later became the site of Carmel Mission. Where was the supply ship *San Antonio* that had preceded them to Monterey? Where was Father Junípero Serra? Till dawn the travelers burned three beacons for the *San Antonio*. For one week they fired guns, and signal lights flared. Then one glad June day a distant cannon boomed. The *San Antonio!* Serra was safe.

In joyous sunshine Portolá, Fages, and Father Crespi crossed the peninsula from Carmelo. Before them they saw the blue lagoon between Point Pinos de Monterey and Point Año Nuevo. It was formed like the letter "o" and filled with barking seals. Two cub whales were at play.

All shouted, "Monterey! Vizcaíno's port!"

Portolá and his company hastened to greet the sea expedition. Heavy storms had driven the *San Antonio* south and north again to the Farallones.

Portolá's camp was transferred to Monterey. As there was no shelter on shore, Father Junípero slept on the ship. The great Cross was constructed. A canopy made of flags of various nations formed a temporary roof for the chapel near Vizcaíno's oak. High winds rose. Father Junípero inserted wax candles in two small hand lanterns and placed them each side of the crucifix. Six lantern poles were stuck in the ground and arranged about the sides of the altar, in the center of which was an image of Our Lady.

Father Junípero blessed the water, sprinkled the shore, blessed the Cross. Assisted by Father Juan Crespi, he sang Mass and preached. There was no music; but muskets volleyed, and the *San Antonio* saluted. It was June 3, 1770.

At the conclusion of Mass, Don Gaspar de Portolá raised the royal standard and took possession of the land in the name of Don Carlos III. There was the customary ceremony of uprooting grass and casting stones and herbs to the four winds. A soldier and a sailor rode at high speed carrying the news to the Viceroy and the College of San Fernando at Mexico City that the Presidio and the second California Mission had been founded on Monterey Bay—San Carlos Borromeo.

San Carlos, the patron saint, was born October 2, 1538, at Arona, Italy. His mother was a Medici, and his uncle was Pope Pius IV. At twelve he received the clerical tonsure; at twenty-two he was a cardinal; at forty-six he died. A fragment of the hat of the patron saint is still preserved in a gold case at San Carlos.

Portolá went south, leaving Lieutenant Pedro Fages in charge at Monterey. He drove building forward. The whole party occupied temporary structures made of poles, filled out with twigs and branches and covered with mud. Fathers Serra and Crespi relied on an Indian interpreter brought by them from Lower California to communicate with the pagans, but for several months the natives avoided Monterey with its booming guns.

Soldiers troubled Serra. Their conduct with Indian women interfered with the progress of the Mission. He asked permission of the Viceroy to transfer Mission San Carlos over the hills southeastward to Carmel Valley near Point Pinos. He also requested more missionaries and obtained them.

Before the transfer was made, Father Junípero had what Father Palóu called an "indescribable jubilee," the first baptism, on December 26, 1770, which was followed by three others. The new building at Carmel was under way in June, 1771, and Serra was living at the Mission in August. He planted a Cross in the center of the plot in-

tended for the quadrangle between the missionaries' house and the
temporary pine church.

Serra was overseer and engineer of work. He gave trifling gifts
to visiting pagans. For children he showed great affection. From him
they learned to salute everyone with the words, *"Amad a Dios!"*
(Love God). So rapidly did the custom spread that it was the Indian
salutation to all Spaniards in the Monterey district.

Serra tried to acquire the Indian language. "The learning of a new
language," he wrote, "is nothing novel to me, but I fear I have little
grace for it on account of my sins."

The Indians were surprised to see Father Junípero toil like a
Mexican peon. He tucked up his habit and with bare feet trod straw
and clay together. He carried stones, mixed mortar, hewed timbers.
His hempen sandals fell from his feet. His habit was torn, and he
girded himself with an old piece of cloth. He cut out diapers for
Indian babies and taught converts to sew. He made shirts for men
and skirts for women. Men gambled away his gifts of clothing. When
they entered Serra's dwelling and the chapel naked, he reprimanded
and sent them away.

At Carmel Father Junípero lived like a hermit in a little shack with
cats as companions. He hoped to secure a large flock of chickens, but
a young son of one of the neophytes shot the first pullets with bow
and arrow and ate them. Serra seldom touched meat. He satisfied
himself with a *tortilla* and some herbs from the field, but he did not
stress his vegetarianism. Fish and fruit, he said, were eaten by the
Virgin. Often he excused himself for not touching meat by saying
that he did not masticate it well. Sometimes he rose from the table
when the meal was only half served and read to his companions.

At times he lacerated his flesh with sackcloth woven with bristles
of broken wire. Continually he was in a state of mental and vocal
prayer.

By gifts and kindness Serra overcame the seven aloof tribes of
Indians. On the coast he found the Rumsen, Sargentruc, Sarconeños,
Guachirron, and Calendaruc. In the interior were the Excelen and
Egeac tribes. The savage Zanjones in the south frequently threatened

to wipe out the Mission. Serra was not alarmed. He would have welcomed martyrdom.

He taught the Indians to play stringed instruments. The males composing the choir sang from square notes written on parchment in different colors to indicate the part followed by each singer. The native musical instrument was a hollow tube from an alder tree.

After Serra came, chiefs gave up plural wives. Women were more faithful than the men. Girls learned to wear skirts and chemises instead of *tule* aprons. The Indians considered possession of a handkerchief a fortune. They believed that after they died, they went West.

Before the end of 1771 Serra saw the buildings and chapel at Carmel completed. He used only the $1,000 allowed from the Pious Fund. For the first time redwood was employed in construction; confessional, benches, and all furniture were made of the new wood. From it was also fashioned the statue of Saint Joseph. At the end of the year there were completed a four-room dwelling for the Fathers, a house for boys, a corral for cattle, a granary, and a kitchen. Canoes now brought the first California salt from Salinas to the Presidio.

Converts came rapidly to San Carlos. The first young people to be married here were Fernando Malaleta and Catharina María on November 10, 1772.

Mexican supplies soon failed. Colonists had only a small amount of milk and a few vegetables from the Presidio garden—the first vegetable garden at Monterey. Presidio soldiers sowed four *fanégas* of wheat and barley to ward off starvation. Beans were planted, and rice is mentioned for the first time in California history. The Spaniards relied on Indians for food.

Fages, who had been made a captain for his untiring activity, went hunting in the Valley of the Bears fifty leagues southward. Monterey was saved by Fages, whose twenty-five pack mules brought back 9,000 pounds of bear meat from the valley near San Luis Obispo of today.

From San Diego rode in a messenger. The *San Carlos* and the *San Antonio* had arrived in violent seas. Serra set out with Fages for San

Diego. There Father Junípero begged Captain Pérez to trust in God and go to Monterey. The *San Antonio* arrived safely with supplies for San Carlos and broke the famine.

At the end of two years Serra described Mission San Carlos. It was a stockade of rough timbers with ravelins in the corner, plastered over with mud and whitewashed with lime. The main house was forty *varas* long and seven wide, and had six rooms. One of the rooms served provisionally as a church.

Fages' military arrogance tormented Serra. He punished neophytes, opened missionaries' mail, drove off cattle from the Mission to the Presidio. He even forbade the foundation of Galvez's favorite Mission San Buenaventura, for which the Visitador-General had packed the church goods.

Padre Junípero decided to confer in Mexico with the new Viceroy, Bucareli, and he sailed October 20, 1772. The Viceroy promised support of the Missions. Liberal supplies were obtained. A general store was to be established at the Presidio. Serra also procured blacksmiths, carpenters, and storekeepers with families for Monterey.

Father Junípero was so eager to visit the California Missions that he left the vessel at San Diego and walked over the five hundred mile trail to Monterey by way of El Camino Real. At San Luis Obispo he met Fages. The *Comandante* was instructed that he could no longer usurp the President's power nor punish Indians without consent of missionaries. Salvos of artillery and pealing bells welcomed Serra to Monterey.

At San Carlos Father Junípero was greeted and gladdened by Father Francisco Palóu, his old friend and pupil of Majorca. Palóu said that after reading Vizcaíno's account of his voyage, he would have given his own soul to convert a single Monterey Indian. Now his life was complete—he was to labor in California.

Famine soon tried this learned missionary. For thirty-seven days the Spaniards and neophytes had no bread, only beans and milk— manna, Palóu called them. Coffee was substituted for chocolate. At first vegetables did not thrive at Carmelo. There was no competent gardener.

Palóu raised lettuce and herbs, irrigating the plants with a gourd.

His artichokes were so large that one lasted three days. The esthetic friar bordered his vegetable garden with blooming azaleas from the forest. In spite of hunger and tattered habit Palóu said that life in California was a "special blessing." Palóu not only grew vegetables with skill, explored and instructed Indians, but he found time at San Carlos to write half of his invaluable history of California.

Comandante Fages set out ten acres of quinces, pears, peaches, apricots, apples—the first private orchard at Monterey. Soon the Mission harvested more than 1,000 *fanégas* of grain. In 1774 San Carlos owned 61 cows, 42 hogs, 14 riding and pack mules, 4 brooding mares, 6 tame horses, 3 colts, and a burro.

When the Anza expedition arrived in 1776, Father Pedro Font delighted the natives by playing on his psaltery. Font was pleased with the church, already adorned with paintings, and the three good-sized rooms where the missionaries dwelt. Palóu's vegetables healed his sore mouth, caused by eating too much meat. Font wrote of Carmel: "It is the most beautiful site...because it is so near the sea and in a country so charming and flower-covered that it is a marvel."

Monterey acquired new dignity—it became the capital of Alta California in the same year that Philadelphia became capital of the colonies on the Atlantic coast. After Rivera was excommunicated at San Diego for violating the Indian's right to sanctuary, Don Felipe de Neve was appointed Governor, and instructed to act in accord with Serra. He advocated Indian self-government: the beginning of secularization of the Missions. Neve told the Indians to select their own *Alcalde*. After acquiring power, Carmel's Indian *Alcalde* began seducing women and urging neophytes to leave the Mission.

Serra scorned honors, but they came to him. On June 17, 1778, he received news that he had been granted the bishop's power to administer confirmations.

Monterey was far from Madrid; but when the King was fighting with England, he remembered the capital of Alta California. He asked contributions for war expenses. Mission San Carlos gave $106. Major-domo Ignacio Vallejo, father of the future General Vallejo, contributed $10 toward the war. Thieves and crows carried off the harvest, but there were 1,660 bushels of wheat, 700 bushels of barley, and 165 of beans.

Governor Neve opposed Mission establishments, and this attitude caused his transfer to Mexico City. He was succeeded as governor by dynamic Pedro Fages. The new Governor's wife, Doña Eulalia, a high-born Catalonian, sniffed at the royal house, "an adobe hut," she called it, with its adobe wall 1,700 feet long, 12 feet high, and 4 feet thick. Naked Indians shocked Doña Eulalia. She proceeded to cut up her own clothing and that of her husband to distribute among pagans. Fages warned, "Soon you will be as naked as the Indians. Women's clothing is not to be purchased in California. Trading with foreign vessels is prohibited."

Doña Eulalia sailed for San Francisco. "Unfaithful!" she called the Governor on her return. "You brought an Indian maid from the Colorado country."

Accusation brought accusation, "You flirted with an officer."

Doña Eulalia poured her Catalonian wrath upon her husband's head. Threatening divorce, she left the house. The Governor sought the advice of the Fathers at San Carlos Mission. Doña Eulalia stormed out her story. "Divorce!" she insisted.

"Not possible, Doña Eulalia," replied the missionaries.

Father Mathias Noriega presided over the ecclesiastical court. There could be no divorce in California, decided the judge.

During church service Doña Eulalia made outcries. The judge sent an officer to seize Doña Eulalia and lock her up in the Mission. She barricaded herself in her private apartment with her children. The Governor forced open the door, carried her to Carmel Mission, took his son, and left for the south. Zanjone Indians were not so violent as the Governor's wife. The missionaries threatened her with flogging and chains.

"The devil may carry me off, I'll never live again with Fages," she declared. She even wrote a letter to the court of Spain urging her husband's removal on the ground that Monterey climate injured his health. Doña Eulalia triumphed.

Monterey missed the energetic Governor, his pockets always filled with *dulces* for the children. To his successor, his old friend Don José

Antonio de Roméu, who had served with him in the Colorado campaign, he left his sheep, goats, and his beloved garden with blooming shrubs, his vineyard, and his six hundred fruit trees. He was justly proud of his orchard, so productive that it maintained itself.

Deep sadness came to Father Junípero on January 1, 1782. He was called upon to administer the last rites to his old Majorcan friend, Father Juan Crespi. Governor Roméu was also soon buried at the Mission.

Serra's own time was not far distant, this he knew. Many years he had triumphed over his infirmities. Nine times he had planted the Cross in the California wilderness. Consumed by desire to redeem souls, he tried to ignore menacing death. Even in the stormy January of 1784, he walked from San Diego on his tour of confirmations. With unusual fervor he celebrated the Lenten season at San Carlos.

Later he went north to Santa Clara. At this Mission he made a retreat and made his confession to Father Francisco Palóu, forty-five years his confessor. The two friends shed tears because they could not take leave of the world together.

Palóu returned to San Francisco. From Monterey again Serra sent for his friend. Palóu found him weak, but in spite of heaviness in the chest Serra insisted upon taking his place in the choir and singing with the neophytes. He made the Stations of the Cross and even cut cloth for garments for Indian converts.

For the last time he went out to gaze upon the blossoming valley of Carmelo. On August 26, he admitted that he had passed a bad night. He made another general confession, took a cup of broth, and lay down, saying that he wished no one to remain with him. Father Palóu next found him holding his breviary. Serra asked for the last rites.

Until morning he slept, usually kneeling with his head against the rough-hewn rawhide bed. Sometimes he sat on the floor resting on the breast of one of the Indians gathered in the cell of "Padre Santo."

Father Palóu asked if he wished absolution. "Yes," he answered.

That night he did not sleep, but there was less suffocation. He spent the day seated in his little rough chair leaning against the bed.

Comandante José Canizares and some officers from a frigate in the harbor came to see him. Serra rose, gave each an embrace, paid them ceremonial compliments, told them he was glad they had come to place a little earth upon his body. Accompanied by officers and followed by Indians, he entered the church, where he prayed.

When Serra returned to his cell, he asked the Presidio carpenter to make his coffin "just as you did for Padre Juan Crespi." He took a little soup but did not lie down. He asked Palóu to sprinkle the room with holy water. "I have come under the shadow of a great fear." Palóu read prayers to him, and Serra said, "Thanks be to God. He has quite taken away my fear." Serra began to pray. Palóu gave him more broth. "Let us go to rest," said the founder of the California Missions.

Father Junípero took off his mantle. He wished to die unsandaled wearing only his habit and hood. He lay on his bed. He had a crucifix a foot long that had always been with him since he left Majorca. Now it rested on his breast as it had when he stretched out on the ground with a blanket and a pillow on a missionary journey. He was setting out on his last journey. He said he wished to sleep.

When Father Palóu returned, Father Junípero Serra was still asleep —at the age of seventy years, nine months, and four days. This was August 28, 1784. With passionate ardor for fifty-three years, eleven months, and thirteen days he had pursued perfection and lived a life of heroic luster.

With double tolling the bells tolled at Monterey and San Carlos. It was necessary to close the doors to place "Padre Bendito" in the coffin. Their arms filled with field flowers and roses from the valley, sorrowing neophytes came to see him in his coffin lighted with six candles. They touched his rosary, his face, his hands, crying out in lamentation, "Holy Father! Blessed Father!"

At night Father Junípero was carried into the church. His only possessions were hardships, pain, and rags. His followers fought for the rags as if they were treasures. People cut pieces from his habit and battled for locks of his hair. The Comandante at the Presidio begged for his hempen sandals. Palóu kept his breviary. He was obliged to cut into pieces the undertunic worn by Serra, so eager were his friends for some trifle that had belonged to him. This garment, two handkerchiefs, and his underclothing were divided for scapulars. In years to come many believed that they had been healed by touching these garments of Serra.

On the day after his death Serra's coffin was borne on the shoulders of officers of the frigate in a procession of officers, soldiers, sailors, citizens, Indians, and candle-bearers which circled the Plaza. When they entered the church, tears, sobs, and wails of those present almost drowned the voices of the singers and of the celebrant, Father Francisco Palóu. Serra was placed on the gospel side of the church at Mission San Carlos, now called Carmel. His neighbor in death was Father Juan Crespi, who had remained with him at San Diego when it seemed that the expedition for the conversion of California Indians had failed.

Father Fermin Francisco de Lasuén of Mission San Diego succeeded him in 1785 as President of the Missions. "Padre Fermin" was a cultured friar, with a fervor for founding Missions as passionate as that of Serra. He catalogued books in the San Carlos library. He erected Stations of the Cross on the trail over the hill through the pine forest from the Presidio Chapel to the Mission; twelve Stations as now are used.

Under Lasuén's administration at the close of 1786 there lived in the Monterey district 2,014 Indians, almost as many as there were at Mission San Diego, which led with 2,654. San Francisco had a neophyte population of 1,110.

Foreigners were forbidden California ports, but the province had its first foreign visitor in September, 1786. This was M. Jean François Galoup de La Perouse, a Frenchman, with an open letter from the ministers of Spain. He brought from Chile the first white potatoes.

Other early foreigners to arrive were John Ingraham, the American, in 1791 on the Spanish corvette *Atrevida*; Captain George Vancouver, the Englishman, on the *Discovery* in 1792; and in 1796 the first Englishwoman, with some escaped convicts from Botany Bay. She swept the streets of Monterey, but one year later was taken back with the other convicts to their prison colony.

The site of the original adobe church erected at Carmel is unknown. After the first flimsy structure was removed, a second church was built nine years after Serra's death. The third church greatly resembled one erected by him in the Sierra Gorda and was probably built around the second edifice. The star window, unique in California Missions, is said to have been his idea. He probably planned the columns, the arches, and the unique Moorish tower. The cornerstone was laid July 7, 1793, by Father President Lasuén.

Manuel Ruiz, a skilled master mason and stonecutter, directed the Indians so well that the sandstone walls quickly mounted. Sea shells were crushed to obtain lime. The stone entrance to the chapel has been much admired. The building was roofed with tile like those manufactured at Mission San Luis Obispo.

The church was dedicated in September, 1797. There were present President Lasuén, Fathers Mariano Payeras, Francisco Pujól, and Antonio Horra. Soon the bells were hung in the tower.

Many possessions of Mission Carmel are at the Royal Presidio Chapel at Monterey: the Stations of the Cross, the original teakwood sanctuary chairs, the sacred silver vessels, the processional Cross. The reliquary, attractively carved and painted, was made by Indians. The contents are listed on the back in Serra's handwriting.

Although on the remote Spanish frontier, Carmel did not escape war taxes. In 1793 Governor Arrillaga notified President Lasuén that contributions would be expected from San Carlos for war with impious France. Diplomatically Lasuén replied that "inasmuch as the Fathers were placed in poverty by their profession, and the Indian wards by their nature, His Majesty would desire only prayer." San Carlos' sole contribution to the war was prayer.

The next decade saw much activity at San Carlos. In 1794 Antonio Domingo Henriquez of Mexico taught cloth weaving. Tanning rooms were built. A wing 300 feet long was added in 1798 to the courtyard. Four years later Fathers Baltasár Carnicer and José Viñals procured a crown of gold and silver, three strings of pearls, and some fine necklaces for the statue of the Virgin.

Before the Mission began to decline, President Fermin de Lasuén followed Serra. On June 27, 1803, he was interred in the chapel erected by him. With his going, Mission-founding seemed to cease.

Distinguished activities have always centered about Carmel. In

1807 it was named as the place where the Fathers of the military district made their annual retreat. Governor Arrillaga appeared here August 10, 1809, to swear allegiance to the new King of Spain, Ferdinand VII.

When revolution began to rumble in Mexico and supplies ceased coming to San Carlos, Father Juan Amoros complained that barefoot neophytes must make shoes for troops.

Monterey, loyal to Spain, arranged a great *fiesta* in 1815 for Governor Solá's inauguration. Twenty Fathers, including those of Carmel, witnessed the military parade in the Plaza. A reception was given by the retiring Governor José Darío Argüello with everyone wearing evening clothes forty years out of fashion. California's most beautiful woman, Doña Magdalena Estudillo, leading twelve *señoritas* from different parts of the province, kissed the Governor's hand. A bear and bull-fight in the Plaza followed. After two days' festivities Solá and his suite set forth from Monterey through the pine forest to attend Mass at San Carlos.

With *fiesta* Solá's administration began. In the third year after he came, however, on November 20, 1818, there sailed into Monterey a black ship flying an unknown flag. It was Bouchard, the buccaneer, of Buenos Aires. Monterey's battery answered Bouchard's guns. The strange vessel appeared disabled and vanished.

Only forty soldiers protected the capital. Montereyans retreated to the Missions of San Juan Bautista and Soledad. The strange craft approached the port again and anchored near the shore. Another vessel following, anchored near by. Questions were trumpeted. A voice answered in English. Nobody understood. At dawn a small boat fired on the shore battery. For two hours conflict raged.

Bouchard sent an officer with a flag of truce demanding the surrender of California: "You may evade the spilling of blood by agreeing to my proposal.... May God keep you many years."

The next day Bouchard landed with fieldpieces and 285 Englishmen, Americans, Sandwich Islanders, Filipinos, Spaniards, Creoles, Portuguese, Malayans, and negroes. Firing went on, but Governor Solá remained at the Rancho del Rey five leagues distant, near present-day Salinas. A naked Sandwich Islander hauled down the colors of Spain. His countrymen rushed ahead with pikes. Monterey was Bouchard's.

The buccaneers ransacked the Presidio, killed cattle, cut down Governor Fages' famous orchard, destroyed the houses of the *Comandante* and the Governor. They fired the fort and departed wearing Spanish finery.

San Carlos suffered less than the capital, which was a sorry spectacle. After Bouchard sailed, Governor Solá ordered San Carlos Mission to contribute $3,500 to defray losses sustained by Monterey.

The Governor's own soldiers, 150 criminals and vagabonds from Mexico, killed Mission cattle. But he expected them to be clothed and lodged by San Carlos. Father Vicente Sarría turned over the Mission keys to the Governor. It was time for him to depart, he said.

In 1819 there were 21,196 neophytes in the twenty California Missions, but only 219 males and 178 females lived at San Carlos. Governor Solá was a rigid disciplinarian. When Ramona, a neophyte, became a mother out of marriage he ordered her head shaved with a razor. On a feast day she was compelled to be seated in the middle of the Plaza with her head uncovered for the public to observe her shame.

Governor Solá was succeeded on November 11, 1822, by Don Luis Argüello, son of Governor José Darío Argüello. California's first native Governor went from San Francisco to Monterey on a whaler to assume office.

The Governor levied heavily on each Mission for clothing, blankets, food, mules, and harness for troops. Already San Carlos' Indians were returning to their *rancherías*. As a tragic climax, Monterey's first legislative assembly proposed suppression of Mission San Carlos.

When the new Governor, José Echeandia, arrived in California, President Sarría and twenty other Franciscans declined to swear allegiance to the Mexican constitution. They were ordered to leave the country within six months. President Sarría was sixty-two years old. He offered to go to the Sandwich Islands. It was discovered, however, that the Missions would be without government if he went. Banishment of the Father President was not enforced.

At San Carlos conditions were desperate. Hungry soldiers refused to cultivate land to sustain themselves. They seized 2,285 bushels of grain harvested by neophytes. Indians fled to the mountains, leaving a population of 234. President Sarría exiled himself to lonely Soledad.

Alone Father Ramón Abella witnessed the death struggle of San Carlos. He tried to be of good cheer. The sleeve of his habit was always filled with apples for children. At Monterey, when he arrived to celebrate Mass, an army of small dusky friends greeted him.

When Governor Echeandia, on July 25, 1826, emancipated all the Indians in the Monterey, San Diego, and Santa Barbara districts that were qualified to become Mexican citizens, conditions at San Carlos worsened. Soon the Governor was obliged to give up his office. He remained in the country, however, and drove out his own successor, Manuel Victoria.

Then came an able Governor, José Figueroa, who brought to California the first printing press. At the beginning of 1834, under Figueroa's rule, William E. P. Hartnell and the Reverend Patrick Short opened California's first college—the Seminario de San José on the Alisal Ranch near Monterey. They taught reading, writing, grammar, bookkeeping, mathematics, philosophy, French, English, German, Spanish, and the Christian Doctrine. Education cost $200 annually. Some of the textbooks of this college are in the possession of the Hartnell descendants at Salinas.

After Father Abella was transferred to San Luis Obispo, Father Rafael Moreno, President of the Zacatecans, was given charge of San Carlos. Each year the Indians worked less; chastised, they did nothing.

In 1836 Edmund Roberts, special agent of the United States Government, found the church dilapidated, "in worse condition than a stable." One year later the French explorer, Abel Du Petit-Thouars, saw the Mission a depressing ruin, with a painting hanging upside down. Only the fruit trees were bearing. Father José del Maria Real was minister. When de Mofras came in 1841 San Carlos was without a priest.

In 1843 Governor José Manuel Micheltorena restored the Missions to the Franciscans. San Carlos, however, was so completely a ruin that when Inspector William E. P. Hartnell arrived, he did not even visit the Mission which in 1834 had been valued at $47,000. In 1845 only 40 Indians were in the vicinity of San Carlos, with 450 scattered through Monterey. There lived Father Real, who came to San Carlos to say Mass. The paintings still hung in the church, which was cared for by a man and his wife, the only residents.

Governor Pio Pico offered the Mission for sale. No one would buy. In 1852 the roof crashed. Settlers and townspeople helped themselves to adobe bricks, tile and timbers. It was said that Joaquin Murietta, the Mexican bandit, hid in the ruins before being shot down in 1853. A young priest at the Mission painted the only picture of him known to exist—a possession of the Bell family at Los Angeles.

Squatters took possession of the Mission, not to be ejected till October 19, 1859, when President James Buchanan signed the patent for the property, returning it to the Catholic Church with 6.25 acres of land.

In 1856 Father Cayetano Sorentini, a parish priest, made an effort to locate the body of Serra. He felt that he had found his grave, but he closed it. Vischer wrote in 1872 that wild clam and chowder parties were held in the Mission. Drunken roisterers made pistol targets of the images.

After the Mexican Government seized Mission Carmelo, the Royal Chapel at Monterey acquired new importance as the parish church. Politically this is the most distinguished building in California. Here worshiped Spanish and Mexican governors, diplomats, and great ladies. Since 1770 its sanctuary light has burned, but the building of today was not constructed until 1794. Its architecture is reminiscent of the Moorish-Gothic Alhambra. The façade is the most elaborate among California Missions, made of stone like that of Carmel. Apparently the same architect planned the two buildings. The first square story is pierced by a small front window. Arches for bells are in the second story. From a carved niche over the ornamental façade the Virgin of Guadalupe surveys Monterey.

Visitors to the Royal Chapel pass over the walk partly paved with vertebrae of whales, reminiscent of Monterey's former whaling industry. Between 1855 and 1858, with money donated by Governor

Romualdo Pacheco, Father Bautista Comellas added the transept to the building and erected an altar said to be a work of Indians.

During the 'thirties and 'forties the great world of Monterey was led by Doña Angustias de la Guerra, wife of Don Manuel Casarin Jimeno. She was one of the Santa Barbara de la Guerras, beautiful and assured. She set the tempo of life at Monterey. When the conquering Colonel John C. Frémont came, Doña Angustias was valiant for Mexico. Californians and invaders battled for an hour at the Natividad Rancho, not far from Monterey. Several Americans were killed. Lieutenant José Antonio Chavez, supposed natural son of Governor Figueroa, was wounded and taken in the night to Doña Angustias' residence. Would she protect him from Americans?

Doña Angustias quickly hid Chavez in her bed and covered him with blankets. She defied the *gringos:* "Search the house!" Chavez escaped.

When Commodore J. D. Sloat raised the Stars and Stripes over the Custom House at Monterey on July 7, 1846, Doña Angustias wept. She was about to become a mother. "My child," she vowed, "shall not be born under the Yankee flag." Doña Angustias spread the colors of Mexico over her bed. Strangely enough, after her husband died a few years later, Doña Angustias married an American, Dr. James L. Ord; and they lived happily.

Monterey, more than any other city in the state, has cherished its old garden and landmarks. The Custom House, scene of many festivities and also the place where Yankee sea captains displayed new wares from the year 1814, survives as a museum. Here is Colton Hall, where the first Constitutional Convention was held, September 1, 1849, a sandstone building erected by *Alcalde* Walter Colton with convict labor. In the first theater, now a museum, in 1848 was produced Monterey's first play—*Putnam; or the Lion Son of '76.* The American Consulate, erected by Thomas O. Larkin, is occupied occasionally by his granddaughter, Mrs. Harry W. Toulmin. Very imposing is the two-story adobe dwelling of Captain J. B. R. Cooper, once the prison of the runaway Doña Josefa Carrillo de Fitch. The Cooper residence is still owned by the family. Oldest of the private dwellings is the Boronda adobe, occupied since 1810 by descendants of Corporal

José Boronda. There is the Vasquez adobe, owned by Louis Hill, birthplace of the bandit Tiburcio Vasquez; the Osio adobe, erected in 1819; and the Munras dwelling, owned by *Excelentísima* María Antonia Field and her brother Stephen. Visitors never fail to make a pilgrimage to the Stevenson house, the old French Hotel, where Robert Louis Stevenson lived in 1879 to be near Fanny Osbourne, whom he had followed from France.

Modern Carmel began with Stevenson and Fanny Osbourne. Their friends Joe Strong, Julian Rix, and Jules Tavernier painted the Mission, whalers, and cypress. They were forerunners of the writers and painters attracted to Carmel by J. Frank Devendorf and Frank Powers, a San Francisco lawyer. Powers took up his residence on the hill among the pines and became an apostle of Carmel. George Sterling, the poet, came there to live in 1904. Jack London paid him long visits. After Upton Sinclair's Helicon Hall burned in New Jersey, he bought a place. His friend Sinclair Lewis followed, and here began his fiction career. Mary Austin wrote in her tree-study— "Aerie." Here Harry Leon Wilson wrote *Ruggles of Red Gap, Bunker Bean*, and *Merton of the Movies*. John Fleming Wilson, Jimmy Hopper, and Fred Bechdolt wrote stories. David Starr Jordan came summers from Stanford University. Robinson Jeffers arrived and with his own hands built a stone tower house and wrote great poetry. Lincoln Steffens and his wife, Ella Winter, lived at Carmel while Steffens produced his autobiography. At Monterey near by was Gouverneur Morris, and at Pebble Beach was Sam Blythe. They have been the magnet of the writing and painting group attracted to Carmel.

Before Carmel became a literary and art center, Father Angelo D. Casanova, rector of the Monterey parish, in 1870 woke California to the grandeur of Serra. Father Casanova obtained funds, removed three feet of debris from the abandoned Mission, and re-roofed the church. He found the graves of Serra and three other Franciscans. Excitedly the Father rode about Monterey on his sorrel horse telling the great news. He announced in a San Francisco newspaper that on July 3, 1882, an opportunity would be offered to view the remains of the missionaries.

It was before the day of automobiles. Tourists were few, but four hundred people from different parts of the state assembled at Carmel. Father Casanova, with his shaggy gray hair, stood at the head of Serra's grave. Holding the burial register, he read aloud the entries: Reverend F. Juan Crespi died January 1, 1782, 61 years old; Reverend F. Junípero Serra, D.D., President of all the Missions, died August 28, 1784, at the age of seventy-one; Reverend Julian López died July 15, 1797, aged thirty-five; Reverend F. Francisco Lasuén, second President of the Missions, died June 28, 1803.

A man descended into each grave and raised the well-preserved redwood coffin lid. Only the skeletons were visible, shrouded in vestments which had been spared by the years. The silk-fringed heavy stoles were like new. A handkerchief binding together Serra's ankles seemed intact, but when it touched air it disintegrated, revealing the bones of Serra's frail, tireless legs. The slab covering his grave had been broken into four pieces.

Father Casanova re-closed the graves and marked the resting place of the missionaries with a tablet which reads:

Here lies the remains
of the Administrator Rev. Father
Junípero Serra
Order of Saint Francis
Founder of the California Missions
and President
Buried in Peace
Died 28th day of August, A.D. 1784.
And his companions
Rev. Fathers
John Crespi
Julian Lopez
and
Francis Lasuén.
May they rest in peace.

Father Casanova made a nonsectarian appeal for funds, supported by Bishop Joseph Sadoc Alemany of San Francisco, Bishop Francis Mora of Monterey, Governor George Stoneman, Mayor Washington Bartlett of San Francisco, and ex-Governors Burnett, Irwin, Downey, and Perkins. Twenty thousand dollars was obtained, and the Mission re-roofed. In July, 1936, the shingle roof was replaced by one of tile. Father Casanova's enthusiasm was caught by Mrs. Leland Stanford, who in 1890 erected a monument to Serra at Monterey.

The late Monsignor Ramón Méstres was filled with a love of Carmel like that of Father Casanova, who is buried at San Carlos. In 1909 Father Méstres rescued from the bay the oak under which Mass had been said by the Carmelites of Vizcaíno's company, and later by Serra in 1770. Father Méstres installed it in the rear of the Royal Chapel at Monterey. In October, 1924, he organized a Serra festival during which the planting of the Portolá Cross was re-enacted on the mesa near Del Monte. On Sunday, October 12, 1924, a handsome sarcophagus made by J. J. Mora was unveiled at Carmel as a monument to Serra, but the founder still rests in his modest earth-house of 1784. A vigil lamp is kept perpetually burning on the marble slab covering his grave by Mrs. Curtis O'Sullivan of Carmel and San Francisco. An Indian placed a natural Cross of wood near the lamp.

Father Méstres determined to assemble the bells of Carmelo. Only one of the original bells hangs in the three-story tower. It bears the inscription: SAN JUAN DE LA CRUZ 1781. (SAINT JOHN OF THE CROSS 1781.) In 1931 one of Carmel's bells was stolen. In the tower is a bell recast by Weed and Kingwell of San Francisco in 1885. It probably consists of one made in the Plaza in 1804, with the addition of several cracked bells, including one that hung on the tree when Serra first said Mass. Father Méstres found two of the missing 1820 bells in Watsonville, where they had been for sixty-three years. One weighs nearly 1,000 pounds and hangs in the south side arch at Carmelo. In defective Latin it is inscribed: AVE MARIA BENESONAN-TIUS LAUDATE. DOMINUM INSINBALIS. RUELAS ME FECE 1807. These bells were made in 1807, but were not brought here till 1820. The smaller bell, weighing 675 pounds, has these words: AVE PURISIMA 1799 SAN ANTONIO. (HAIL MARY MOST PURE. SAINT ANTHONY. 1799.) Another bell, made in 1690, was given to Carmelo in recent times by Mr. George Barron. A third of Spanish make bears the date 1805. Two other bells came from Russia.

At San Carlos Museum is Serra's missal and a portion of his stole taken from his grave by Cristiano Machado, who opened the grave for Father Casanova. Vestments are difficult to identify, but the blue, cerise, and black were doubtless worn by the founder; they are of Jesuit cut, having been brought from Jesuit Missions.

In recent times Serra's cell has been realistically restored by Harry Downie, who for eight years has had charge of the Mission and has rebuilt the Indian cemetery. Serra's cell was eleven and a half feet by eleven and three-quarters, with the ceiling eight and three-quarters high. His own Latin Bible is in the room, and on the small table with a candle is a wooden skull described by Palóu as having been used by Serra for meditation. The first three rows of floor tile are the same as in the original cell. Other objects of furniture are a wooden pallet, a wire scourge from Mexico similar to Serra's, a picture of Our Lady in a tin frame, and a large rosary such as he wore.

In the church are the original crucifix, one of the windows of the first church, the statues of San Carlos, the Virgin, Our Lady of Carmelo, Saint Michael, San Buenaventura, and several living-room chairs. Part of the baptismal font was taken to Santa Cruz for a garden seat, and the bowl was buried near the church. The base was returned from Santa Cruz, fitted to the bowl, and they are now in the baptistry. An effort is being made to have the 1,000 books of the library now at the Royal Chapel returned to Carmel to be the nucleus of a library.

For fourteen years Serra labored at Carmel. Here he made more than 1,000 converts. His hand began the registers of baptisms, marriages, confirmations, and deaths—the oldest records in California. Here he trod clay and made adobe bricks. His footprints are indelibly impressed in the soil. His blessing is on the valley of Carmelo.

It is said that at midnight on the eve of San Carlos Day, a spectral friar appears in the chapel of the rose-gray adobe building at Carmel. Dark wraiths ascend from the *campo santo* to keep him a yearly tryst. Velvet-clad Dons and Doñas of distant days and a ghostly train of men of the sword are on their knees before the altar. Faint incense is in the air. *Sanctus, sanctus, sanctus,* is intoned. Bells ring out that once more the day of San Carlos has dawned. The pale friar lifts his hand in benediction and is gone.

III

San Antonio de Padua

NEARLY twenty years ago, on San Antonio's Day, Fremont Older, Evelyn Wells, and I motored to Mission San Antonio de Padua for the first time. We found this third Mission erected by Father Junípero Serra, a mellow ruin in Monterey County on the abandoned Camino Real at the base of purple Sierra of Santa Lucia, now called Mount Junípero Serra. Doña Perfecta Encinal was then alive, a skeleton in rags, with a skin like burned leather. She was said to have been one of the builders of the last Mission. She and other Indians had decorated the altar with wild flowers and greenery. During Mass in the Mission ruin a snake coiled close to the feet of the priest. This Mission I used as background for the novel *Savages and Saints*.

The Viceroy Marqués de Croix selected the name for Mission San Antonio de Padua. San Antonio, who lived in the thirteenth century, was a favorite devotion of Father Junípero Serra and of his own Franciscan Order. The saint was called the Wonder-worker. Father Junípero needed the strength of workers of wonders. No sooner had he set men to hewing timbers for Mission San Carlos Borromeo than he left Monterey with Fathers Miguel Piéras and Buenaventura Sitjar to found San Antonio de Padua. With them were a few Indian workmen, some Lower California neophytes, three sailors, and an escort of eight soldiers.

Father Junípero rejoiced as he went over the hot dusty trail carrying an immortal message to Indians thirty-five leagues distant. He did not mind that they passed near the savage Zanjones. Up the Salinas River and the Arroyo Seco they went, camping under trees several nights until they reached the Indians' *Texhaya*—Portolá had named it La Hoya de la Sierra de Santa Lucia. For the oaks draped with gray rags of moss, Serra christened the valley *Los Robles*. He called the river San Antonio and ordered goods unpacked.

"Let us suspend bells from the oaks!" said Serra, grasping the cord of the bell as he rang and shouted, "Hear, oh gentiles! Come! Oh, come to the Holy Church of God!"

Father Miguel Piéras protested, "Padre Junípero, why tire yourself? Pagans cannot hear. It is useless to ring the bell."

"Padre Miguel, let me give vent to my heart's desire," said Serra. "I would that these bells were heard all over the world."

The natives understood only a strange tongue variously called *Tatché*, *Telamé*, and *Sextapay;* but that mattered not to Serra. Soon a large Cross was raised and blessed. A brushwood shelter was erected for the altar table.

On July 14, 1771, Father Junípero Serra celebrated Mass in honor of San Antonio. During the service a nude Indian, matted hair hanging to his waist, approached. Father Junípero, noticing the native, said during his sermon, "We see what has not been observed in any other Mission. At the first Holy Mass a pagan is present."

Father Junípero approached the Indian, caressed him and gave him gifts. By signs and gestures he made the man understand that the Fathers had come to remain.

For a month Serra remained at San Antonio. He drew up the baptismal book, and on August 14, 1771, Father Piéras recorded the baptism of a boy four years old who was dying in the camp of his parents. Father Francisco Palóu wrote the first page of the marriage register. Father Piéras married the first Indian couple on May 1, 1773. On June 14, 1773, Alejo Duarte wedded an Indian girl, María Gertrudis. Father Palóu arranged the burial register. A white child, María de la Concepción Duarte, was the first to be buried, on August 28, 1774. She was also the first white child baptized.

Father Sitjar, the Superior, mastered the harsh guttural idiom at San Antonio so well that he wrote a manuscript of four hundred pages on the subject, now in the Smithsonian Institution. He taught the Indians to pray in Castilian and in their own tongue. Immediately a humble little church was built. Near by were houses for the Fathers and their servants and quarters for the soldiers.

Until the missionaries came, these Indians' writing consisted of lines drawn on the earth when they wished to remember something. Notched sticks recorded harvests or the number of people in their tribe. To them wealth was a blanket, a change of clothing, a few turquoise beads.

San Antonio Indians married and divorced lightly. Some had several wives. In the pagan state bodies were cremated on a pyre of firewood, while friends and family wailed. One of the guiding native precepts was, "What you do not want done to you, do not do to another."

The Indians revealed to the missionaries a large cave in the hills, with hieroglyphics on the walls. Their shrine was filled with strange figures of wood and stone. The natives gave these images to the missionaries and painted a large Cross over the hieroglyphics on the walls. This cave now belongs to William Randolph Hearst.

When the soldiers came, the Indians said the musket-bearers were immortal. They also called the missionary Fathers immortal.

During 1772 only 19 natives received baptism at San Antonio, but at the end of 1773 there were 163 baptized. One of these pious little Indian maidens, Loreta, prayed:

San Antonio Bendito!
Tres cosas te pido:
Salvación y dinero,
Y un buen marido.

Saint Anthony, thou blest!
Just three things I request:
Salvation, money too,
And a husband ever true.

There was a legend in this valley that long before, Fathers with crucifixes dangling from their cord-encircled waists had come, not on foot but flying. These winged Fathers also taught the faith of the Cross. It is believed that the natives heard of Christianity from the Carmelite Fathers who landed at Monterey with Vizcaíno in 1602. Notwithstanding the patron saint, San Antonio's first harvest failed. Two bushels of grain planted in 1773 brought no result. The next year two bushels produced thirty. Then the river went dry. There was no drinking water. Discouraged, the Fathers planted nothing for three years.

The Mission was moved about a league and a half up the same *cañada* in which the first establishment was founded to the Arroyo San Miguel, the permanent Mission site. In the driest season there was running water.

A church was erected with a building for the Fathers, quarters for the guard, and adobe workrooms. The missionaries encouraged mixed marriages; soldiers married Indian women, and houses were erected for the couples.

Building was soon paralyzed by *Comandante* Pedro Fages. He arrived with Father Junípero in August, 1772, and displaced soldiers and sailors with men who refused to work.

At the new Mission site the fertile soil was easily irrigated, but first crops were killed by frost and snow. Acorns fed livestock brought to San Antonio in 1773: 38 cattle, 11 mules, 30 pigs, and 9 horses. In those days the Mission depended largely on food supplied by Indians: pine nuts, acorns, rabbits, and squirrels. The neophytes even journeyed to the coast, a day and a half from the Mission, to catch fish.

Buildings were made of oak, pine, redwood, and limestone. From Monterey were brought carpenters' and masons' tools, field implements, kitchen utensils, as well as altar bells, vestments, and sacred vessels. Scholarly Father Sitjar assembled a good library. The missionaries indulged in what they thought a great extravagance—a large painting of San Antonio de Padua.

Angered by the Fathers' success in converting natives, pagans fell upon Mission San Antonio in 1775 and shot an Indian about to be baptized. "San Antonio! San Antonio!" moaned the wounded man. In spite of several arrows in his body he recovered. Such incidents increased the zeal of converts and stirred the Fathers to greater activity.

The church had adobe walls and was roofed with beams covered with mud. Rooms were added in 1776, lengthening the building thirty feet. Tiles were put on the roof. Quarters for soldiers were built. The little street with adobe dwellings on either side was completed. Enough supplies were raised to sell a surplus. The Fathers fattened shoats on pine nuts and acorns. When Anza came with his soldiers in 1776 meat was given to the soldiers and muleteers.

Father Piéras marshaled workmen and dug irrigation ditches. Storerooms and Indian quarters were enlarged. In 1781 San Antonio had 1,086 neophytes, the largest Mission community in California. With the exception of Santa Clara, it had the finest church.

During a visit in December, 1778, Father Serra arranged the register of confirmations, wrote the title page, and confirmed 332 neophytes. Three years later he returned to confirm 166. In the following year 26 were added. On his final visit in December, 1783, 726 Indians, besides a few whites and half-whites, had been confirmed.

At San Antonio in 1790 a large building divided into rooms for Indian families was erected with a tile roof.

In December, 1801, Father Francisco Pujól of San Carlos Mission received information that San Miguel Indians had attempted to poison his own colleague, Father Marcelino Cipres, while a guest of Fathers Juan Martín and Baltasár Carnicer at San Miguel. Father Pujól hastened to aid. All recovered, but he himself fell victim to the poisoners. He was brought back to San Antonio, where he died on March 15, 1801. Notwithstanding the Father's death, San Antonio saw added authority given to Indians. They elected *Alcaldes*.

In the early part of the nineteenth century Mission San Antonio was fortunate in obtaining two remarkable men, Father Juan Bautista Sancho and Father Pedro Cabot. They had come from Spain together, and for a quarter of a century they labored here. Father Cabot's manner and deportment recalled the courts of Europe. Father Sancho worked in shops and fields with the neophytes. He taught the Indians catechism in their own tongue. Often he forgot to eat, stopping work only in storms. When Father Cabot protested, he answered, "If I eat, I must work." Father Sancho's last years were spent in high fever and pain, but his activity never diminished.

These dynamic missionaries erected a water mill, a horsepower mill, and a large tannery with four tanks. Granaries nearly two hundred feet long, made of adobe and roofed with tile, were built. A guest house was added. Houses for Indians were erected. A cemetery was laid out away from the church and walled in like the garden.

Neophytes numbered 1,296 in 1805, and then population decreased. From the founding of the Mission until 1810 3,555 Indians were baptized.

At this time was undertaken San Antonio's most notable construction, a new church. In two years it was nearly completed. The edifice was blessed in 1813. Material of the old church was used for a dwelling for Fathers Sancho and Cabot.

Deaths among the Indians were almost as frequent as baptisms. Soldiers brought *mal Galico* to ravage the natives. Fathers Sancho and Cabot wrote in 1814 in the baptismal book that during the last two years they had not baptized a single pagan.

The nearest Indians, Tulareños, were thirty leagues distant; they had a distinct language and made beautiful baskets. Occasionally they brought their work to San Antonio and asked that a Mission be founded in their country.

San Antonio's most important product was flour, known throughout California. Flour, corn, and pigs were exchanged with Monterey ships for iron, from which tools were forged. A Lima ship supplied pickaxes, plowpoints and plowshares. Vestments and nine brass chandeliers were acquired.

San Antonio's harvests were unfailing, and 6,045 bushels of grain were garnered in 1821, necessitating new granaries. Weaving rooms, carpenter and shoe shops, and stables were added on two sides of the patio, almost completing the quadrangle.

The King of Spain was no longer king in California. Mexico, now independent, determined to discontinue the Missions. For the first time neophytes voted for a representative in the Mexican Congress. Indian *Alcalde* Saba Panilla met with *Regidores* Sinforiano Fernández and Damian Sembrano at Mission San Antonio and selected as elector José Aruz for Missions San Carlos, San Juan Bautista, Soledad, San Miguel, and San Luis Obispo. They signed their names with a cross. Aruz voted for Governor Pablo de Solá as delegate to the Mexican Congress.

At other Missions in this period life was stationary, but as long as Father Sancho lived, San Antonio, although neglected by Mexico, was well kept. It had decently clad Indians. Horses and sheep multiplied at the Mission Ranchos San Carpoforo, San Bartolomé, El Tule, San Lúcas, San Benito, San Bernabé, San Miguelito, Los Ojitos, San Timotéo, and San Lorenzo. A new silver censer and two paintings of Saints Rosa of Lima and Rosa of Viterbo were obtained.

Then Father Sancho succumbed to an infirmity from which he had suffered many years. His colleague, Father Pedro Cabot, interred him in the Mission on February 11, 1830. During the next thirteen years only 136 Indians were baptized, but between 1771 and 1832 the number totaled 4,419.

Like Father Sancho, Father Cabot declined to support the constitution of Mexico, but as late as 1833 he contributed a hundred bushels of grain to the Monterey Presidio. He was displaced by Father Jesus Maria de Mercado, one of the native Franciscan friars brought by Governor Figueroa to California. Father Cabot retired to Mission San Fernando. Records of crops at San Antonio ceased.

Father Mercado lived in one room without kitchen or dining room. The rest of the building was occupied by Administrator Manuel Crespo and his friends. The priest's salary was $1,000 from revenues of the ex-Mission. The Father often traveled sixty miles to visit the sick and dying. He asked permission to use a small cart for driving. *Alcaldes* and their women roistered in the Mission. Neophytes became vagabonds existing on roots and seeds. Hunger caused three deaths to one birth. Don Florencio Serrano opened a school in the Mission, but closed it for lack of pupils.

When Inspector William E. P. Hartnell arrived early in August, 1839, he found San Antonio's accounts and buildings equally confused. Church expenses were unpaid. Neophytes stole and killed, then fled. The Administrator lashed the Indians and placed them in stocks for petty offenses. There was no wool for weaving, nor were there any weavers. Father José Gutiérrez, last of the Franciscans, was paralyzed. He wrote to the bishop from "my solitude and exile in this desert of San Antonio."

Four years later there were only four head of cattle at the Mission. Fifteen converts lived in roofless dwellings, with 70 Indians near by. The property decreased in value from $90,000 to $8,000. A garden survived with 65 fruit trees, and the vineyard had 4,000 vines.

Much of San Antonio's story in the early 'forties is blank. José Pico, Manuel Soberanes, and Manuel Manso were in charge. In 1845 Governor Pio Pico ordered the Mission sold. Although there were still buildings with a library of two hundred volumes, and five bells, a sawmill, fruit trees, and a vineyard, no one would buy.

When the United States took possession of California in 1846, Governor R. B. Mason tried to protect the Mission. In 1849 he wrote Don Mariano Soberanes to restore the roof tile taken by him. Soberanes replied that his own ranch house had been burned by order of Lieutenant-Colonel John C. Frémont, and permission had been given him to take tile from roofs of uninhabited dwellings to compensate him for the loss. Soberanes was forbidden to remove more tile.

On October 19, 1858, the United States Land Commission gave the Catholic Church title to the San Antonio Mission property, 33.19 acres. On May 31, 1862, the patent was signed by President Lincoln.

Before San Antonio was abandoned, it was given temporary life by its last priest, Father Doroteo Ambrís, a Mexican Indian reared and educated by the Fathers. American pioneers recall him with affection. Father Ambrís gathered about him thirty-five Indian families and they raised good crops and had an attractive garden of marguerites, four-o'clocks, pinks, poppies, and hollyhocks. Each evening at six o'clock three of the five bells were rung as one. Two neophyte sacristans, Fruto and Jacinto, made up the choir, daily sweeping the corridors with tarweed brooms. Once Father Ambrís gave Fruto a pair of shoes, but the Indian slung them over his shoulder and continued going barefoot. When the priest asked why he did not put on the shoes, Fruto replied, "Padre, my foot got a crack.

A cricket live there. It sing. If I put on my shoe, him stop singing."

After thirty years at San Antonio, Father Ambrís died at the adobe house of Sostenes García, a descendant of Don José Francisco Ortega, discoverer of San Francisco Bay. His last words, on February 5, 1882, were, "The soul to God, the body to the adobe (earth)."

Father Ambrís was placed in the sanctuary near Father Francisco Pujól, Father Buenaventura Sitjar, and Father Bautista Sancho.

Native herbs were studied by Father Ambrís, and he left many notes concerning them with Father Alexander Garriga of San Luis Obispo:

Parsley root relieves bladder trouble. California fuchsia, *balsamillo*, is good for spleen or syphilis. Cascara as a purgative helps rheumatism and poison oak. Maiden hair, *culantrillo*, stops hemorrhages. Leaves of rosemary boiled in red wine till reduced two-thirds prevent consumption. Rosemary also helps epilepsy. It also soothes weak eyes as does the water of Castilian rose blossoms. Even poison oak has virtues. It will cure a felon. Gravel is allayed by drinking tea of tassels of ears of corn. Fits of insanity may be relieved by a poultice of laurel leaves, nutmeg, cinnamon, and olive oil boiled together and placed on the head until abundant perspiration starts. For insomnia drink a cup of boiled milk with sage or salvia before going to bed. Crushed soap root applied to the breast relieves sunstroke. Chewing squash seeds is good for tapeworm. If the head comes up, smoke tobacco. For tetanus or cleaning wounds *yerba de pasmo* is used. Swallow weed, *yerba de la golondrina*, relieves coughs, dropsy, jaundice and snake bite.

After the death of Father Ambrís, services were held annually on San Antonio's Day. A few faithful *rancheros* and Indian families came to visit the Mission with its ragged garden and orchard. The Indians walked twenty-five or thirty miles to say their prayers and to decorate the ruin with flowers and green branches.

During these desolate years timbers vanished from the Mission and roof tile disappeared. This did not cease until Father Alexander Garriga was given charge of Mission San Antonio and Soledad. On June 23, 1900, he celebrated the feast of San Antonio in the vestibule of the roofless church which furnished standing room for a few settlers and Indians.

In 1903 the California Historic Landmarks League began holding outings at San Antonio on the day of the patron saint. For the first time since the departure of the last Franciscan in 1844, the Mission saw the return of the Order of the founders. Father Zephyrin Engelhardt, O.F.M., the historian, celebrated Mass. Father Garriga preached in Spanish. Preservation and restoration of Mission San Antonio began. The Native Sons supplied $1,400 for the fund. Tons of debris were removed from the interior of the chapel. Breaches in the side wall were filled in. Between five and six thousand bricks were used, many weighing fifty pounds. In some places the walls were six feet thick. The west wall was completed, the east wall was well under way, and thirty feet of roof-line had been erected in the winter of 1904, when five vaulted arches over the chapel vestibule collapsed because they were not protected by a roof. A break also occurred in the west wall, doing considerable damage.

Daughters of California Pioneers, Monterey Sons of the Golden West, and the California Historic Landmarks League, under the able leadership of Congressman Joseph R. Knowland, raised nearly $1,400. The southwest abutment of the arch over the vestibule was taken down to the foundation and then rebuilt. The front gable was restored. A temporary shingle roof forty feet long was built abutting upon the southwest side of the chapel and extending to the front to protect the reconstructed adobe work.

Great damage was wrought by the earthquake of April, 1906, but the new patched wall remained intact. For two years restoration went on. Ten thousand of the old adobe bricks were used in rebuilding. Almost $4,000 was spent on the Mission.

San Antonio's oldest woman, Doña Perfecta Encinal, aided in the rebuilding. This descendant of the neophytes brought her sons, daughters, and grandchildren to labor at the Mission. Soon she joined the vanished tribe of her forefathers. At the *fiesta* on San Antonio's Day in 1937 Dan and Mary Mora were the only surviving Indians.

Gertrude Atherton, the novelist, half a century ago came as a bride to the Milpitas Rancho surrounding Mission San Antonio, but the Atherton adobe was destroyed by a fire. The Milpitas property is now a part of William Randolph Hearst's San Simeon Ranch. Near the Mission, Mr. Hearst has built an imposing ranch house in the style of early California.

Mission San Antonio de Padua singularly retains its original beauty. The façade, built in advance of the front end of the church and made of burned brick, is almost as perfect as when erected. The recessed window arches and the curious doorway, square on one side and rounded on the other, are pleasing. Although it has been eroded by weather, part of the brick colonnade still stands; but if not protected it will crumble—the fate of the colonnade in the Fathers' garden.

In the patio are some anise plants of the missionaries' herbal garden. This same innocent anise mixed with *aguardiente* became a fiery drink, *anisado,* dangerous to the peace of the community when there were many Indians. At the entrance to the church on the right are plumed tamarisks and two ancient olive trees transplanted by Father Ambrís from the orchard. A few feet from the church survive six large olive trees, all that remain. Against the colonnade on the left of the church and in the rear of the building, flame four pomegranate trees. Two unpruned century-old pear trees stand in the patio ruins, still bearing fruit.

Over the altar are statues of San Antonio, Saint Francis, and Saint Joseph. There are also a figure of the Virgin and a large mutilated image of Saint Michael. Father Tiburcio Wand at Mission San Miguel has charge of San Antonio's copper baptismal font. He has also beautiful vestments, a statue of San Buenaventura, and one of San Antonio. In recent time he has found two ship's heads brought by sailors in gratitude to San Antonio and placed in front of the Mission. Eventually all these will be returned to their original home. Several hundred of San Antonio's roof tiles lent by the Mission to the San Francisco Midwinter Fair in 1894 now cover the Southern Pacific station at Burlingame, California. For these the railway company has offered to give $700 toward restoring the Mission.

Once San Antonio had eight bells. Now it has none. At one time a large bell hung in the main bell-cote in the picturesque gable over the front entrance, and one in each of the square bell-cotes on either side. Three smaller bells were suspended from a beam over the church. Later one of the three bells was removed to a schoolhouse at Jolon, where it summoned the children to classes and called worshipers to the community church. That bell disappeared, as did the second. For years the third bell was in the church at Watsonville, but it melted in a fire in 1927.

For more than twenty years Mission San Antonio has had one faithful devotee, Brother Hans, in the brown habit of the Third Order of Saint Francis. He usually works for his board on the Mission ranches. If he is paid, the money is given to the Mission. He may be thirty miles distant from San Antonio, but he always arrives to decorate the altar. He serves at Mass and is major-domo at *fiestas*. Brother Hans is certain that the Mission will find its Wonder-worker.

Father Tiburcio Wand, who has spent his youth at remote Missions, is in charge of both San Antonio and San Miguel, where he resides. At San Antonio he has built an adobe caretaker's house and installed a man to look after the Mission. Twice a month Father Wand appears to say Mass. He has vigor, enthusiasm, and the faith of Father Junípero Serra. He says San Antonio must be restored. Perhaps the Mission has found its Wonder-worker.

IV

San Gabriel, Arcángel

And every note of every bell
Sang "Gabriel!" Rang "Gabriel!"

So WROTE Charles Warren Stoddard of this stately building, celebrated in verse and story, more often, perhaps, than any Mission in California.

San Gabriel began when Portolá and his company in 1769 camped not far from La Brea pits on Wilshire Boulevard of modern Los Angeles. Near by were the Indian village Yang Na and the Ranchería Yabit.

Father Junípero Serra petitioned Viceroy Carlos Francisco de Croix to establish a Mission in California under patronage of Arcángel San Gabriel. The request was granted. Captain Pedro Fages, who had been one of the Portolá expedition, and Father Junípero decided that the site should be near the *Río de Nombre de Jesus de los Temblores* (River of Earthquakes), also known as *Río de Santa Ana*. Fathers Angel Somera and Pedro Cambón were selected to found San Gabriel. Escorted by fourteen soldiers and four muleteers, the missionaries set forth from San Diego, August 6, 1770.

The pack train reached the River of Earthquakes, today called the San Gabriel. The Fathers were pleased with the arroyo lined with blackberries, roses, grapevines, willows, and cottonwoods. The missionaries planned to graft cuttings brought from Mexico onto the wild grape stock. Less than a league distant was an oak forest. A well-wooded and well-watered site was quickly selected. The Fathers prepared the foundation.

Suddenly crashed through the wilderness two Indian chieftains leading howling armed savages. Quickly the missionaries unfurled a canvas picture of the Virgin. Her ethereal loveliness startled the Indians. Necklaces, bows, and arrows were laid at her feet. Then they sped to neighboring *rancherías* and brought back friends. To their surprise the offerings were untouched by the fair dazzling stranger.

When Spaniards struck fire from flint, again the natives were awed. Gods, they called the strangers. The natives helped hang bells on a tree, the first bells of San Gabriel. They gave their strength toward erecting the high Cross.

On September 8, 1771, the day of the Nativity, Mass was said in a brushwood shelter on the first site of Mission San Gabriel, Arcángel. The following day Fathers, soldiers, and muleteers built an arbor of boughs and *tules* to serve as a temporary church. Joyously the pagans worked for the beautiful Lady. They helped construct dwellings for the Fathers and the guards, and corrals for cattle and horses. A stockade was erected.

These Indians were of the Beñeme Ranchería and of the Jeniguechi tribe. The small round-faced, flat-nosed women wore in their ears abalone rings from which hung hawk feathers. Around their necks were chains of black stones, beads of whale teeth, and boas of wild flowers. In winter they wore cloaks of deerskin, otter and rabbit skins. The Fathers gave them dresses. To the men the missionaries offered tobacco, clothing, and food. The Indians liked the tobacco, but they buried the food. Corn sprouted—white witchcraft!

Two months after foundation day a boy was baptized, November 27, 1771. He was from the Ranchería Guivichi. Fernando Salvador de los Santos he was christened.

The Spaniards began shooting birds; and at last the Indians knew they were not gods. The natives soon found that white men were most mortal: they bound a chieftain, lassoed his wife, and dragged her into the forest. The husband pursued. An arrow sped. A soldier shot the husband. The Indians fled. Triumphant soldiers set the chieftain's head upon a pole.

Sixteen guards were now necessary at San Gabriel. Fathers Somera and Cambón retired to Mexico. Fathers Antonio Paterna and Antonio

Cruzado arrived. The Indians returned to the god of their fathers, Qua-o-ar, who was so sacred that his name was seldom uttered. Instead they called on *Y-yo-ha-riv-gnina*—"that which gives life."

Comandante Fages took the offending soldiers to Monterey; but for some time Indians spoke of Spaniards as being "of a nasty white color with blue eyes." Indian women violated by soldiers had to undergo long purification. A child showing white blood was strangled.

Gradually, however, natives became friendly. There was rejoicing when the murdered chieftain's widow offered her child for baptism. Other women brought infants to be blessed. But when San Carlos had 250 converts, San Gabriel had only 96.

Four tribes speaking four different idioms furnished neophytes: Kokomcar, Quiguit-amcar, Carbonanga, and Sibamga. Their poets recited their legends. They thought they came from the north. Apparently of delicate constitution, they lingered in the south. The moon was their calendar. Summer was when the maguey plant matured, or when frogs began to croak. Fall was when they harvested sweet *guaatta*. Winter was marked by acorn-gathering. Mourners for the dead cut off their hair, threw beads into the air, placed seeds with the body, fasted several days moaning. They had a great feast with dances. The body was burned, and the dead forgotten. These Indians believed in good and evil spirits and in returning good for evil. Heaven was a country where acorns abounded. They had a legend of making a flying machine out of reeds and soaring to the sky to become stars.

A chieftain had one or two wives. When he wished to marry, he gave twenty-five cents in shell bead money to each of the wife's relations. Soon they brought the bridegroom baskets of *chia* and distributed them. Decked out in strings of beads and fantastically painted, the bride was carried by the strongest of her tribe to her husband, her family dancing around throwing food and seeds at her feet. The relations emptied upon the bride and groom baskets of seeds, like the custom of rice-throwing. If the husband abused his wife, the relations gave back the money paid and found her another husband—"part of my body."

Many of the men were tattooed, a mark of land-owning. The medicine man was wizard, seer, healer, rain maker, prophet, interpreter of the Great Spirit. His great accomplishment was expertness in collecting poison for arrows.

At first natives lost caste with their tribesmen by baptism— *soyna*, or bathing, they called it. More and more, however, returned to the Mission and laid bows and arrows at the feet of the Fathers.

A year passed before Father Junípero Serra was able to visit San Gabriel, but he came September 11, 1772, with Fages on his way to San Diego. Serra drew up the title pages of books of baptisms, marriages, and deaths. Even a few converts delighted him. Father Junípero gave gifts to gentile parents. "Precious creatures," he called the children.

Soldiers again impeded San Gabriel's progress. Serra reported to the Viceroy that "a soldier committed lewd acts with a pagan.... Not even boys were safe from soldiers."

Later famed for its harvests, San Gabriel's first wheat was destroyed by floods. The garden was also swept away, but in the creek grew wild celery, onions, plants similar to lettuce, and parsnips. Fishing was impossible because war was being waged among *rancherías* between the Mission and the sea. Occasionally the Indians killed and ate a bear, but more often deer, coyotes, rabbits, squirrels, gophers, skunks, raccoons, birds, even snakes—rattlesnakes excepted. Roasted grasshoppers were a delicacy.

Father Francisco Palóu, Acting President of the California Missions during Serra's absence in Mexico, brought experienced men in 1773 to teach Indians to plant wheat, corn, and beans. Soon Mission San Gabriel had the first vegetable garden in the vicinity of today's Los Angeles.

For two years the Fathers lived in shelters of poles with thatched roofs. Serra appealed to the Viceroy, who sent tools, implements, and beads and clothing for the Indians. A large painting of San Gabriel was placed in the log chapel. Thirty-eight head of cattle, 30 sheep, 17 mules, 12 goats, 6 horses were the beginning of the Mission herds. Twenty pigs fattened on acorns. Soldiers declined to work. Father Paterna plowed. Both he and Father Cruzado retired.

Missionaries were wearing ragged vestments, living on three corn cakes a day, and tightening their girdles when Captain Juan Bautista Anza with Father Francisco Garcés and thirty-four men arrived from Sonora on March 22, 1774, to demonstrate the feasibility of a direct route to Monterey. Garcés left Anza at San Gabriel and returned to the Colorado River, the first man to cross Tejon Pass. He was later killed in a Yuma massacre.

Serra came in December, 1776, to San Gabriel and baptized Indians while on his way to found Mission San Juan Capistrano. He returned on November 4, 1778, and confirmed 362 neophytes.

About 1776 probably, the Fathers decided to move San Gabriel Mission five miles north to higher ground near the Ranchería Sibagna. After the American occupation, for years *Misión Vieja* was a neglected ruin. Later, Japanese used the fields for growing flowers, and these gave way to oil derricks. On July 31, 1921, a tablet was placed on the dwelling at the corner of San Gabriel Boulevard and Lincoln Street, Pico, California, by Walter P. Temple, owner of the land, commemorating the first San Gabriel.

At the new establishment the Fathers built a three-room house 150 feet long and 18 wide. One room was for the missionaries, another for tools, the third for seeds. The chapel was 30 feet long by 18 wide, roofed with *tules*.

On the far side of the *acequia* lived Indians in *tule* huts, resentful of proselyting. They had their own religion, their legends of a flood and heaven.

Mission San Gabriel acquired neighbors, the second civic settlement in California, the Pueblo de la Reina de los Angeles. Probably its birthday was September 4, 1781. The Viceroy and the Governor were so pleased with the northern Pueblo San José, now four years old, that the second pueblo was inevitable. Los Angeles was so christened because Portolá and his men passed this way on the feast day of *Nuestra Señora de los Angeles;* they named the large stream *Rio de los Angeles de Porciuncula* for Saint Francis Jubilee.

Solemnly the Fathers from Mission San Gabriel dedicated the Plaza of California's second pueblo. Governor Felipe de Neve made a speech. A procession carrying the standard of Spain and bearing the image of the Virgin encircled the square. Salvos of musketry were fired while all rejoiced.

This original Plaza was not that of today, which only touches its corner. The first Plaza began at the southeast corner of Marchessault and Upper Main or San Fernando Street, continuing along the east line of New High Street, and thence to the north line of Marchessault and back to the beginning.

Forty-six persons settled in the pueblo: Indians, negroes, with here and there a trace of Spanish blood. The government gave each colonist a house, a tract of land, and $116.50 annually for two years, and $60 for the next three, the amount to be paid in supplies. Settlers had four leagues of common land northwest of San Gabriel, and were to be free from taxation and tithes. Each colonist received a pair of oxen, a cow, a horse, a burro, sheep, goats, mules, mares. Tools were supplied, and soon were erected a town hall, twenty-nine dwellings, barracks, guardhouse, and granary.

There was a *mañana* spirit in Los Angeles, but the colonists harvested 4,500 bushels of grain, excelling all Missions except San Gabriel, which not only supported its own neophytes and fed troops, but proudly sent $134 to aid the war Spain was waging against England in 1782.

Late in March of this year Father Junípero Serra arrived at Los Angeles on foot from Monterey. He was sixty-eight and so weak from fasting that he feared he would never reach the pueblo. Early next morning he set out on foot for San Gabriel. When he returned in 1783, he had already confirmed 866 neophytes at the Mission. He departed for Monterey looking ill, but he walked all the leagues north.

In this period San Gabriel had a modern woman, a neophyte, the only one of her sex in California Mission history to lead an insurrection. "Kill the *padres!*" she shouted to the Indians. Twenty conspirators were captured and given three years' imprisonment.

Governor Fages was summoned from Monterey; he sentenced the woman to perpetual exile. "Lazy, cowardly!" Fages called San Gabriel Indians. In 1792, however, they carded, spun, wove, even made spinning and warping frames. Antonio Domingo Henriquez and his Indian wife were their teachers.

About this time San Gabriel excelled all Missions in farm products—6,833 bushels of grain were harvested. There were 10,233 livestock on the ranges. Neophytes numbered 1,078.

San Gabriel grew in grandeur. In 1790 or 1791 the cornerstone was laid for a new stone and mortar edifice 108 feet long by 20 wide. The building was half finished in 1795. Four years later it was not completely roofed.

Although the San Gabriel Indians' native art consisted of figures of animals drawn on tree trunks, artists developed. In the museum are Stations of the Cross painted in 1798—crude, garish, imperfectly drawn, but unique in being the only pictures of their time done by California Indians.

In 1795 San Gabriel acquired two bells of heavy make. One, crown-topped, is dated 1795 and inscribed: AVE MARIA ME FECIT RUELAS SAN JUAN NEPOMUCENO. It is said that a young Mexican, while watching the casting in the Ruelas Foundry, threw a silver coin into the molten metal of the bell. He himself came as a Franciscan to San Gabriel. At the ringing of the Angelus he recognized the tone of the bell with his silver coin. Another bell of superior make lent by San Gabriel to the church of Our Lady of the Angels in Los Angeles is inscribed: ANO DE 1795 LA PURISIMA CONCEPOYON DE NS. (YEAR OF 1795. THE IMMACULATE CONCEPTION OF OUR LADY). San Gabriel's third oldest bell hangs in the *campanario* and is lettered: AVE MARIA PURISIMA. S. FRANCO. PAULA RUELAS ME FECIT. (HAIL MARY MOST PURE. SAINT FRANCIS. PAUL RUELAS MADE ME.) A staid New England bell reads: 1828. MEDWAY BOSTON. HOLBROOK.

San Gabriel's bell of poetry and romance, weighing nearly a ton, hangs in the lower right-hand corner of the *campanario*. For more than a century it has rung the Angelus. It is said that a *señorita* in Spain, on hearing that her soldier lover had died in Alta California, threw all her gold and silver ornaments into the cauldron where a bell was being recast for California. This bell bears the inscription: FECIT BENITUS A REGIBUS. ANO DE 1830. (MADE BY BENITO REGIS. YEAR OF 1830.)

San Gabriel's church building of today was begun in 1800. For nearly thirty years Fathers Antonio Cruzado and Miguel Sanchez had looked forward to having a glorious church of stone, mortar, and brick, but death took Father Sanchez on July 27, 1803, and Father Cruzado followed on October 11, 1804. In spite of earthquake damage to the church in 1804, the first Mass was said in the new building on February 21, 1805.

New life had come to the Mission: Father José Zalvidéa. This tall, commanding Spanish friar spoke the Indian idiom so well that he used it in preaching. He worked like an Indian mixing adobe clay for brick. Food, sweet and sour, was blended by him to annul pleasure of the palate. Father Estévan Tápis in 1803 had vainly tried to grow cotton, but all was possible to Father Zalvidéa. He brought water from a distance and laid out a flower garden before the Mission with a sundial in the center. He planted citrus, fruit, and olive orchards. From his Vina Madre of 2,000 vines came all other Mission vineyards. Father Zalvidéa was the father of California viticulture. San Gabriel vines were interspersed with flowering shrubs. Father Zalvidéa planted rose hedges, but most famous of all was his cactus hedge fencing hundreds of acres of cultivated land against wild horses. A portion of the cactus hedge twelve feet high exists at San Gabriel.

Everywhere on the wide acreage was felt Father Zalvidéa's force. In 1811 the largest wheat crop known at a Mission was harvested—18,710 bushels. A year later San Gabriel outdid itself and garnered 32,618 bushels of grain. The Mission establishment owned Ranchos Santa Anita, San Pasqual, Azusa, San Francisquito, Cucamonga, San Antonio, San Bernardino, San Gorgonio, Yucupa, Juropa, Guapa, Rincon, Chino, San José, Ybarras, Puente, Misión Vieja, Serranos, Rosa Castila, Coyotes, Sabonería, Las Bolsas, Alamitos, and Cerritos. Most important were Santa Anita and San Bernardino. All ranch animals were branded with the old Mission mark, the letter "T" for *temblores*, or earthquakes.

Building marched with agricultural activity in Father Zalvidéa's time. The large quadrangle was enclosed with dwellings for the Fathers, forty-seven houses for Indians, weaving rooms, carpenter shops, storerooms, granaries, and a tannery. Tile and pitch were used for roofing. As early as 1807 San Gabriel Mission was designated as the Retreat House of the district.

Once San Gabriel Church had a bell tower on its northeast corner; but at sunrise on December 8, 1812, it was destroyed by the great earthquake which overthrew the main altar, damaging the sacristy. No reproduction of the bell tower exists. San Gabriel acquired an august *campanario,* a solid wall pierced with arches corresponding in size with the bells to be hung in them.

Ten buttresses with pyramidal copings support San Gabriel's walls. In some of these buttresses are niches embellished with pilasters sustaining and completing the entablature. At the base of the niches is a projecting sill to give greater space for statues. The stairway to the choir gallery has served as a model for many California buildings and has often been painted by artists.

Father Zalvidéa in 1825 erected a water-power gristmill, the first in the vicinity, manning it with Indians who made coarse, unbolted flour of corn, wheat, and barley. Soap and tallow candles, as well as flour, were sold to vessels entering San Pedro harbor. Father Zalvidéa became so ambitious for his Mission that he purchased great quantities of iron for fencing. This transaction, without the approval of his Superior, caused him to be transferred to Mission San Juan Capistrano, where he died, it was said, half demented.

Los Angeles asked the government for a church for its eight hundred inhabitants, to replace the small chapel erected in 1784. Stately San Gabriel was twelve miles distant. Los Angeles heard the Mission bells, but it was inconvenient, especially at funerals, to go to San Gabriel; *pueblaños* had to travel in *carretas,* ride, or walk. They usually sang sacred songs on the journey. A funeral occupied two days.

The cornerstone of the new church, a branch, or *asistencia,* of San Gabriel, was laid by Father Luis Gíl y Taboada on August 13, 1814. Workers went on a strike, the first in California history. The master builder demanded six *reales,* seventy-five cents, for each day's labor, besides board and a barrel of wine every six months.

All Missions helped build the new church. La Purísima, San Luis

Obispo and Santa Inés each gave six mules and two hundred head of cattle. Church goods came from San Buenaventura. San Juan Capistrano and San Luis Rey supplied laborers. San Gabriel donated two barrels of white wine. San Fernando Rey, Santa Barbara, and San Gabriel added several barrels of brandy, later sold to the Presidio for $575.

An architect, José Antonio Ramírez, was found. Mechanics were supplied by San Luis Rey. Neophytes worked as master carpenters and masons at one *real*, twelve and a half cents, a day and board. The strike was broken. Work went on—slowly.

Eleven years after the chapel was begun it was formally dedicated, December 8, 1822, under the name of the Church of Nuestra Señora Reina de los Angeles. It was also known as Our Lady, Queen of the Angels, Church of the Angels, Church of Our Lady, Father Lievana's Church, the Adobe Church; but it is usually called the Plaza Church. From materials of the first building the present church was reconstructed in 1861. It is still the center of colorful life, the most interesting landmark in Los Angeles, aside from San Gabriel.

The new church received three bells from San Gabriel Mission. The first, made in 1795, was lent by Father Joaquin Nuez in 1821. It was used in dedication services and has served the church ever since. It is said that two other Holbrook bells were sold to the Plaza Church in 1827. Father Tomás Esténaga's price for the bells was "seventy head of fat cattle." In 1843 the bells were not paid for. Another sweet-toned *campana* of the Plaza Church was inscribed: G. H. HOLBROOK 1828. This is the bell that Captain Henry Fitch presented to the Plaza Church as a penance for eloping with *Señorita* Josefa Carrillo. For many years there was another bell in the storeroom back of the church. During the *fiesta* of 1931 it was returned to San Gabriel Mission.

On August 15, *fiesta* of Our Lady, patroness of the pueblo, there was always a procession around the Los Angeles Plaza where lived the Carrillos, Sepúlvedas, Olveras, Lugos, Avilas, and Picos, families from Mexico and Spain who had taken the place of the early settlers.

The earthquake of 1812 caused havoc at San Gabriel's Rancho

San Bernardino in the Valley of Guachama—Place of Plenty to Eat and Drink—near San Gorgonio Pass. Temperature of hot springs increased. Tremors continued. The gods were angry, said the Indians. Led by medicine men, the pagans destroyed buildings and killed many of the Christianized Indians and whites.

In 1819 the Guachamas requested the Fathers to re-build the Mission Chapel San Bernardino. Gladly the missionaries returned. Grain was sown. A vineyard and olive orchard were planted. Sheep and cattle roamed over the ranch.

In 1831 desert Indians destroyed grain and stole stock. This time the Fathers built on cobblestone foundations, a new adobe structure 225 feet long and 125 wide.

In October, 1834, famine brought the Paiutes over the Sierra. Perfecto, a Christian Indian chief, gathered the sacred vessels and fled toward San Gabriel. The Paiutes followed. Defeated at Cucamonga, they retreated over the Sierra, driving off stock.

In the following year San Gabriel neophytes set fire to the chapel and carried Father Esténaga to the mountains. His captors released him, fearing that as a powerful medicine man he would work them harm if slain.

Soon bricks were carried away from San Bernardino Chapel. The lumber was made into Los Angeles buildings. Mormons bought the ranch from Diego Sepúlveda in 1851 for $750. Their Bishop Nathan C. Tenney lived in the chapel, where his wife kept a school. From 1860 to 1867 the building, which was in time called an *asistencia,* was occupied by Dr. Benjamin Barton's family.

In recent years San Bernardino County Supervisors saved the chapel from obliteration by purchasing the land on which the ruins stood. Private persons financed restoration work. The square adobe building occupied by the caretaker is original. The restored *asistencia* is between Urbita Springs and Colton.

Like other Missions, San Gabriel was scourged by venereal disease brought by soldiers. Fathers José de Miguel and José Maria Zalvidéa established a hospital near the Mission and treated Indians. It was 600 feet long and roofed with tile. Despite disease and war, few Missions excelled San Gabriel in spiritual and material success. Between 1810 and 1820 more Indians were baptized here than at any other Mission except San Francisco and San José. Its herds numbered 38,489. San Luis Rey alone surpassed the Mission in agricultural products.

San Gabriel, however, had some scandalous young people. When Anastasia Zuñiga and a Los Angeles widow disgraced the Mission, Governor Solá ordered that their hair should be clipped and one eyebrow shaved. Then they should be exposed to the public during Mass. Afterwards they should be imprisoned at the Presidio for six months.

Smiling Joseph Chapman, reformed American pirate, however, had rather a pleasant life at San Gabriel. He had been pressed into piracy at Boston, and in 1818 was brought to California by Hypolite Bouchard, the buccaneer. Doctor, blacksmith, carpenter, "Pirate Joe's" versatility captivated the *padres*. He hewed timbers for the Los Angeles Plaza Church. Directed by Father Bernardo Sanchez, he built a sixty-ton ship, the *Guadalupe*. From a canyon fifty miles distant timbers were carted to San Pedro, assembled and launched. Pirate Joe's gristmill, *Molino Viejo*, was finally used as a private golf house by the late H. E. Huntington.

San Gabriel's most unusual woman, Victoria, owner of the great Santa Anita Rancho, was one of the few Indians to marry a cultured Saxon. Hugo P. Reid, a Scotsman, came in 1834, married Victoria, took possession of her land, and built her a two-story house with walls four feet thick. She refused to go upstairs, fearing earthquakes, and dared not ride behind horses. Dressed in black satin, over her shoulders a bright Manila shawl, she sat on the floor eating with her fingers, directing her Indian servants. She was worried because her husband insisted that their children be educated.

All Victoria's fears were realized. Earthquake destroyed her house. Oxen ran away and upset the *carta* in which she was riding. The guardian appointed by her husband robbed her. With a quilt over her shoulders, she died wearing a print dress. Reid wrote many valuable papers on Indians and their customs.

Father Zalvidéa's work was carried on by Father José Bernardo Sanchez, who explored California, wrote an excellent diary, and was

President of the Missions. Father Sanchez kept two fieldpieces, two six-pounders, and two two-pounders, to protect the Mission against uprising. In his time Indian women dressed gaily and men wore bright sashes. After Mass they were given *panocha*, molasses, honey, and wine from the stores, and a few *reales* to spend. They had races, games, and played ball. An Indian orchestra of two violins, a bass viol, and a trumpet performed in the square.

Hospitably Father Sanchez welcomed the American Jedediah S. Smith, who in November, 1826, led a ragged band of trappers over the Sierra, hitherto considered impassable. Smith and his company settled down at the Mission, rested and drank brandy. Glowingly they wrote friends in the United States of San Gabriel. When they left after six weeks, Father Sanchez gave them an order for all the supplies they could carry from the Rancho San Bernardino.

San Gabriel became the hospital for the battle between former Governor José Echeandia and his successor, Manuel Victoria, who was at Monterey. Echeandia remained at San Diego stirring up revolt in 1831. Captain Pablo de la Portilla, the leader, was joined by some troops and Pio Pico, José Antonio Carrillo, and Juan Bandini. Victoria marched south from Monterey to quell the insurrection. At Santa Barbara he was reinforced by José de la Guerra and Captain Romualdo Pacheco. The Governor and his men met the rebels near Cahuenga Pass.

Victoria, wounded, was carried to San Gabriel Mission, and it was a day of glory for Pirate Joe Chapman. He treated the Governor. Life was too stormy for Victoria, however; he surrendered to Echeandia and promised to leave California.

About this time two strangers added drama to life at San Gabriel: Father Juan Alexis Bachelot, Prefect Apostolic of the Sandwich Islands, and Father Patrick Short. Six years before, these missionaries had gone to preach in the Sandwich Islands. Queen Kaahumanu ordered them banished "because their doings are different from ours, and because we cannot agree." On Christmas Day they were put aboard the *Waverly* to land on January 21, 1832, at San Pedro. On the barren strand thirty miles from any habitation they were found by an Indian seeking shells. Between them they had only two bottles of water and a biscuit.

San Gabriel housed the strangers. Father Bachelot became first resident pastor of the Plaza Church, Los Angeles. Father Short went to Monterey, where he taught at William E. P. Hartnell's Seminario de San José.

Romance is often crime in the past tense; and in March, 1836, young and charming Doña María del Rosario Villa de Félix brought romance to San Gabriel—she and her lover, Gervasio Alípas. Doña María was the wife of Don Domingo Félix, a great *ranchero*.

The name Félix meant happiness, but it seemed a curse. Don Domingo's grandmother was first of the Anza expedition to die when they set out in 1775 from Tubac. Doña María fell under its dark sway when Gervasio came from San Diego.

Don Domingo discovered his wife's guilt. On condition that she abandon her lover, she was pardoned by her husband; but a new surge of passion swept away her promise. To be near Gervasio, Doña María fled to San Gabriel. The Fathers urged her to go back to her husband. Don Domingo appeared before the Administrator of the Mission and demanded her. Doña María returned to her husband. Félix placed his wife before him on his horse and triumphantly set out for their *rancho*.

Concealed in an arroyo, Gervasio tossed his *reata* over the head of Don Domingo, dragging him from his horse. A stiletto gleamed. Doña María helped cover her husband's body with earth and leaves. The lovers fled.

Some children found Don Domingo in a glade which cut across a road some distance from the town. There were bloodstains and footprints of a man and woman in the soft earth. Doña María and Gervasio were arrested.

In furious session the Los Angeles *Ayuntamiento* met. A meeting was called at the residence of Don Juan Temple. Fifty citizens demanded delivery for immediate execution "of the assassin, Gervasio Alípas, and the faithless María del Rosario Villa.... Let the infernal couple perish.... Public vengeance demands public example.... Death to the murderers!"

The *Ayuntamiento* refused the crowd's demand. Seizing the jail key, indignant citizens swept aside the guard.

The lives of the guilty lovers were spared until Holy Week had passed, but no priest was called to shrive the doomed man and woman. When the crowd entered the prison, it was found that Gervasio had nearly filed off his shackles. He was taken from the jail and shot. Less than an hour later Doña María held her proud Spanish head against the prison wall and met her end.

All the City of the Angels came, and for two hours gazed on the lifeless lovers at the entrance to the jail. This was on April 7, 1836; Vigilantes had arrived in California. Doña María was the first woman executed in the territory.

Nearly one hundred years after Doña María and Gervasio died, the owner of the ranch killed his wife. After a term in prison he gave the property to the City of Los Angeles, and it became Griffith Park. Still standing in the park is an adobe house that once belonged to Don Anastasio Félix.

Quite different was another woman in the story of San Gabriel, Doña Eulalia Pérez de Guillen, nurse and midwife, once owner of the present site of the city of Pasadena. About 1800 she taught spinning, weaving, and tailoring to the Indians, clothing 4,000 natives. She held the store keys and paid bills. When in 1832 Governor Echeandia's messenger demanded $20,000, Doña Eulalia refused. The money was taken by force from San Gabriel and never returned. For her services Doña Eulalia was given the San Pasqual Ranch, sometimes called *La Sábana de San Pasqual* (the altar cloth of San Pasqual) because of the brilliant display of poppies that could be seen for miles. Doña Eulalia died at Los Angeles in 1885, supposedly 120 years old.

In 1834 blight fell upon San Gabriel's 163,000 vines. The large orange orchard, the only one in California—containing 2,333 trees—bore gnarled and scant fruit. It seemed to matter little when, on August 9, 1834, Governor José Figueroa completed the secularization of the Missions.

San Gabriel became a curacy of the first class, the priest receiving a salary of $1,500 annually, to be paid by the Indians. The Franciscans declined the money. Colonel Nicolas Gutiérrez, ambitious to become

Governor, was Administrator. San Gabriel Indians went to northern Missions. The first year after secularization, only 400 remained here, although 8,060 had been baptized.

Father Tomás Esténaga gave his own meager stipend to the Indians, allowing them to live in brush houses which they could burn. One morning, however, when the Indians entered the church there was no priest. Father Esténaga could bear the life no longer; he had gone to Sonora on the same vessel with Father Francisco Ibarra of San Fernando. Temporarily Father Bachelot attended San Gabriel, once called Queen of the Missions.

Now the Queen had not a tallow candle nor tallow to make candles. Buildings were unroofed. Timbers and lumber were burned for firewood. Juan Bandini, who was in control in 1838, opened a dram shop in the Mission, sold brandy to the Indians, and then punished them for being drunk. In 1841 Prefect Santiago Argüello wrote to José de la Guerra of Santa Barbara that Major-domo Pérez had converted San Gabriel into a brothel.

Governor Juan Bautista Alvarado began distributing San Gabriel's land. In 1842 he granted the Rancho de la Puente to John Rowland and William Workman. Father Narciso Durán, President of the Missions, protested to the Mexican Minister of the Interior. The new Governor, Manuel Micheltorena, from Los Angeles, on March 29, 1843, decreed that the Missions should be restored to the friars.

One year later the Governor established primary schools at Los Angeles for children of both sexes with a teacher at $40 a month. San Gabriel had no school until after American occupation, when the first school was made of branches of mustard and stood under an oak.

Father Esténaga could not remain away from San Gabriel. He returned to a sad home-coming: workshops without laborers, strangers on the land. Only aged Indians and some widows and orphans remained. The establishment was expected to pay one-eighth of the income for maintenance of three hundred soldiers and for governmental needs. At last Father Esténaga consented to swear allegiance to the new constitution of Mexico.

Soon Micheltorena was banished. Pio Pico, born at San Gabriel in 1801, son of a Mission guard, became Governor. On June 8, 1846, the Governor sold the Mission to Hugo P. Reid and William Work-man for debts. No tools or implements remained, only thirty head of cattle. Already Pico had confirmed to himself and his brother Andrés 532,000 acres of land.

Father Esténaga withdrew from San Gabriel to San Fernando, where he soon died. In 1847 Father Blas Ordáz, who had explored California to the far north, took charge of the Mission and minis-tered to the few Indians until his death. The last Franciscan at San Gabriel was Father Francisco Sanchez, the Father Salvierderra of Helen Hunt Jackson's *Ramona*. With him was Father José J. Jimeno. In the 'fifties the Indians lived two miles from the church in *tule*-thatched huts at the side of a lake near Pasadena. They grew corn, beans, chilies, flowers, and attended Mass at the Mission. On August 15, 1852, Father Sanchez recorded his last baptism. Both he and Father Jimeno retired to Santa Barbara.

San Gabriel's bells were muted. Indian men sank into drunkenness and thievery, Indian women wallowed in degradation. For a time Joaquin Murietta the bandit is said to have stopped at San Gabriel, where his sister lived. In this vicinity his countrymen still hum a Spanish air declared to be Murietta's own song—a lament for his broken life. Aged Spanish-Californians wistfully say, "In those days bandits were gentlemen."

After American occupation the United States Land Commission declared invalid the sale of Mission property to Reid and Workman, and it was returned to the Catholic Church. On November 19, 1859, President Buchanan signed the patent.

In the 'sixties there sprang up a wildling grapevine in a near-by canyon, one of the largest in the world, with a circumference of five and a half feet. It now belongs to the Mission Play House property where Congressmen John S. McGroarty's *Mission Play* was presented twenty-one years for the benefit of the restoration of California Missions.

Father Joaquin Bot served the Mission in 1868, also from 1872 to 1887, and again from 1890 to 1902; but the Mission had no regular minister.

In February, 1908, San Gabriel was turned over to the Missionary

Sons of the Immaculate Heart of Mary, who also have charge of the Plaza Church. Four years after arriving, the Superior, Father Oñate, founded a school which was dedicated on October 6, 1912. The Mission in 1923 became the headquarters and preparatory college of the Claretian Fathers.

No Mission in California is better known than San Gabriel—104 feet long, 27 wide, and 30 high. At the floor some of the walls are 6 feet thick. Limestone and cement were used as far as the windows, and then brick. Back of the altar are original statues from Mexico: San Gabriel, Saint Francis, Saint Anthony, San Joaquin, Saint Dominic, and the Virgin. The organ loft and railing, as well as the roof tile, are as in ancient days. Best preserved is the sacristy with vestments of silk tissue, embroidered velvet, and cloth woven by Indians. A pair of tall, massive doors once turned on pivots in the main portals of the church. Among San Gabriel's treasures are its hammered copper font of 1771, the original holy-water bowl and sprinkler, and the silver baptismal shell.

In 1886 the ceiling was paneled in oak, and the windows were enlarged. Most of the floor tiling is modern. Father Rafael Serrano in 1921 erected a monument before the interior doorway in memory of Father Junípero Serra.

Father Andrés Resa in 1935 began excavating the San Gabriel courtyard, which is interesting with its old bake ovens where Indians made bread, and its kilns for manufacturing *ladrillos*, floor tile. The Father uncovered the ruins of the smithy, tannery, wine vats, soap works, the foundations of original buildings, also water jars and urns.

San Gabriel's forges and shops are stilled. The idyllic gardens and vineyards have vanished; the leagues of land belong to strangers; but San Gabriel remembers Father Zalvidéa, resting at San Luis Rey. Here in the Mission sleep Fathers Gerónimo Boscana, the scholar; Antonio Cruzado, who gave twenty-eight years to the establishment; zealous José Bernardo Sanchez; and Blas Ordáz, the explorer. The Mission still seems a strong fortress for progress. It is deep-rooted in the warm rich soil of the south. Above jangling streetcars and automobile sirens, San Gabriel's bells still sound their clear, inspiring message and are a solace to the heart of a troubled, bewildered world.

V

San Luis Obispo de Tolosa

MISSION SAN LUIS OBISPO, fifth in California, is in the heart of the city of San Luis Obispo; but its symbol should be the figure of a bear. Near this place, on September 2, 1769, while seeking Monterey, the Portolá company killed a bear weighing 375 pounds. Portolá named the locality *La Cañada de los Osos*, the Valley of the Bears. Officially it was known as *La Cañada de la Natividad de Nuestra Señora*.

As heroes the Spaniards arrived at Chief Buchon's *ranchería*, not far from Pismo Beach of today. Often the natives had been scarred by hungry bears. The chief gave the Portolá company gifts of *pinole*, *atole, tamales*, and fish. The Indians sprinkled wild seeds over mats and requested the strangers to be seated. Chief Buchon was so named for his immense goiter. The Santa Lucia Mountains begin in Mount Buchon. Point Buchon and a street in San Luis Obispo still bear the chief's name.

The site of San Luis Obispo, however, was first marked not by Portolá but by Vizcaíno. From his ship, on December 14, 1602, he beheld the highest point of the coast range, La Sierra de Santa Lucia— so-called because the preceding day, December 13, was Santa Lucia's feast.

In the fall of 1770, the new establishment, San Luis Obispo, was planned and named for San Luis Obispo, the young Bishop of Toulouse, France. He was the son of King Charles II of Naples and the nephew of Louis IX of France; but in 1294 he donned the habit of Saint Francis.

Establishment of the fifth Mission was delayed because supplies failed Mission San Carlos. Chief Buchon's bear-land, however, saved the northern Missions. From this district Lieutenant Pedro Fages and his soldiers carried 9,000 pounds of bear meat on pack mules to famine-stricken San Antonio and San Carlos.

President Junípero Serra journeyed southward in 1772 with Fages to establish the new Mission San Luis Obispo. Father José Cavaller, who was to be in charge of the Mission, accompanied them. Their mule train bore church goods, supplies, and agricultural implements.

Fifty leagues southeast of Monterey, and about three leagues from the ocean, on a slight elevation, an arbor was erected for a chapel. A high Cross was planted and venerated. Serra celebrated the first Mass in the arbor on September 1, 1772. *Tixlini*, the natives called the Mission site. For several years the establishment was known as San Luis Obispo de Tixlini.

Two Lower California neophytes were assigned by Serra to build the chapel and dwellings. After a day's stay at San Luis Obispo, Fages and Serra departed, leaving Father Cavaller alone guarded by three leather-jacket soldiers, three Catalonian volunteers, and a corporal. They had as supplies three pecks of seed wheat, fifty pounds of flour, some chocolate, and a box of brown sugar to barter with Indians for wild seeds.

Among the Nochi Indians at San Luis Obispo, Father Cavaller found a language different from those at San Antonio and San Gabriel. Here were fourteen idioms, but the villagers understood each other. Father Cavaller communicated with the Indians by gifts of beads and sugar. There was a head man in each village to whom tribute was paid, usually fruits and beads. Land was held by families, and wars resulted from taking wild fruit that did not belong to them.

On October 1, 1772, Father Cavaller baptized a boy, Francisco Maria, son of native parents. Three days later the child died. To impress pagans the infant was buried with pomp.

Natives were slow to accept the faith. They lived in *tule* and mat houses. When seeds and wild fruit ceased being plentiful, they moved to another place. New huts were quickly constructed. Father Cavaller found it difficult to till the soil with two poor mules and worn harness. Winter came, and clothing was the only enticement that the Father had to offer the Indians.

As usual, there were trouble-making soldiers; an Indian woman was found with one of the guards. Baptisms ceased for a year.

Indians helped cut timber for the little chapel which served as a temporary church. For their work they received beads and sugar. Lilila, a woman living till 1874 at San Luis Obispo, helped build the first church: a structure of poles roofed with *tules*. A few rooms served as a dwelling for both missionaries and soldiers. Hastily a granary and other buildings were erected; the rainy season was approaching.

At the end of the year Father Cavaller was joined by Father Domingo Juncosa, and later by Fathers Antonio Murguia, Juan Prestamero, and Tomás de la Peña.

In the beginning San Luis Obispo had only 18 head of cattle, but 41 were acquired in one year. The establishment also had 4 mares, 4 tame horses, 5 pigs, 2 riding mules, and 14 pack mules, with implements for the fields and tools for building.

Irrigation from two arroyos was easy. Two *fanégas* of beans were harvested from a plate of seed planted in the fertile soil. Grain, however, was scarce. The missionaries said they lived like birds.

Lower California Indians came to till the soil. Inhabitants were increasing when an Indian shot an arrow with a burning wick into a dry grass roof. A large part of the Mission was destroyed, and the furniture was damaged.

After a year Father Francisco Palóu, friend and later biographer of Serra, came from Lower California bringing four Christian families and five Indian youths to teach neophytes. The women were to instruct girls in spinning, weaving, and sewing. Missionaries were relieved of the necessity of dressmaking for converted females. Indian youths learned agriculture and mechanical arts, but they never excelled as carpenters as the women did as weavers.

At the close of 1774, 103 persons lived within the sound of Mission bells. Twenty-eight marriages had been contracted. Three soldiers of the guard had married Indians, and one neophyte maiden was the wife of a white servant.

Chief Buchon was a stalwart supporter of the Mission. One of the chief's concubines became a Christian and married a soldier. Their son went to Mexico with Anza. After Buchon died, the natives recognized his widow as chieftess and paid her as tribute a portion of their wild seeds.

Back from Mexico in 1774, Serra walked overland hundreds of miles from San Diego to counsel and bless the Missions. San Luis Obispo had a harvest of 472 bushels of grain. Livestock numbered 109. Serra was delighted with the progress made in 19 months by the new establishment. After baptizing some Indians, he went on to San Carlos. Soldiers and corporals acted as godparents to Indian converts. Even Captain Pedro Fages, military commander of Upper California, served.

Captain Juan Bautista de Anza of the Presidio of Tubac, Sonora, came here twice. His first visit was in April, 1774. His second picturesque expedition arrived on March 2, 1776, on the way from Sonora to found the Presidio and Mission on San Francisco Bay. Father Font, the chaplain, wrote of the luminous black eyes of the San Luis Obispo native women. They were fair, with hair flowing over their shoulders—"little Spaniards," he called them. They wore earrings, and at the waist had a girdle from which hung a bear or otter skin. Legend said that years before strangers dressed like Spaniards had been wrecked on the San Luis Obispo coast, where they lived and died. Perhaps European blood contributed to the good looks of the San Luis Obispo Indians.

Anza was presented by Father Cavaller with fine baskets, beaver and bear skins, and shells. While at San Luis Obispo he stood godfather for an Indian child, Carlos Antonio, baptized by Father Pedro Font on March 3, 1776.

At this time the Mission had a patio surrounded by buildings with a square hall in the middle. A shed served as a church. At one side were small huts, where converted girls slept in charge of an aged soldier's wife who taught them sewing.

In front of the Mission were the guardhouse and *ranchería* shacks. Father Font remarked that *tule* and logs used with adobe walls created fire hazard. In November, 1776, the Father's dwelling blazed. Soldiers and Indians fought the fire. The church and granary were saved, but furniture and farm implements were destroyed.

Couriers dashed to San Francisco. Captain Rivera delayed establishing Santa Clara Mission and hastened to San Luis Obispo. He discovered the incendiaries, hostile pagans. Two ringleaders were taken as prisoners to Monterey. Again fire broke out on Christmas Eve while the Fathers were saying midnight Mass, but it was smothered.

These repeated fires made history for Mission San Luis Obispo. Roofing tile must be made. No one understood the process of manufacture, but the missionaries experimented until in 1786 they succeeded. It was said that the first tiles were fashioned with Indian legs as forms, but doubtless wooden figures were soon substituted. Tiles were rapidly made in great quantity, and other Missions imitated San Luis Obispo. Since that time, not only California Missions, but public buildings and private houses in the West have employed this method of roofing.

On November 30, 1778, Father Junípero Serra drew up the title page of the confirmation register, and during his visit in December confirmed 265 neophytes. He came again in March, 1782, and also in May. His last visit was on November 28, 1783. Before he died he rejoiced that 616 natives had been baptized at this Mission.

San Luis Obispo was never one of the prosperous establishments, but in 1782 Father Cavaller was able to send $107 to help the King of Spain prosecute his war against England. After having served the Mission seventeen years, he died on December 9, 1789, and was buried by Father Miguel Piéras on the gospel side of the altar.

So well had Father Cavaller built, that even after his death activity continued. Here was the olive orchard, of importance in California. Some of the trees still survive. In 1791 the Mission contributed to the newly founded establishments, Santa Cruz and Soledad, giving vestments and oil.

San Luis Obispo suffered considerable turbulence. The first Indian *Alcalde* seized a friend's wife and fled. In 1794 several neophytes of San Luis Obispo and La Purísima were arrested for inciting revolt at San Luis. Five of the culprits were condemned to work at the Presidio. Now 946 persons lived at the Mission. Workrooms, barracks, guardhouse, and missionaries' dwellings were completed. A portico was added to the adobe church. In 1798 a water-power mill was erected that supplied flour for other Missions.

In this same year there came to San Luis Obispo unique Father Luis Antonio Martínez, with his large twisted nose and thickset body. Sometimes he wore a habit five years. Speaking the native idiom, he kept the Indians in order. Himself hospitable, he was liberal in furnishing supplies to the Monterey Presidio. He entered the capital with a train of Mission produce drawn by sleek mules with gaily decked Indian drivers. From a cart at the head of the procession he beamed on the inhabitants.

When neophytes were of special service, Father Martínez rewarded them with gifts: blankets, breechcloths, pants of soft skin, cloth jackets, and a cotton shirt. Women received blue or white petticoats and blouses. He called his Mission "San Luisito." As early as 1829 Indians brought balls of California gold to the Father.

For the Spanish Government, Father Martínez described San Luis Obispo Indians. Indian women in their native state supported their husbands by seed gathering. They were kindly; when the Father fell ill, they cared well for him. The Indians used no fermented drinks, only a mixture of tobacco, lime, and water.

The Indians' native music was a wind instrument made from the branch of an elder tree. From the Spanish they learned to play the violin, flute, guitar, and bass viol. The Indians called spring, flower time; summer, fruit time; autumn, seed time; winter, water time.

The natives never named the dead, and so their history could not be learned. Some Indians thought the dead were transformed into bears. If a native died, his beads were distributed among relatives to pay for wailing. Women lamented for nothing for the poor, for three days and nights. If the deceased was of rank, lamentations were long.

Father Martínez built much at San Luis Obispo: an adobe granary and weaving room, a long brick wall, thirty-five tile-roofed houses, a gristmill run by water, and a large reservoir. At the Rancho de la Playa a granary 115 feet long and 34 feet wide was erected. This Mission supplied the Monterey Presidio with excellent livestock.

In 1804, although 2,074 neophytes had been baptized, only 832 survived. It was necessary to have a hospital 115 feet long.

Fathers Martínez and Rodríguez renovated the church in 1812 and finished the sanctuary in Roman style. They procured an altar bell and erected stone pillars in the corridor of the Fathers' dwelling. The inner court of the Mission was paved with brick. Even pigeon houses were made of brick and mortar. Indians were well housed. Two old pepper trees in front of the church afforded shade.

San Luis Obispo had no bell tower, but three bell arches were over the front of the building and two at one side. In 1818 Father Martínez obtained two bells from Lima, Peru. The smaller one bears the inscription: ANO D 1818 MANUEL VARGAS ME FECIT LIMA MISION D SAN LUIS OBISPO D LA NUEBA CALIFORNIA. (MANUEL VARGAS MADE ME IN 1818. MISSION SAN LUIS OBISPO IN NEW (UPPER) CALIFOR-NIA.) The next Vargas bell reads: MANUEL VARGAS ME FECIT ANO D 1818 MISION D Sn LUIS OBISPO. D NUEBA CALIFORNIA. A smaller, nameless bell was made in San Francisco of two broken bells that were recast in 1878 by Bishop Mora.

San Luis Obispo Mission bells have their romance. Ramón loved Tonia, but he had no money. He waited to rob Padre Lorenzo, who was leaving to seek gold. A dark form approached. Ramón's knife flashed. A Mission bell rang out. Ramón had killed his beloved, who was wearing a man's cape. Ramón flung the bell far into the sea. On the coast above San Luis Obispo people thought they long heard its dirge-like sound.

In 1815 squirrels and mice destroyed San Luis Obispo crops, although the acreage was fourteen leagues long and a league wide. In 1818, however, the Mission had its largest harvest, 6,620 bushels of grain. Indians resented supporting soldiers—bearers of disease—but in 1821 Father Martínez gave 80 horses and saddles and 50 blankets to Monterey troops.

On the north side of the Sierra de Santa Lucia, not far from the Santa Margarita River, Father Martínez built a large sandstone and brick chapel, Santa Margarita de Cortona. Here was a large Indian population. Deer abounded, also antelope, quail, ducks, geese, rabbits. In 1938 the chapel exists as a hay barn. Its only furnishing, undestroyed, a painting of the Virgin Mary that once hung over the altar, belongs to Mrs. William R. Whittier of Sunnyvale, California, whose grandfather, the late Martin Murphy, in the 'fifties owned the ranch.

Mission San Luis Obispo shared the fear of Bouchard, the buccaneer, in 1818. Governor Solá sent the alarm of the attack on Monterey. Father Martínez was ill in bed, but he said, "If I had only two little cannon, I would capture the pirate's two ships!" He sent twenty-five Indians to Santa Barbara with a message for his friend Captain de la Guerra. Accompanied by thirty-five Indians, the Father followed. They all hastened to Mission San Juan Capistrano, the last point attacked by the pirate. Viceroy Juan Venadito informed King Ferdinand VII of Father Martínez's valor, and also of his support of the soldiers during nine years when they received no wages.

But Governor José Echeandia called the missionary "one of the furious enemies of our system." The Father refused to celebrate Mass in thanksgiving for Mexican independence. Nor would he swear loyalty to the constitution. He was also charged with burning candles before the portrait of the King.

In 1827 the Mexican Congress decreed the expulsion of all male Spaniards under sixty years of age, and this included Father Martínez. The President of the Missions, Vicente Sarría, however, begged the Father not to leave San Luis Obispo, and he remained temporarily. During the Solis revolt in 1829, the Governor accused Father Martínez of sympathizing with the rebels, and although the missionary was suffering from inflammatory rheumatism, the soldiers carried him on horseback to Santa Barbara. Governor Echeandia himself became jailer of the priest and locked him up in the de la Guerra house, presiding at the missionary's court-martial. Father Martínez was banished to Lima, Peru, and thence to Spain.

Father Joaquin Jimeno, of Mission San Luis Rey, was directed to take charge of the orphaned establishment in 1830. Soon the Mission was decaying with poverty. Sheep dwindled from 5,200 to 1,000. New Mexican traders carried off the few cattle. For several years there were only five or six baptisms annually.

Father Jimeno was succeeded by Father Luis Gíl y Taboada of Mission Santa Cruz, who spoke Indian languages, had medical knowledge, and even performed Caesarean operations. He was needed; pulmonary trouble and venereal disease were laying low the Indians. Father Gíl restored the health of the neophytes, built a new belfry, acquired a sanctuary lamp and vestments. San Luis Obispo's bells, however, had a tone of doom. Father Gíl died in 1833 at the Santa Margarita Rancho and was buried in the church at San Luis Obispo.

About this time earthquakes shattered the Mission Church and destroyed ranch buildings at San Miguelito. Walls of houses at Santa Margarita were also rendered unsafe. Only 265 Indians still lived at the Mission.

Don Juan Bautista Alvarado, later second native son of California to become governor, was appointed Commissioner at San Luis Obispo. He headed a clique of revolt against the new Governor Victoria, who had on taking the oath of office suspended Echeandia's secularization decree. Soon Alvarado and his friends caused Victoria to depart. Neophytes at San Luis Obispo suffered for necessities.

Two able but enfeebled missionaries now came to San Luis Obispo, Father Ramón Abella, who had served nearly a quarter of a century at San Francisco, and Father Felipe Arroyo de la Cuesta, a cripple in a wheel chair. Father Abella endeavored to have neophytes maintain a decent life, but they roistered wildly. Horse and mule traders from Sonora seized cattle. It mattered little when, on August 9, 1834, the Missions were secularized.

San Luis Obispo became a parish of the second class with Manuel Jimeno in charge as *comisionado*. Neophytes robbed the church. Domingo Amado, a drunken schoolmaster, sold whisky and lived with two women. Nearly all women at the Mission drank too much. "Father, I was drunk," they apologized. "I did not know what was done." Father Abella sent the women away.

When Manuel Jimeno took over the property in October, 1835, it was valued at $70,769; but the Mission rapidly bled to death. *Alcaldes* and Indians gave away wheat. When the Commissioner protested, they hurled objects at him. The Commissioner entreated Governor Alvarado to send soldiers. Armed expeditions recovered 1,000 horses stolen by the Chaguanaos Indians.

When Eugene de Mofras, the French traveler, visited San Luis

Obispo in 1841, there were barely 100 Indians. Some of them still cherished *rebozos* made under the direction of the banished Father Martínez. Herds and flocks were greatly reduced, and all tillable land and the Ranchos Santa Margarita and Asunción had been given to private individuals.

Father Ramón Abella, the last Franciscan at the Mission, was at that time the oldest California missionary. At San Francisco he had entertained Rezánov, Kotzebue, and Chamisso, who named California's poppy, *Eschscholtzia*. In his last days here he was compelled to be host to the ex-friar Angel Ramirez, embezzler of Customs funds at Monterey. Dying of syphilis, the ex-friar arrived with his mistress at the Mission, seemingly to torment Father Abella. He was cared for by the missionary till he died. Exhausted by his activities, Father Abella withdrew from San Luis Obispo to Mission Purísima. He died in 1842 at Mission Santa Inés.

In this same year Governor Alvarado directed Administrator José Mariano Bonilla to parcel the Mission lands among the Indians. After Governor Micheltorena displaced Alvarado, for a brief time the Mission was in charge of Franciscans, who presided over a few aged neophytes.

When Pio Pico became Governor in 1845, looting began. Indian land was sold for whisky and a blanket.

On December 4, 1845, Wilson, Scott and McKinley bought Mission San Luis Obispo for $500 at public auction. Vainly Father José Miguel Gómez asked Governor Pico for the products of the vineyard and orchard. The new owners had everything.

Mission San Luis Obispo shared in a dramatic incident of the American occupation. To the Mission in 1846 came Lieutenant-Colonel John C. Frémont and his soldiers. Don José Jesus Pico had been arrested and brought here in December for breaking his parole and supporting Flores in the Natividad campaign. Frémont tried Pico and condemned him to death.

Señora José de Jesus Pico and her fourteen children lived at the Rancho Piedra Blanca. She heard that her husband was sentenced to death. Quickly she assembled the children and hastened into San Luis Obispo. She called upon all the most beautiful women. Arrayed in their loveliest *mantillas* and *rebozos,* the *señoras* attended Mass at the Mission entreating aid of San Luis. Then women and children appealed to the American commander. Frémont could not resist their pleas. He pardoned Don José de Jesus and they became fast friends.

Father José Miguel Gómez, first secular priest ordained in California, on November 22, 1856, took charge of San Luis Obispo as secular priest. A year later Don Dolores Herrera ceded a piece of land to Bishop Thaddeus Amat of Monterey and Los Angeles, to found a convent and school on the old Mission ground. A generation passed before the convent was opened on August 16, 1876.

Until 1875 Mission San Luis Obispo had a corridor in front with unornamented columns with a square base and topped with a square molding supporting the roof beams which held the tile roof. But the columns were removed. San Luis Obispo, creator of California's roof tile, was first to adopt shingles. In the 'seventies Father Apollinarius Rousell erected a frame tower. Wood painted gray covered the adobe walls. In 1934 a cement bell tower replaced the one of wood, and three years later the corridor was rebuilt on the original lines.

The façade of the church retreats twenty feet from the front line of the corridor. At the entrance are doors from ancient days with the old hinges, and ornamented with interesting panels. Over the altar is the original statue of San Luis, the patron saint; the ceiling is ornamented with blue stars undimmed as when they came from the brush of the Indians.

In the rear sanctuary is visible the original construction: old rafters connected with bamboo and plastered with mud. The slender sapling ceiling was brought twenty miles from Cambria by Indians, solidified with lime, crushed abalone shells, and juice of cactus blossoms.

The Mission atmosphere survives in the adobe building once used as barracks, now occupied by the pastor. Here are large cool rooms with deep-recessed windows and high ceilings. Upstairs in the museum is the oldest roof tile in California, clappers of recast bells, wooden bells used during Holy Week, shining copper kettles, Indian corn grinders. There is a chair with arms worn from long use by Indian lace makers. Highly treasured are the copper baptismal font and the original vestment case. The redwood crucifix was carved by the Indians. Also of redwood is the first little crib that served the Mission at its foundation in 1772. Of much interest is the painting of the patron, San Luis Obispo, brought about 1774 by Father Junípero Serra from Mexico.

Fronting the courtyard is a corridor where the priests meditate. In the *plazita* is an old blacksmith shop of brick and boulders now serving as a garage. Lavender, heliotrope, cacti, roses of Castile, and the largest pomegranate tree in California recall Mexico and Spain. Grapes on the cruciform arbor never fail—the longest arbor to remain of those built by Franciscans at California Missions.

The Fathers often think of Chief Buchon, who came to seek the new faith; Father Cavaller, who starved on sage and wild mountain seeds; Father Junípero Serra toiling into the Mission from El Camino Real; dynamic Pedro Fages riding in from Monterey; Anza and the San Francisco founders; Father Martínez's exile; but sometimes in this tranquil garden they hear the rumble of the brown bear that later adorned the banner of the state of California.

VI

San Francisco de Asis (*Mission Dolores*)

LIKE the city of San Francisco, the Mission San Francisco de Asis has always been a child of fortune. Precisely where buccaneer Francis Drake unfurled the flag of England in 1579 on the northern coast of California is uncertain, but probably near Cermeñon's Bay of San Francisco. Nearly two centuries later, fear of England and Russia stirred Spain to establish three Missions in Upper California: San Diego, San Carlos, and San Buenaventura. Of Visitador-General Don José de Galvez, Serra asked, "Is there to be no Mission for our Father Saint Francis?"

"If Saint Francis desires a Mission," answered Galvez, "let him cause his port to be discovered."

By chance the port was found. Don Gaspar de Portolá and his sixty men from San Diego lost their way while seeking Monterey and stumbled north. Guided by Sergeant José Francisco Ortega, from an elevation now called Montara, on October 31, 1769, they saw the Farallones of today. Drake had christened the rocky islets the Saint James. Ortega led the travelers along the bay shore until four white cliffs were distinguished. They were looking at the Indians' Strait of Yulupa, Sunset Strait, about 1,450 feet wide, now known as the Golden Gate. This was November 1, 1769.

In March, 1772, Lieutenant Pedro Fages, future Governor of California, with Father Juan Crespi and twelve soldiers explored San Francisco Bay, arriving from Monterey by way of Alameda County. Fages named the Golden Gate *La Bocana de la Ensenada de los Farallones.* The purple mountain to the north, today called Tamalpais, Fages christened *La Sierra de Nuestro Padre de San Francisco.*

Captain Fernando Rivera y Moncada was the next explorer. He

left Monterey with Father Francisco Palóu and sixteen soldiers on November 23, 1774. Five days later Palóu described a great redwood, *madera colorada,* that from a distance looked like a tower—Palo Alto's famous tall tree. The company camped on the Arroyo de San Francisco, covered with poplars, willows and laurel—San Francisquito Creek of today. Palóu thought this a good place for a Mission. In the native idiom of Monterey, the friar spoke to the Indians about God; but in his diary he confessed, "I am not satisfied that they understood me."

The explorers visited what later were called Seal Rocks. They climbed Sutro Heights and raised a huge Cross on a sharp declivity above the Golden Gate. Rivera opposed the settlement on San Francisco Bay, but Palóu urged the Mission establishment. Viceroy Bucareli demanded not only a Mission but a fort.

To prepare the way for the new foundation, Captain Juan Bautista de Ayala was sent from Mexico on the transport *San Carlos,* sometimes called *El Toison de Oro,* or the *Golden Fleece.* The travelers set sail from Monterey July 27, 1775. For nine days they invoked Saint Francis. On the evening of the ninth day the *San Carlos* reached *La Boca,* the Golden Gate.

Pilot José Cañizares drove an intrepid little redwood *cayuco* (dugout) through the rocky channel. After dark the frigate followed. The next morning, Saturday, August 5, the *San Carlos* and the launch, uniting, sailed to the island named by the explorers *Nuestra Señora de los Angeles,* Angel Island. Hoisting the Spanish flag, they gave three cheers for the King of Spain. Chaplain Vicente de Santa Maria celebrated Mass.

Forty days the *San Carlos* lay in San Francisco Bay. Ayala discovered Alcatraz Island and named it for its pelican inhabitants. At some distance to the southeast, three Indians were found weeping in a cove—*La Ensenada de los Llorones*—the Bay of the Weepers, later Mission Bay.

On *tule* rafts Indians came bearing gifts and fresh fish. Native offerings were repaid with red beads and baubles.

Before leaving, Captain Ayala and Father Santa Maria buried at the foot of the Cross erected by Rivera two letters intended for the land expedition which was expected.

At San Carlos there was alarm over Ayala's long stay in the north. Don Bruno de Ezeta (Heceta), accompanied by Fathers Palóu and Campa, set out in September, 1775, to find Ayala. They carried a small canoe on a mule. The dugout filled with sand and water was discovered, but not Ayala. Palóu returned enthusiastic about founding the northern Mission.

Captain Juan Bautista de Anza, thirty-seven, born in Arizona, son and grandson of fighting frontiersmen of the same name, was ordered to lead the overland expedition of colonists from Sonora to San Francisco. For the first time women, children, families were to be sent to Upper California.

The standard of the Anza expedition which founded San Francisco was raised at San Felipe de Sinaloa. San Miguel de Horcasitas, then residence of the Governor of Sonora, was the place of rendezvous. In September the company assembled; on the twenty-ninth they began the seventy-league march to Tubac, to meet the commander.

Hitherto, only $1,000 had been allowed to found a Mission; but aside from monthly pay each family of the Anza expedition cost $800. The Pious Fund contributed $10,000. Luxuries made the venture attractive: six yards of ribbon for women, four for the hair of men; even children had ribbons. There was brandy and wine. Nor were Indians forgotten. Tobacco attracted men, and red beads and handkerchiefs the women. *Panoche* enticed children.

Daily pay began with enlistment. Colonists numbered 240, including 160 women and children—all descendants of soldiers of Cortés. Besides officers and colonists there were 825 head of stock, 320 head of cattle, 340 horses. One hundred and forty mules carried supplies and baggage; 20 mules, the luggage of the commander and officers.

The night before departure from Tubac, Father Pedro Font of the College of Santa Cruz, Querétaro, with Anza's tankard summoned the travelers to devotion. The next morning he sang High Mass, assisted by Fray Francisco Garcés and Fray Tomás Easaire. The Holy Virgin of Guadalupe, Saint Michael, and Saint Francis of Asis were

invoked for protection. At eleven o'clock on October 23, 1775, the
bugle sounded; the epic march began.

Four scouts rode ahead. Anza led with a vanguard. After him came
the priests, then the colonists. Travel was slow; cattle fed by the
trail. At each departure Chaplain Font struck up the Alabado; the
people responded.

The first day out from Tubac, Anza acted as midwife. The wife
of José Vicente Félix died in childbirth. Fray Garcés took her remains
to his Mission San Xavier del Bac. With four motherless children the
widower continued the march, nursing mothers suckling the baby.
Eight infants were born on the journey.

Each morning Father Font said Mass. After the evening barbecue
he played his psaltery by the campfire. The colonists passed through
sun-tortured deserts so desolate that not even birds dwelt there. Indians forded them over the Colorado River. Once across the desert,
even Anza shoveled sand all night to find water for the cattle.

Anza celebrated discovering water by giving the travel-worn colonists brandy. Father Font protested, but the colonists had a *fandango*.
California love began.

There was a widow in the expedition, a laughing, dancing woman
in the twenties, mother of two little girls—María Feliciana Arballo
de Gutiérrez. Even on this grim pioneer journey she sang and danced.

"Naughty," Father Font called her songs. To his horror the
fandango lasted all night. A jealous admirer of Doña María tried to
chastise her. Anza interfered. "The man is quite right," declared
Father Font, denouncing the raucous levity of the expedition.

"Not while I am here," declared the gallant soldier, who had just
torn himself from his own lovely wife, Doña Ana, in Tubac.

Through the snows of San Sebastian the colonists toiled in cold that
killed even horses. Weeping, they went over the Sierra Madre in a
furious storm. Near San Gabriel the earth shook. Doña María's jealous
suitor called it punishment for her coquetry.

Impatient of reproaches and weary of travel, at Mission San Gabriel, reached by the company on January 4, 1776, Doña María
married Juan Francisco López, a soldier of the guard. Father Francisco
Garcés, the famed pioneer missionary, performed the ceremony.

With her husband Doña María remained at San Gabriel to embellish California history and art. One of her descendants was beautiful Josefa Carrillo, who eloped with Captain Henry Delano Fitch; another was Governor Pio Pico; still another was Governor Romualdo Pacheco, the only Spanish governor since American occupation. General Vallejo's lovely granddaughters have her blood. This faraway dancing woman gave to the cinema of our own time Leo Carrillo; and to the stage William Gaxton.

North-northwest the Anza expedition fared. Oaks and pines appeared. Soldiers found rocks showing signs of minerals. Scarlet seed pods of wild roses were eaten. The travelers called the San Jacinto Valley of today, Paradise. In Santa Ana Valley they found grapevines, blackberries, sunflowers, lavender, tulips, heartsease. They feasted on wild lettuce and onions. Larks sang. It was like Spain.

Indians fled from the travelers, but Anza tried to attract them with gifts of cigarettes and glass beads.

At Mission San Gabriel, Don Fernando Rivera y Moncada with Father Antonio Paterna came to welcome them. The Mission guard fired a volley. Fathers Antonio Cruzado and Miguel Sanchez rang bells.

But there was brief joy for Anza. Mission San Diego had been wiped out. Immediately he set out with Rivera, Font and twenty soldiers to pacify the Indians.

Although self-sustaining San Gabriel was not prepared to entertain 200 guests indefinitely. Couriers were sent to Anza, politely inviting him to depart with the colonists. They must go forward, or all would be lost. Forward they moved—Anza was that kind of a man.

On Sunday, March 10, 1776, they arrived at Monterey dripping wet. Father Junípero Serra came from San Carlos to bid them welcome. Desolating news from Captain Rivera awaited Anza. Neither Presidio nor Mission was to be established on San Francisco Bay. The colonists were to await further orders at Monterey.

Anza's groin was griping with pain, but even in chill wet March he mounted his horse and rode forward. With him went Father Font, Lieutenant Moraga, Corporal Robles, eleven soldiers, and six servants.

The colonists were left at the Presidio, the stock pastured at Point Pinos.

The travelers passed through Santa Clara Valley of the present time and camped on the Arroyo de San Mateo. Natives were friendly but filthy. Anza gave beads even to the women, who wore petticoats of dried grass with wooden ear- and nose-rings. The company moved toward San Francisco Bay, camping at Mountain Lake on the southern edge of the Presidio reservation.

Anza found Rivera's Cross raised in 1774 near the site of the Legion of Honor Building later erected by Mr. and Mrs. Adolph Spreckels. He designated the tableland where the fort was to be established.

Father Font called San Francisco Bay, with its spouting whales, tunas, seals and otters, a "prodigy of nature." In his diary he wrote:

Although I have seen many beautiful lands, I have yet seen none that pleased me so much as this.... If it could be well populated ... there could be nothing more pretty in the world; this place has the best accommodations for founding on it the most beautiful city ... the port being exceptional ... for dockyards, docks ...

Anza and his company early the next morning crossed to the edge of the white rock that forms the end to the gate to the port where the bay begins. Font described it: "One can spit into the sea."

Anza and Font sent the pack train the following day to the Arroyo de San Mateo. Accompanied by Moraga, they set out to determine the Mission site. Near Arroyo de los Dolores, or Dolores Creek, was a *laguna* from which they plucked blue lilies. Father Font filled his tent with them. Anza and Font decided to build the Mission near here at the foot of two hills, *Los Pechos de la Choca*—the breasts of the Indian maiden—now called Twin Peaks.

Font's diary describes the Arroyo de los Dolores, its banks overgrown with manzanita, camomile, and wild violets. Near by, on March 29, 1776, Moraga began San Francisco gardening when he planted maize and chick-peas to test the soil.

On their return journey at today's Palo Alto, where the Anza expedition camped, Father Font, on March 30, measured the towering redwood tree 140 feet high and 15 ½ feet in circumference—the first measurement of the kind in California. He used a graphometer borrowed of Father Palóu. The redwood tree still stands.

After exploring the southern end of the bay, Anza decided to return to Monterey. With ringing bells San Carlos received the travelers. Serra believed that a way would soon open for establishing the northern Mission, but Rivera's permission did not arrive. Anza refused to turn his company back to Sonora. Placing in command Lieutenant José Joaquin Moraga, he rode southward with Father Font.

On May 28, 1776, Moraga received word from Rivera to proceed to San Francisco and establish the Presidio on the spot selected. Serra believed that the new Mission would soon be founded, and so he was happy when he saw Moraga and his company set out.

Down the pine-covered slopes they rode at two o'clock in the afternoon of June 17, 1776. With Moraga were Fathers Francisco Palóu and Benito Cambón, a sergeant, 2 corporals, 16 soldiers, 7 colonists, 7 servants, and 3 unmarried neophytes. Moraga's wife was in Mexico, but all other married persons had their families. The company went slowly because of pregnant women. A mule train carried provisions and utensils, and there were 286 head of cattle.

The founders of San Francisco passed over the brown-coated Gavilán range and traversed the plain of San Bernardino, Santa Clara Valley. They feasted on meat of strange animals, elk "as good as beef," they declared. Indians in turn wondered at the strange animals, cows, brought by colonists. Milk the Indians distrusted; they would not drink it.

On the tenth day from Monterey the colonists pitched camp on the bank of the blue-lilied lagoon. San Francisco consisted of fifteen tents on June 27, 1776—the embryo of a great metropolis.

The commander ordered a small bower made. On June 29, 1776, the feast of the apostles Saint Peter and Saint Paul, five days before the Declaration of Independence on the Atlantic side of the continent, Father Palóu said Mass in an *enramada*. San Francisco was born; at last Saint Francis had his Mission.

For an entire month the colonists waited for the supply ship, the *San Carlos*, but it did not come. Finally the transport arrived at

Monterey with great tidings. The Viceroy ordered the *San Carlos* north with all implements and property belonging to the new Mission and Presidio. Rejoicing, Serra called it the reward of faith.

Most of the colonists at San Francisco were moved from the *Laguna de los Dolores* to the site of the temporary barracks. There remained at the Mission, San Francisco's cradle, only Fathers Palóu and Cambón, six soldiers, three servants, two colonists, and the cattle.

The first house at the Presidio was ten *varas* by three and had a *tule* roof. On July 26, 1776, Moraga began work on the barracks. A *tule* structure was thrown up for a chapel. Father Palóu wrote in his diary on July 28, "I celebrated first Holy Mass."

On August 1, 1776, aided by six soldiers and two colonists, Father Palóu began building Mission San Francisco de Asis. He laid the cornerstone.

At last the *San Carlos* came through the Golden Gate, August 18, 1776. Wild seas had driven it off its course. Two thousand miles it had traveled sailing from Monterey to San Francisco.

Pilot José Cañizares drew the Presidio plan. Within a walled stronghold 253 feet square were to be erected a church, warehouses, guardhouses, barracks, and dwellings for colonists and officers.

Captain Fernando Quíros sent two carpenters and a squad of sailors from the *San Carlos* to expedite the work. Within a month the Presidio commander was housed, and soldiers were in their quarters. On September 17 Father Palóu celebrated first Mass in the Presidio Church assisted by Father Tomás de la Peña. Officers entered the church singing the *Te Deum*. Bells rang. There were volleys of pistols and muskets, and salvos of cannon. The transport in the harbor boomed response. Lieutenant Moraga and the officers took possession in the name of the King. At the feast following the ceremony toasts were drunk to the King and the Viceroy.

While Captain Quíros, Father Cambón, Pilot Cañizares, Lieutenant Moraga, and eight soldiers surveyed the port on a launch, the missionaries and workmen began the permanent Mission. Soon the Fathers' building was completed, 28 feet long, 14 wide, clay-plastered and *tule*-roofed. To this was added a church 50 feet long and 14 wide, with a small sacristy. The ship's carpenter built the altar, made the doors of the church and dwellings, and left a fishing boat and net as gifts to the Mission. Flags, bunting, and pennants from the *San Carlos* adorned the building.

Mission San Francisco de Asis was blessed on October 3, but not formally opened until October 8, 1776. Fathers Cambón, Nocedal, and Peña assisted Father Palóu at High Mass. After preaching, Palóu led the procession which bore an image of Saint Francis, and placed it on the altar. Firecrackers and rockets were discharged. Salvos sounded from soldiers' muskets and from a small ship's cannon. While guests banqueted on two beeves, terrified natives fled southward.

Saint Francis, patron of the new Mission, is the world's most popular saint. Born in 1182 at Assisi, Italy, the son of Pietro Bernardone, a wealthy cloth merchant, he passed a worldly youth. Soon he renounced patrimony, donned beggar's garments, kissed lepers' sores, hid in a cave, and said he was wedded to lovely Lady Poverty. The merchant called his son mad for dwelling with his disciples in huts near Assisi, the site of the first Franciscan monastery.

Francis lived on raw food sprinkled with ashes, calling his body Brother Donkey. Rabbits nestled in his habit. Frozen bees crawled to him to be warmed. For him nightingales sang their sweetest melody. The sun was his brother. Stars were his sisters. Covered with a borrowed habit, he died on the bare ground on October 3, 1226. His last words were, "Bring my soul out of prison."

At Saint Francis Mission four sailors, left by Captain Quíros as laborers, began the San Francisco water works by digging an irrigation ditch near the Mission. Impelled by curiosity, gradually Indians came.

In fury San Mateo pagans attacked San Francisco Indians, burning their huts. Both sides had dead and wounded. On *tule* rafts the San Francisco Indians moved to the shore facing the Presidio. They avoided the Mission, but they returned to hunt ducks on the lagoon which they exchanged with the Spaniards for beads.

For several months no converts were made at the Mission. Indians threatened the lives of a sergeant and the Lower California neophytes. At San Francisco is the only record of an Indian attempting to kiss a Spanish woman.

Soldiers tried to frighten the natives by discharging their muskets. Indians left but returned. A settler, wounded by a native, killed him. There was shooting from behind rocks. Another Indian was wounded. Natives pleaded for peace, but the soldiers flogged two. If the Indians behaved, the Spaniards promised friendship; if they threatened the Mission, they should die.

Father Palóu drew up the title page of the baptismal, marriage, and death registers. The first entry was on August 10, 1776; Francisco Soto, son of Ignacio Soto and María Barbara Lugo, was baptized.

On June 24, 1777, Father Palóu felt that life at the new Mission had blossomed: three pagans were baptized. Later seventy-two *rancherías* were represented in the baptismal book; but Chamis, a youth of twenty-two, was first—from the Ranchería Chulchui, by Spaniards called *La Asumpción*. Francisco Moraga he was called, honoring Don José Joaquin Moraga, the *Comandante*. Lilote, eleven years of age, was the first Indian girl baptized. On July 9, 1777, she was christened María Francisca. At the close of the year neophytes numbered thirty-five.

Palóu performed the first marriage ceremony on January 7, 1777; Juana Francisca Pinto, daughter of Pablo Pinto, became the bride of Mariano Antonio Cordero, a Monterey soldier. Francisco Moraga, the first Indian baptized at the Mission, wedded Indian Catarina de Bononia on April 27, 1778—the first Indian marriage. The wedding ceremony was a novelty to Indians. In paganism they had no ceremony. The husband divorced his wife saying, "I put her out." Children belonged to the mother.

On December 21, 1776, the burial register was opened when María de la Luz Muñóz, wife of the soldier, José Manuel Valencia, was buried in the Presidio Church. The first interment at the Mission was that of Francisca Alvarez, on March 4, 1777. The first Indian burial at the Mission church took place October 20, 1777. Pedro, four-year-old child of pagan parents, had died from falling into a kettle of hot water.

Father Francisco Palóu, who laid the Mission cornerstone and served here nine years, made Dolores the literary shrine of California. Here he wrote the first book in the state. As early as 1773 at

Monterey he had copied original documents and recorded current events. At San Francisco he continued his labor, and also began his admirable biography of Father Junípero Serra. It was completed in 1785 and published in Mexico in 1787. Palóu apologized for its imperfections: "It was written in the heathen surroundings of San Francisco." His historical notes were virtually unknown, although printed in Mexico in 1857, until John T. Doyle of San Francisco brought them to light by publishing them in 1874.

Palóu is one of the best authorities on the five native tribes around San Francisco Bay. In cold weather men daubed themselves with mud. When sun appeared, they washed it off. As protection against cold, women and girls wore a *tule* skirt and cape. Women gathered black seeds, crushed them into flour, and made ball-shaped *tamales* the size of an orange. Men fished, hunted deer, quail, rabbits, geese, ducks, and thrushes. They relished fat whale and seal meat. Both Indians and Spaniards liked hazelnuts growing in the ravine, but especially they enjoyed strawberries thriving in the sand dunes. Palóu said the berries were larger and more delicious than those of Spain. *Amole* bulbs, the size of an onion, served the Indians for soap and food. Certain individuals were believed to send rain, make acorns grow, or cause whales to approach.

When a relative died, the natives cut their hair. Ashes were thrown over their faces, heads, and bodies. They beat themselves with rocks. The dead were cremated.

Hunters and fishermen were called "great men" by the San Francisco Indians; when they hunted and fished they planted a stick surmounted by feathers and wild seeds. While hunting they themselves abstained from meat.

Wrongs were righted by a man and his relatives. Shouting they went into battle. They thought that when they died they sailed out to sea. Questioned about the after-life, they answered, "Who knows?"

Pioneer Don Ignacio Arteága arrived on May 12, 1777, at San Francisco, bringing supplies from San Blas on the *Santiago*. His was the first vessel to make the voyage direct from a Mexican port to San Francisco Bay. Small boats floated on the tide through the narrow channel to Dolores.

Impatient to see the new Mission, Serra also came. Late on October 1, 1777, he surprised Father Palóu by arriving unannounced on foot from San Carlos. Sixty-three years old, with a lame leg, he had come fifteen leagues through rough country, forded creeks, and completed the journey from Santa Clara in a day and part of a night.

Serra wished to be in San Francisco to say Mass on October 4, feast day of Saint Francis. His sermon delighted not only missionaries but troops. Indians gazed at him in awe. After five days at the Mission Father Junípero went to the Presidio. Looking out on the port, he said, *"Gracias a Dios!* Our Holy Father Saint Francis with the Cross of the Mission procession has reached the extreme end of the continent of California. To pass farther on a ship will be needed."

Two years later Father Serra again walked from Monterey to confirm and baptize neophytes. The sore on his foot was so inflamed and his leg so swollen that a ship's surgeon declared it a miracle that the President of the Missions could walk. Serra would accept no remedy, leaving the healing to the Divine Physician. He remained at the Mission from October 21 to November 6, 1779. Back he came on October 28, 1781, and only a few months before his death he arrived, May 5, 1784, to take leave of the Mission. Before departing, he confirmed 146 adults and Indian children, including a few infants from the Presidio.

Father Francisco Palóu, on April 25, 1782, laid the cornerstone of the present church. At the ceremony were also Father Vicente de Santa Maria, Father José Antonio de Murguía of Mission Santa Clara, Surgeon Joseph Davila, Don José Joaquin Moraga, his son Don Gabriel Moraga, Ensign Ramón Lazo de la Vega, and Mission guards and troops. In a receptacle in the pit of the cornerstone were placed an image of Saint Francis, several coins signifying the church treasure, five medals of various saints, and relics of Saint Pius and other martyrs. The new church edifice was 114 feet long, 22 high, with walls 4 feet thick.

For a year the Mission was cut off from supplies, but planting was begun near today's San Bruno. There 3,183 bushels of grain, corn, peas, and beans were garnered. The four-acre Mission orchard began to flourish, yielding San Francisco's first fruit—figs, apricots, peaches, apples, and pomegranates.

Mission products were needed. War was raging between Spain and England. The *Santiago*, fearing attack by the English, declined to deliver freight at San Francisco. Pack mules were sent to Monterey for supplies for two hundred Mission Indians. This condition continued till 1792.

Converts came from afar to Mission Dolores: Suisunes, Petalumas, Olompalis, and Ululatos. Native polygamy was a problem of Father Palóu's. Frequently an Indian married an entire family. The friar baptized three children born within two months of each other to a pagan father. The man had married three sisters, all happy. He then married his mother-in-law. The adults were converted. Palóu had the neophyte put away all his wives except the first. The others were married to neophytes.

In 1784 death struck down Serra, and in 1785 the founder and first commander of the San Francisco Presidio, Lieutenant José Joaquin Moraga. He was interred by Palóu in the Mission cemetery.

The new church was dedicated on April 3, 1791. All admired the arched, carved wooden doors, the Doric columns supporting a balcony with an iron railing which has since disappeared. They marveled at the tile roof resting on rough-hewn timbers lashed together with rawhide. They were charmed with the ceiling that the Indians had decorated with vegetable colors. The bell summoning them to Mass cast a new enchantment over the neophytes.

Mission San Francisco de Asis had three pierced openings in the wall arch for bells. Soon after the dedication, a bell was bought which has hung there ever since. It has the King's crown on one side and is inscribed: DMAN MENDOSA ALA M.N.D. LA. CA FRANCISCO D. MONTEREI ANO D. 1792 N. S. P. SS. (DAMIAN MENDOSA. FOR THE MISSION OF THE DOLOROSA. FRANCIS OF MONTEREY. YEAR OF 1792. OUR SERAPHIC FATHER ST. FRANCIS.) This is the smallest and oldest of the trio of bells, being the "ringing bell." It is suspended from its handle by rawhide thongs still secure. Two other larger bells in the arches are rung instead of swung. The north bell is lettered: RUELAS ME FECIT 1797 IMEYAMOS JOCP. AVE MARIA PRUSSIMA. (RUELAS MADE ME. 1797. AND I AM CALLED JOSEPH. HAIL MARY MOST PURE.) The south bell reads: AVE MARIA PURIS. S. IMA VIVA JESUS IMEYAMOS S. MARTIN 1797. (HAIL MARY MOST PURE. HAIL JESUS. I AM CALLED ST. MARTIN. 1797.)

Five days after the church was dedicated, on April 8, 1791, the remains of Lieutenant Moraga were transferred to the new building.

Captain Nicolas Solér did not like the Presidio climate, and he was in favor of abandoning the fort. Outweighing chilling fogs and wind, however, was the necessity of protecting the port. Although foreigners were forbidden entrance, on November 14, 1792, the English Captain George Vancouver came through the Golden Gate from the Sandwich Islands on the *Discovery,* defying roaring Presidio guns and the thundering cannon of Fort Point. Vancouver blandly took soundings and awaited day in front of Yerba Buena cove.

Comandante Hermenegildo Sal and his family decided to entertain the Englishmen. Vancouver and his officers enjoyed strawberry picnics, *meriendas,* quail hunting, and a trip to Santa Clara. Vancouver was pleased with the gift of a fat ox, sheep, and vegetables, but he was not impressed by the low thatched houses at the Presidio with windows, holes in the wall without glass, nor with the white-washed church.

Mission Dolores he found more attractive, with its larger houses, enduring and better finished. The vegetable garden, however, was overrun with weeds. The Indians lived in conical mud huts, but they wove cloth for their own garments "by no means despicable."

Vancouver's unwelcome visit brought about the building of the new Castillo de San Joaquin at Fort Point. Begun in August, 1793, it was completed the next year. It was shaped like a horseshoe and measured 120 feet. Torbidio Ruiz, architect, superintendent, and builder, was a roving mason from Monterey. Thirty neophytes with twenty-three yoke of oxen from Mission Santa Clara erected the fort. That Mission also supplied tile at $20 a thousand. On December 8, 1794, the fort was blessed and placed under the protection of San Joaquin.

Spaniards were obliged to endure fog and wind, but shivering Dolores neophytes took refuge on the Oakland coast—the first commuters. In 1796 there were 1,889 converted Indians. They harvested 6,505 bushels of wheat, barley, and corn. Soldier Lozero taught them to make pottery, but they wearied of their task and fled.

President Lasuén requested missionaries not to send neophytes after fugitives. Father Antonio Dantí, however, ordered fourteen Mission Indians to cross the bay and bring back deserters. Seven fugitives were killed, and then two hundred neophytes, scornful of work and discipline, fled to delightful pagan dances. Even Raimundo, a Lower California neophyte who crossed the bay with thirty Mission Indians on a *tule* raft, could not induce them to return. Governor Diego Borica sided with the Indians.

Sergeant Pedro Amador was warned to avoid bloodshed, but he was sent to capture the deserters. Near Mission San José the soldiers overtook the fugitives and killed nine Indians. Amador lost two soldiers, but he captured eighty-three Christians and nine gentiles and took them to Mission San José. Seventy-nine deserters were returned to Mission San Francisco and set to work on the Presidio.

In an endeavor to keep neophytes at the Mission the Fathers erected adobe dwellings, roofed them with tile, and built new bathhouses at Rancho del Rey.

California's first high romance entered Mission San Francisco de Asis February 26, 1791, with the baptism of María de la Concepción Marcela, infant daughter of Don José Darío Argüello, Captain-Commander of the San Francisco Presidio. At fifteen this girl had the loveliness of a woman. So thought the Imperial Chamberlain of Russia, Nikolai Petrovich Rezánov, who arrived on April 4, 1806, commanding the *Juno*. He was head of a great fur company with a grant which divided large profits among the Imperial family, and he had been Ambassador Extraordinary to Japan. At Sitka, Alaska, he found his scurvy-stricken countrymen starving. He had to choose between eating eagles and devil fish or venturing to California, defying the Spanish law that forbade trade with foreigners.

Rezánov purchased an old vessel from the American Captain Wolfe for $8,000, filled it with supplies to barter, and set sail for California.

In a dense fog he entered San Francisco Bay and went ashore, accompanied by Lieutenant Davidof and Dr. Georg H. von Langsdorff, surgeon and man of science. In Latin they spoke with Father Joseph Uria and Father Martín Landaeta of the Mission, who served them with wine of the country and "super-excellent chocolate." After admiring the asparagus, potatoes, peas, beans, corn, cabbage, lettuce, and onions in the Mission garden, the Russians were guided by Father Uria over the sandy road to the Presidio. *Comandante* Argüello was absent, but he was represented by his son, Don Luis.

Fifteen-year-old Doña Concepción was hostess. Rezánov, a middle-aged widower, charmed by her unspoiled beauty, forgot starving Sitka. She was dazzled by his tales of the great world of St. Petersburg and the court. Looking out on the Golden Gate they were betrothed.

"Russians are heathens!" protested the Argüellos. Don Luis took his sister to the Fathers at the Mission. Concepción still declared that she would marry the Russian.

Couriers summoned Governor Arrillaga from Monterey. The Governor, a bachelor, spoke with Rezánov in French. He wished Rezánov well in romance, but no flattery on the part of Rezánov could prevail against Arrillaga's refusal to sell food save for cash. Romance was the Russian's sole coin.

The marriage contract was drawn up. Rezánov and Doña Concepción were formally betrothed. The diplomat would appeal to the Spanish court. Obstacles must melt. Kneeling before the altar in Mission Dolores, Rezánov and Concepción made their last vows of love. On the *Juno*, laden with food and grain, Russia's Court Chamberlain Rezánov sailed past the port on May 21, giving and receiving salutes and swung out of the Golden Gate to save his countrymen at Sitka.

The Argüellos prayed that Concepción would forget the heretic; but even during long silent years she remembered, although she did not know what had become of Rezánov. He succored his starving countrymen, started through Siberia overland for St. Petersburg.

On the way he was stricken with violent fever. Weakened, he fell from his horse and died at Krasnoyarsk.

Concepción Argüello was nearly fifty when she learned from an English traveler why Rezánov had failed to return. The gold era entered California. At Monterey the Dominican Sisters established a convent of Santa Catarina of Siena. There, on April 11, 1851, she received the white habit of Saint Dominic and became California's first nun, Sister María Dominica.

In 1854 the Sisters moved to Benicia. The convent journal recalls her last hours. On Christmas Day, 1857, she died. She was buried dressed in her white habit as a nun. Sister María Dominica lies in the Dominican cemetery on the hillside overlooking Benicia Bay. After more than eighty years, flowers almost daily are brought by strangers and placed on her grave.

Early in the nineteenth century California had many earthquakes. *Comandante* Argüello wrote, June 21, 1808, that in three weeks the Presidio had suffered eighteen shocks, cracking walls. He feared for Fort San Joaquin. Most California Missions suffered from the great earthquake of 1812, but San Francisco was spared. The Mission was even embellished by Father Abella, who remained twenty years. Silver sacred vessels were obtained. Saint Michael's statue was procured. Four large paintings were presented to the Mission. Saint Roch was the subject of one picture, and the birth of Christ of another.

Spring was called by the Indians flower time; summer, rest time; winter, wild seed time; autumn, wild geese and acorn time. In acorn time, October 2, 1816, Mission Dolores had a visitor, Otto von Kotzebue, commander of the Russian ship *Rurik,* who brought to the notice of the world California's state flower, the golden poppy. Hills covered with these blossoms had caused the region to be called the "land of fire."

Kotzebue and his friends, the French nobleman Adelbert von Chamisso, and Herr Doktor Johann Friedrich Eschscholtz, both botanists, tented on the shore of San Francisco Bay. Even in October Chamisso discovered the poppy, called by the Spanish *copa de*

Royal Presidio Chapel now Parish Church at Monterey

Courtesy Society of California Pioneers

Mother Mission San Diego before restoration

San Diego de Alcalá, founded July 16, 1769. First California Mission

San Cárlos when Vancouver came in 1792

San Carlos Borromeo (Carmelo) where Serra is buried

Mission San Gabriel Arcángel, 1771

Mission San Gabriel in Los Angeles

San Antonio de Padua. View before restoration, 1902

San Antonio de Padua after completion of new roof

Courtesy Gabriel Moulin

San Luis Obispo de Tolosa, 1772

Courtesy San Luis Obispo Chamber of Commerce

San Luis Obispo de Tolosa

San Francisco de Asis, 1776

Mission Dolores Church after earthquake of 1868

Interior of Mission San Francisco de Asis (Dolores)
San Francisco

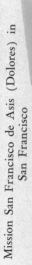

Mission San Francisco de Asis (Dolores) in
San Francisco

Ruins of Mission San Juan Capistrano before restoration

Mission San Juan Capistrano, California's oldest building. Serra's church

Campanario, Mission San Juan Capistrano

Mission San Buenaventura before restoration

Mission San Buenaventura

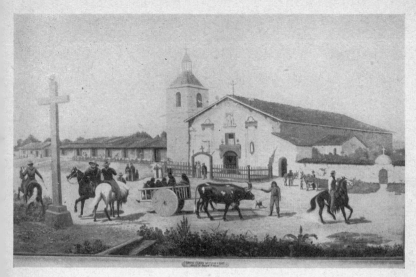

Mission Santa Clara de Asis in 1849 from painting by Andrew P. Hill

Earliest picture of Mission Santa Clara de Asis

oro, or *el capitán de las flores*. It was also known as the *dormidera*, sleepy-one, because of closing its petals late in the afternoon.

In 1820 Chamisso gave his discovery the terrifying name *Eschscholtzia Californica*, in honor of the "very skillful, very learned, very amicable Eschscholtz."

Kotzebue was entertained by Governor Solá, who came from Monterey. A bull and bear fight was given at the Presidio, but the Russian complained that he was received in a dirty little room at the Mission. A sermon in Spanish placing Saint Francis on an "equality" with Christ offended him. Half-clothed Indians could not understand the Christian language. The neophyte orchestra of violin, violincello, and two flutes played out of tune. Louis Choris, artist of the expedition, however, found everything pleasant.

About this time baptisms numbered 5,807. Neophytes studied at the Fathers' school, but after thirty-five, Indians never learned Spanish. They mastered the violin, bass drum, and bass viol. One neophyte made a cornet. The Indians irrigated their garden from a stream of water flowing through the Plaza. Twenty looms whirred in the weaving shops, and two mills were operated by mule power. In 1814, 11,190 bushels of grain were raised.

Although the Indians lived in substantial houses with tile roofs, they had little stamina. Measles cost the Mission 236 neophytes, and venereal disease was devastating.

Governor Solá suggested transferring some Indians across the bay to a milder climate. On the northern shore they improved in health, and so, on December 14, 1817, the *Asistencia* of St. Raphael, the Archangel, came into existence. Out of this foundation grew Mission San Rafael. At first it housed 282 Indians.

One year later only 600 neophytes were living at Mission San Francisco de Asis—mostly the decrepit, the infirm, and small children. Thirty-two were staying at Mission San José. Eighty-four had run away to *rancherías*. San Francisco's death rate was alarming. Finally only fifty-eight able-bodied men could be depended upon for labor. Women did men's work.

In this period Mission and Presidio were greatly perturbed. On May 18, 1822, General Agustín Iturbide, declaring Mexico independent of Spain, was crowned Agustín I. Monterey knelt in loyalty. San Francisco was expected to do the same. Fireworks exploded. Artillery thundered. The new constitution was cheered. Captain Luis Argüello became Governor.

Argüello informed the Father *Comisário Prefecto* Vicente de Sarría that he was expected to take the oath of allegiance. Father Sarría replied that he considered himself a citizen of Spain; he did not wish to be molested any more than a citizen of the United States would be.

So much of the land near the Mission was covered by a creeping mint-like vine that Governor Borica, in a letter to Engineer Alberto Cordova on April 4, 1797, called the locality *Yerba Buena*. Here in the 1820's in today's Grant Avenue near Clay Street, three miles from the Mission, was built the first house of modern San Francisco by William A. Richardson, a native of London. Richardson had several schooners and became the founder of shipping on San Francisco Bay.

Nearest neighbor to the Richardson family was Jacob P. Leese, a native of Ohio. On July 4, 1836, he celebrated completion of his frame dwelling with the first reading in San Francisco of the Declaration of Independence and the first raising of the flag of the United States.

In 1823 Mission San Francisco de Asis was commonly called Dolores to distinguish it from Mission San Francisco Solano in the north, founded by Father José Altimira. Death had reduced the population of Dolores until in 1827 there were only 241 Indian men, women, and children. They harvested 500 bushels of wheat, 600 of barley, 85 of beans and peas. There was no sale for their 4,000 lean cattle, 5,000 sheep, 470 useless horses, and 18 pack mules.

At the Presidio officers rode bareback. *Comandante* Martínez tried to obtain 50 saddles from Mission Santa Inés, which excelled in leather manufacture. Father Blas Ordáz refused credit, demanding cash; Mission Santa Barbara had given him a worthless draft for $10,000.

Demands were made upon the Mission in the 'thirties by the juvenile *Comandante* Don Mariano Vallejo. For his soldiers he obtained grain, tallow, tools, and livestock. Santa Clara contributed butter. Corn, vegetables, and soap were donated by Mission San José. In 1832 Mission Dolores' fields yielded only 300 bushels of wheat, 250 of barley, 101 of peas and beans, and 30 of corn. Fifty families did the work. They received nothing for their labor.

Near the Presidio on a small ranch lived Juana Briones de Miranda, a modern woman. She appeared before the *Alcalde* and asked to have her husband exiled leagues from San Francisco. She not only sustained her large brood in her adobe at the foot of Telegraph Hill near Washerwoman's Bay, but she befriended mistreated runaway sailors by secreting them in her house until their ship left port. Later she guided them down the peninsula and obtained work for them. Much of the lumber hewn in the 'thirties and 'forties near what later became Redwood City, was supplied by the adzes of these seamen.

Doña Juana herself was one of the few Spanish-California women to acquire a Spanish land grant. Near today's Los Altos in the western foothills of Santa Clara County, still stands her adobe dwelling on the Rancho La Purísima. It is the property of Mrs. Edith Eaton.

Last to be lost by Mission Dolores was its wide acreage: Ranchos San Pablo, San Antonio, Nuestra Señora de la Merced, Buri-Buri, and El Potrero, where horses were raised. Rancho Las Pulgas fell into the hands of Governor Luis Argüello, and at his death became the property of his widow, Doña Soledad Ortega de Argüello.

When Governor José Figueroa came in 1833 and brought ten Mexican friars to displace the Spaniards, Father Tomás Esténaga surrendered the Mission to Father José de la Concepción Quijas and withdrew to Mission San Gabriel. Father Quijas found that 6,536 Indians had been baptized, besides 448 Mexican children. There had been 1,961 Indian and 79 Mexican marriages; there were recorded 5,037 Indian burials, and 150 Mexican. Only 204 Indians lived at the Mission. They harvested 1,100 bushels of grain. Herds numbered 5,000 cattle, 1,000 horses, 3,500 sheep, and 18 mules.

Mission Dolores was one of the first establishments to be secularized. When Governor Figueroa issued his decree on August 9, 1834, the property was valued at $60,000. The library was appraised at $522. There were 114 fruit trees, and a fenced orchard was valued at $334.

In the inventory the church was described as an adobe structure of one nave, 122 feet long and 37 wide, roofed with tile. Adjoining the rear of the church was a sacristy 42 feet long and 25 wide with adobe walls and a tile roof.

After the Mexican Government seized the Mission, José Joaquin Estudillo was appointed administrator, and he was succeeded by Ignacio del Valle. Mission San Francisco de Asis was called Pueblo de Dolores. Indians were supposed to own the property, but they were too feeble to assert their rights. Only nine or ten were capable of hard labor.

When William E. P. Hartnell, Inspector of the Missions, reached Dolores in January, 1839, the Indians had no clothing. Tiburcio Vasquez, son of one of the first colonists, was administrator. Most of the neophytes were living at San Mateo. Herds had dwindled to one-quarter of what they had been at the time of secularization.

The Presidio was equally desolate. Corporal Joaquin de la Peña said a ship could easily send in launches to land on the beach at its foot, and unknown to Mission guards roll the eight cannon down the cliff.

In 1841 de Mofras, the French traveler, reported that Mission dwellings had fallen to pieces. Two years later eight old Indians presented a petition to the authorities for support. The church was served by Father José M. del Mercado of Santa Clara. Occasionally Father José Maria del Real came. Father Miguel Muro remained only a few months in 1845.

On his confirmation tour in 1844, Bishop García Diego, California's first bishop, did not visit Dolores. Indians had abandoned religious instruction and become drunkards, robbers, and murderers. To Governor Pio Pico the Bishop gave his reason for remaining away from San Francisco: "There would be no hospitality. Only a missile would pierce me." There was a rumor that when the Bishop arrived at Monterey, a musket was discharged at him in the dark.

In 1845 Governor Pico warned Indians that they must return to

Dolores, or the property would be sold. No purchaser could be found; the establishment remained in the hands of the state.

In February, 1846, a twenty-four-year-old priest, Father José Prudencio Santillan, was curate of the Mission with a salary of 1,000 pesos a year, which he was unable to collect. The Mission cemetery served the growing town of Yerba Buena, "the place where the Yankees lived," which in ten years had acquired 250 inhabitants, mostly Americans. The last entry in the register of the dead was made by Father Real, when an American, William Alexander Leidsdorff, owner of the first steamer used on San Francisco Bay, passed away on March 8, 1848.

After the United States flag was raised over Yerba Buena July 9, 1846, more Americans came on the *Brooklyn*, Oregon-bound, July 31, 1846. Two hundred Mormons, led by Samuel Brannan, an Elder of the Utah Church, held the first non-Catholic religious services at Yerba Buena. Sam Brannan's *California Star*, January 9, 1847, was Yerba Buena's first newspaper. On January 30, 1847, the *Star* made an announcement: the name Yerba Buena was changed to San Francisco.

Father Santillan soon ceded Mission Dolores property to Bishop García Diego and left California. In 1848 he returned and presented to the United States Land Commission a claim to the Mission and three square leagues of land, alleged to have been granted him February 10, 1846, by Governor Pico.

Like many Pico grants, it was suspected of having been pre-dated. Although approved by the United States Land Commission and the District Court, it was declared invalid in 1860 by the United States Supreme Court. Already, on March 3, 1858, President Buchanan had signed the patent granting Mission property and 4.51 acres to the Catholic Church.

In Father Santillan's time confusion controlled Dolores. Major-domo Vasquez was selling wine; cattle were tramping down the garden. Suddenly overnight near the Mission sprang up the world's largest mining camp. Gold-seekers squatted even on Mission land. Sand hills were overspread with tents of canvas, blankets, and boughs. In one year San Francisco had 25,000 inhabitants.

Many newcomers were Roman Catholics. English, French, German sermons were required. California's Catholic clergy spoke Spanish. Administrator José Maria Rúbio invited assistance. Father J. B. A. Brouillet came from Walla Walla but, finding the Mission unfit to live in, moved to Santa Clara. Father Anthony Langlois arrived from Oregon. Father Rúbio authorized Father Brouillet to erect the parish church of Saint Francis in San Francisco. In a house belonging to Major James A. Hardie, commander of the United States troops at San Francisco, on June 17, 1849, Father Brouillet, aided by Father Langlois, held the first Catholic services in new San Francisco. Soon $5,000 was collected, and St. Francis Church was erected on a lot 70 by 140 feet.

Mission Dolores took on new life. On Easter, 1849, small boys were sent with castanets through the streets. Indians plunged into the *laguna*, giving themselves unwonted baths, gathered blue lilies, and, gaily bedecked with flowers, marched into the church to the strains of the violin. After services worshipers went out to witness the torturing and execution in the Plaza of a stuffed figure representing Judas.

During this period Mission Dolores was an amusement center for gold-seeking San Francisco. In the summer of 1850 Colonel Charles L. Wilson built a plank toll road connecting city and Mission. Omnibuses ran every half hour. Saturday nights there were *fandangos* at the Mission, where the von Witzleben brewery stimulated gaiety. There were several saloons and two race tracks. Duels were frequent. Bear and bull fights enlivened Sunday afternoons. Mission Indians began begging from gold-seekers, and soon were rolling by the wayside in drunken stupor. Young Indian women, however, worked in Spanish families and were excellent domestics.

In June, 1850, the Pope appointed the Reverend Father José Sadoc Alemany, O.P., as Bishop of California. He came on the steamer *Columbus* on December 6, 1850. In 1853 the Pope designated San Francisco as a Metropolitan See and appointed Bishop Alemany of Monterey to fill the new office. Archbishop Alemany took up his residence in San Francisco.

With Father Brouillet arrived the founders of California's first enduring college: two Italian Jesuits, Fathers Michael Accolti and John Nobili, who came by way of Oregon. In 1851 they established Santa Clara College at Mission Santa Clara with Father Nobili as president.

Mission Dolores also had a new school in an adobe building north of the Mission Church. It was founded by a tall dark-haired Frenchman, Father Flavian Fontaine, one of the Picpus religious from Valparaiso. Three teachers presided over twenty pupils in three rooms.

One year later Father Flavian acquired and cleared two blocks of land covered with sagebrush, wild blackberries, toyon, and scrub oaks for the school. He erected a brick building for boarders and day pupils, but he could not raise funds to continue the work. Despairing, Father Flavian returned to Paris.

Father Nobili of Santa Clara College began paying Father Flavian's creditors. Father Francisco Veyret of Santa Clara was president and the only teacher. The school was difficult of access and had little ground for games. The boys scorned housework. Father Veyret fetched wood and water, cleaned, and washed dishes. Six mouths were to be fed, and he said, "They ate like ogres." Only two boys paid, rarely in cash, often in promises. Father Veyret abandoned the project to Father Nobili.

After Father Fontaine left, in 1855 the buildings were bought by St. Ignatius College, later the great University of San Francisco.

In this period Lola Montez, the dancer, former favorite of King Ludwig of Bavaria, married Editor Patrick Hull at Dolores. Casey and Cora, victims of San Francisco Vigilantes, were also brought here to be buried.

The United States Government tried to protect Dolores and all Missions, but Moraga's work at the Presidio was largely demolished in 1853 by Major J. G. Barnard to make way for new buildings. Only one of the original Presidio structures remains: the greatly remodeled Officers Club. Probably it is the oldest building in San Francisco, but its date of erection is uncertain. In 1792 *Comandante* Sal reported to the Viceroy that all buildings begun at the Presidio in 1776 were destroyed by storms in 1779. Possibly the Officers

Club was begun in that year; when it was completed remains a matter for speculation.

Six pieces of Spanish artillery still exist. Two stand at the entrance to the Officers Club. Two are mounted on the lawn bordering the parade ground, the former site of the garrison dwellings. Two grace the grounds at Fort Mason.

In a long adobe building, formerly the living quarters of the Fathers at Mission Dolores, there was founded in 1853 the first diocesan school, the Seminary of St. Thomas Aquinas. The Superior, Father Richard Carroll, who was later interred in the Mission Church, had fifteen students. The seminary was closed in 1866, when Father John J. Prendergast found himself with only two students. The seminary building was partly modernized in the 'sixties and served as parish house until the present residence was erected by Father Brennan.

Father Prendergast, who became a Monsignor, made several changes in the Mission church. It seemed in danger of crumbling, and he covered the building with clapboards and placed windows in the south wall.

During Monsignor Prendergast's time a white altar was installed in the church. In September, 1903, Miss Nora H. Fennell, who organized the first American choir at Dolores, herself playing the little yellow melodeon, asked daughters of pioneers to restore the sanctuary. When the white altar was removed, the original altar appeared, soft green embellished with gold flecked with red, as it was brought from Mexico. It was discovered that the altar statues carved out of redwood were made in California: the images of the Virgin Mary, Saint Francis, San Joachim, Saint Michael, Santa Clara, and Saint Anne.

At Dolores was established the first parochial school, during the 'seventies. It was in the workshop on the west side of the quadrangle which had housed the Mission weaving industry. Notre Dame Convent was founded in Dolores' orchard. The Holy Family Day Home stands on the site of the Indian village.

The modern church at the side of the Mission crumbled in the earthquake of 1906, but the ancient adobe building passed unharmed through the ordeal. The spirit of Saint Francis seemed to stay the flames one block away.

In 1917 Monsignor John W. Sullivan undertook restoration work and engaged the architect Willis Polk. The rough-hewn beams held together by rawhide thongs were giving way. Steel beams were placed in grooves on the exterior of the adobe walls. The space was filled and covered with cement so that beams inside and out were invisible. Steel trestles were added to support the heavy roof. Interior walls were redecorated, but the original ceiling paint was left. When floor tiles in the body of the church were badly broken or missing, cement was used to make repairs. A wrought-iron rail replaced the one of wood, and an iron rail was installed in the gallery. New glass was set in the windows. A rough cement coating took the place of clapboards.

Mass is still said at Dolores on Decoration Day; June 29, Founders Day, feast of St. Peter and St. Paul; and October 4, feast of St. Francis. The Mission is used largely as a museum. Tourists are attracted by the ciborium brought by Father Palóu in 1776; the French monstrance of 1757; the original chalice, the silver missal stand, the books of baptism, marriage, and death; antique vestments, paintings, confessional doors, the revolving tabernacle, and the hand-carved altars which came from Mexico in 1780. Aside from the redwood statues there are those of Our Lady of Mercy, San Luis Rey, St. Joseph, San Buenaventura, San Juan Capistrano, and St. Francis Solano.

In 1938, while workmen were transplanting palm trees from Notre Dame convent garden, formerly the Mission orchard, to the Exposition grounds, several valuable relics were discovered. Doubtless more could be found by excavation.

Many changes have come to Dolores since the day in 1776 just before the colonists on the Atlantic coast declared their independence, when the little group of gray friars and blue and red uniformed soldiers first tented on the field of lupines by the *laguna* of the blue lilies, but interest in the Mission increases. Thousands annually visit the building and stroll through San Francisco's oldest garden of death where flowers bloom seemingly of richer hue for growing in sacred ground. Here is the tomb of Don Luis Argüello, California's first native son to be Governor. Near by are Casey and Cora. One breathes the same air with Lilote, the first coppery-skinned daughter of San Francisco to be baptized at the Mission; Father Palóu beginning California literature; Father Serra limping in from San Carlos; Moraga clanking back from battle; Concepción Argüello and Rezánov on their knees vowing eternal love—all these incongruous beings had the compassion and understanding of him who embraced even lepers, and in humility called himself the world's greatest sinner—Saint Francis.

VII

San Juan Capistrano

HERE at the swallows' Mission San Juan Capistrano is California's oldest building, Father Junípero Serra's church. Alone of all the California Missions these walls beheld Father Junípero while he re-enacted the sacrifice of Calvary. Every brick of Serra's church seems to recall that moment, and the air still reverberates with his prayers. That is why the heart catches a little in the singing garden planted by the late Father St. John O'Sullivan, who revived the beauty of the spot and celebrated the invisible presence of Serra.

When Portolá passed here in 1769 he called it a "most inviting valley": trees, water, pasturage, and so many wild grapevines that it looked like a vineyard. Near by was a village of fifty Indians, their bodies painted with red and white ochre. San Francisco Solano, the place was christened by Portolá. Viceroy Antonio Maria Bucareli chose as patron saint of the Mission, San Juan, surnamed Capistran, one of the few lawyers canonized.

In this delightful valley where the Arroyo Trabuco meets the Arroyo de la Misión Vieja, on October 30, 1775, Father Fermin Francisco de Lasuén of San Carlos and Father Gregorio Amúrrio of San Luis Obispo, guarded by Lieutenant Francisco Ortega and soldiers, began the Mission foundation. The Cross was raised. From timbers were suspended two bells. The chapel was begun. Father Lasuén said Mass.

Swift-riding couriers from San Diego interrupted with news, "Indian revolt!" Hurriedly bells were buried. Portable objects were taken to San Diego. Temporarily San Juan Capistrano was abandoned.

Father Lasuén was made senior missionary at San Diego. A year later Father Serra, accompanied by Fathers Pablo de Mugártegui and Gregorio Amúrrio, with an escort of soldiers, set out to found the Mission. On October 30, the octave of San Juan Capistrano, they arrived. Still upright was the Cross planted by Lasuén. Serra disinterred the bells and rang them to announce to the Indians the missionaries' return.

Natives warmly welcomed the Fathers. Quickly a bowery for a chapel was constructed. Father Serra offered up the first High Mass at San Juan Capistrano. The feast of All Saints, November 1, 1776, was the day thereafter celebrated as the formal founding of the seventh Mission.

Serra left for San Gabriel to procure Indian laborers and native interpreters. On the return journey the train of supplies and cattle proceeded too slowly. In spite of his lameness, Serra went eagerly ahead, accompanied only by a soldier and a neophyte.

A few leagues from the Mission suddenly Serra was surrounded by painted, armed savages yelling frightfully. His last hour had come, he thought. The convert shouted to the pagans, "Don't hurt the old *padre*. You will be killed."

The pagans desisted. Serra bade them approach, presented them with beads, gave them his blessing, and left them friends.

When he reached the Mission he learned that soldier Manuel Robles had assaulted the wife of an Indian chief. Why the natives had menaced Serra on the trail was clear. He demanded removal of the soldier, but would not aid in punishing him.

During the month that Serra remained at the Mission, he drew up the title pages of baptismal and burial books in his definite, singularly modern handwriting. The baptismal register begins: "Praise be Jesus, Mary, Joseph!" The Mission was called San Juan Capistrano de Quanís-sajivit.

Although they did not understand the strangers, the Indians repeated with fervor and tenderness the words faith, hope, and charity uttered by Fathers Mugártegui and Amúrrio. Soon the first temporary chapel was completed. It stood on a stream that never ran dry and was sheltered by a rugged mountain.

At other Missions Indians asked for eatables and gifts, but at San

Juan Capistrano they requested baptism. Father Amúrrio recorded the first, December 19, 1776: a child Nanojibar, about six years old, from the Ranchería Guillucome, was given the name Juan Bautista. The first marriage united Brigida and Saturnino, Mission neophytes. Father Mugártegui performed the ceremony on January 23, 1777. He also officiated at the first burial on July 13, in the same year: Sinforosa, child of pagan parents.

San Juan Capistrano met obstacles usually attending young establishments: the Alocuachomi Ranchería threatened neophytes in June, 1777. Corporal Mariano Carrillo killed three and wounded four of the offenders. A chieftain was punished for furnishing women to the Spanish guard. Painted for war and vengeance-bent, San Gabriel Indians appeared at the Mission. The Fathers held up the image of Our Lady. Down upon their knees fell the Indians, weeping and embracing the missionaries.

The following year came new trouble. A chieftain's wife eloped with a native of Lower California. The chief appealed to his friends. Spaniards were devils, he said: they brought drouth to destroy crops. Several months later Spanish soldiers bearing messages to the Governor were attacked near San Gabriel and a corporal was killed.

Even in this turmoil the missionaries erected dwellings for themselves and their Indian servants. An adobe church was built, and on December 2, 1777, there was a baptism. Father Serra came and observed that the church was too small to accommodate neophytes. Following his advice, the front part was extended, built higher, and the rear half correspondingly raised. This portion of the building in the rear is California's oldest structure; it has seen 161 years. It is the only church in California where the founder of the Missions not only celebrated Mass but also administered the sacraments of baptism and confirmation. His last record in the Mission register was: "I set out from the Mission San Juan Capistrano on the fifteenth day of October, 1783."

At the end of 1784 Fathers Mugártegui and Amúrrio had recorded 566 baptisms, 126 marriages, and 99 burials. In the same year they harvested 2,883 bushels of corn, 665 of wheat, and 100 of beans, requiring erection of two granaries. There were 1,353 goats, 703 cattle, 904 sheep, 59 horses, and 12 mules. Forty cabins were erected for neophytes, all of adobe and *tule*-roofed until tiles could be manufactured. After the garden was surrounded by an adobe wall in 1795, new quarters were erected for the military guard and weavers.

The thriving new Mission donated to Mother Mission San Diego peas and beans for planting. In return San Diego gave several colts and sackfuls of wood. Fifty pounds of iron for plowpoints were much appreciated, as were the expert weavers lent to assist in cloth making.

When once land was cleared of brushwood, the soil was fertile. Domestic grapes grafted onto wild roots were grown successfully.

In 1797 at San Juan Capistrano the most splendid building of the Mission period was begun. Fathers Fuster and Santiago assembled the neophytes, explaining how God had ordered Moses to build Him a great tabernacle, and how women had offered jewels and fine linen to adorn it.

The Indians agreed to quarry stones and haul them to the Mission. Indian women, thrilling over the story of the service of women of ancient time to Moses, felt heavy of heart because only stone was to go into their great structure. Large rocks they could not carry, but they walked six miles to fetch small stones from the quarry. Some carried them in a net on their backs. Others suspended them from their heads in small sacks. Weaker ones carried a few in their arms. Men dragged large rocks from the quarry with chains; these chains are still to be seen at the Mission museum. Pine logs for beams and sycamore poles for rafters were brought from Trabuco Canyon.

The cornerstone was laid March 2, 1797. Isidro Aguilár from Culiacán, Mexico, directed the work. He remained nine years. Skilled artisans fashioned the baptismal font and holy-water receptacle. Leading into the sacristy were well-carved arched doorways with stone facings more elaborate than those at any other Mission.

After the death of the master builder in 1803, for three years the Fathers continued the work alone. Father Fuster did not live to see his church dedicated. On October 22, 1800, he was buried on the epistle side of the main altar by Father Pedro Estévan.

The new building was in the form of a Roman Cross with six

domes, one over the sanctuary, three over the transept, and two over the nave beyond the transept. Its roof was vaulted like the sky. The building was 146 feet long and 28 wide with a vestry 28 by 19 feet. Its boulder foundation was from 2 to 7 feet thick. Walls were of concrete, sandstone, and adobe. Ceilings were of *tule* woven together with rawhide strips bound to hand-hewn rafters and plastered. From a point ten miles to the north the high bell tower could be seen. Perched on the tower was a gilded cock, and from the dome of the transept rose a narrow spire of square Mission tile. From the august tower the sound of the bells carried even farther than eye could see.

When the building was dedicated, September 7, 1806, neophytes and even missionaries regarded with awe the beauty of their own creation. Father Estévan Tápis, President of the Missions, officiated at the dedication, assisted by Fathers José Faura, Norberto de Santiago, José de Miguel, José Zalvidéa, Antonio Peyri, and Pedro de la Cueva. Father Marcos Vitoria said Mass, and Father Juan Urresti preached.

Governor José Joaquin Arrillaga arrived for the dedication. With him were San Diego and Santa Barbara soldiers in glittering uniforms. Neophytes from distant *rancherías* crowded the church. A *fiesta* followed which became a legend in Southern California.

The first baptism in the new church took place on October 18, 1806. Many others followed. There was a great activity in fields and factories. Neophytes feasted on strange new fruits, pomegranates, peaches, quinces, nectarines. Sparkling wine was made, "almost as good as that of Mexico."

The abundant wool clip supplied other Missions. Under government contract at $30 a month, Mariano Mendoza of Monterey taught Indians weaving. If he neglected his work, missionaries warned, he would be chained up. Forty crude looms rattled and clattered. Owing to lack of lemons, there was difficulty in dyeing a satisfactory blue. Substituting vinegar, Mendoza wove a carpet 18 yards long for the church, 40 blankets, 60 yards of cloth for neophytes, and 80 half-size blankets for Mission Santa Clara. After the Indians learned all Mendoza could teach, he was dismissed. There still exist bird skins that were dressed and leather that was tanned by neophytes.

Building was resumed on a large scale in 1807. A corridor 150 feet long was erected for the new church, and a side altar added. Thirty-four adobe houses for neophytes were constructed.

After serving San Juan Capistrano for eleven years, Father José Faura, one of the builders of the stone church, retired in October, 1809. Father Norberto de Santiago, who had lived at San Juan Capistrano for twenty-one years, followed his friend. They were succeeded by Fathers José Barona and Francisco Suñer. Under the new missionaries there was increased speed in the soap factory, and the wagon and carpenter shops. A watercourse was continued 1,400 feet. The population reached 1,361.

On a summer-like morning, December 8, 1812, Mass was being celebrated. What was that distant roar? Was it the sea? The tower tottered. Several persons left. Fathers Suñer and Barona were in the sanctuary. They implored the congregation to take refuge in the sacristy. People fled to the side door. Again the tower tottered. The Fathers and neophytes escaped to the sacristy. Bells swayed, tolled, were silenced, and then crashed to earth. With them fell two Indian bell ringers. The door had been twisted by the earthquake, and could not be unlocked. Nearly forty neophytes were buried under the stone and mortar of the fallen tower.

This magnificent church of San Juan Capistrano had been in building more than nine years. It endured six years and nine months. Gradually the old ruins were cleared away. One woman was taken out alive.

Among those who died, legend says, were Indian Teofilo, the artist, and Magdalena, the half-breed. Wishing to forget her Indian blood, she claimed she was the daughter of a Spanish soldier. The Father feared her influence over Teofilo and said he must marry Ana, an Indian girl. He told Magdalena to carry a penitent's candle in front of the Indian women. This she did on the day of the earthquake. Teofilo hastened to her side and was buried with her. Faded Indian frescos commemorate the lovers.

After December 8, 1812, Serra's church was again used for services. The iron railing along the sanctuary of the ruined church still serves as the balustrade of the gallery in the old church.

Bravely the Fathers in three months re-erected the baptistry on the cemetery side of the former church. Its remains still exist. Here, on March 21, 1813, the first baptism was administered, the subject being the infant Benito Niceto. The following year Father José Barona and Gerónimo Boscana built a hospital.

The new *campanario* was a pierced bell wall joining the two buildings. Here since 1813 have hung San Juan Capistrano's four bells. Two suspended from sycamore beams were made in 1804. Their inscriptions read: AVE MARIA PURISIMA SN ANTONIO 1804. (HAIL MARY MOST PURE SAINT ANTHONY 1804.) And: AVE MARIA PURISIMA SAN RAFAEL 1804. (HAIL MARY MOST PURE SAINT RAPHAEL 1804.) One of the smaller bells is lettered: AVE MARIA PURISIMA ME FECIT RUELAS I ME YAMO S. JUAN 1796. (HAIL MARY MOST PURE. RUELAS MADE ME AND MY NAME IS SAINT JOHN 1796.) Largest and oldest is the benediction bell that has been here since the beginning. It is inscribed: VIVA JESUS SN VICENTE ADVON DE LOS RRS PS MIROS F VICTE FUSTR IF JN SN TIAGO 1796. (PRAISED BE JESUS, SAINT VINCENT. IN HONOR OF THE REVEREND PADRES MINISTERS FRAY VINCENT FUSTER AND FRAY JUAN SANTIAGO 1796.)

This coppery green bell, in which two original bells were recast, commemorates the Fathers who built San Juan Capistrano. At this Mission the bells have their own message in being rung. On feast days and for the last Mass all four clang boisterously. Death is denoted by immediate tolling, provided it is before the evening Angelus. Night is never disturbed by an announcement of death. By the manner of ringing townspeople know whether man, woman, or child has passed away. San Juan Capistrano believes that when Matilda, the Indian maiden who cared for the sanctuary, died, although no hand touched the bells, they rang.

The sunny Mission of San Juan Capistrano was not overlooked by Bouchard, the buccaneer. In 1818, after looting and burning the Ortega Rancho Refugio nine miles from Santa Barbara, he arrived. The Fathers and all families took refuge at the Rancho Trabuco. Aside from burning a few Indian straw houses and emptying wine, Bouchard did little damage.

At this time, however, the Mission had harvested 14,662 bushels of grain. In 1819 herds of cattle were at their largest, and numbered 31,263.

When the new Mexico constitution was adopted, October 4, 1824, Fathers Barona and Zalvidéa refused to swear allegiance. The next Mexican governor, Don José Echeandia, sent Lieutenant Romualdo Pacheco to promise San Juan Capistrano Indians equal rights with Spaniards. Young neophytes told the corporal of the guard to put the Fathers in stocks or "we will put you in stocks." They began to rob. At Spaniards they hurled the supreme insult, "English!" Neophytes refused to work; the land was covered with tree-like mustard. Herds died of thirst.

On March 20, 1829, Father Boscana and his associates were informed by the Mexican Government that they must leave California in one month. The missionary had buried thirty-nine victims of the earthquake of 1812, he had been hurled under a horse by a soldier in 1817; banishment by the Mexican Government found him benumbed. Snuff-taking was his only solace. The Mexican decree was not enforced, because no substitute for Father Boscana could be obtained. On July 6, 1831, he was buried at San Gabriel.

Father Boscana left a manuscript concerning the natives and their god Chinigchinich. Indian women varnished faces, breasts, and arms brown, the exposed parts being painted, black, red, and white. Women hung beads and shells from their necks. Every morning they were supposed to bathe—"The moon can see you get clean."

An Indian mentioned mother before father. He had plural wives to supply him with food. A bride was brought to her husband in gay apparel. Women tore off her clothing. The chief himself dressed his wife in the costume of the chieftess: a wig and skirt of feathers.

During the eclipse of the sun or moon Indians shouted, beating on the ground, on hides, on mats with sticks to manifest pain. Music was made with rattles of turtle shells, palm seeds, or wild cherry pits.

Months were counted by the moon, hours by the sun. Indians thought the sun had twelve palaces at equal distances around the earth and passed a month at each dwelling.

Some Indians pretended to be descended from coyotes. San Juan Capistrano natives believed a brother and sister who married in sin had borne rocks, trees, plants, the entire world. The human race was destroyed in a deluge, a few taking refuge on a mountain top. Chinigchinich promised never to destroy the world again.

When the god died, his followers offered to bury him. "No," he said, "I will go to the stars. From there I shall see you. To those who keep my commandments, I will give all they ask. To those who disobey my teachings, I will send bears to bite and serpents to sting."

Dancing, Chinigchinich ascended to the stars. In a round temple natives kept a figure made of a sack of coyote skins filled with arrows and feathers. Here day and night they danced, propitiating their god. The Indians believed, "As the moon died and came to life, so shall we die and live again."

During the twelve years Father Boscana spent at San Juan Capistrano, he selected the library. It contains Spanish translations of Bossuet and Massillon, and a revolutionary book of 1785, *The Critical Theater* or *Various Discourses on all Kinds of Matter for the Reproof of Common Errors* by the Very Illustrious Señor Don Fray Benito Gerónimo Feyjoo y Montenegro.

Captain Pablo de la Portilla arrived in 1834 at San Juan Capistrano to carry out Governor José Figueroa's emancipation of the Mission Indians and to organize three pueblos of ex-neophytes; San Dieguito, Las Flores, and San Pascual. When he began parceling out Rancho San Mateo, drunken natives committed robberies and murders shouting, *"Soy libre!"* (I am free).

An inventory at this time valued San Juan Capistrano buildings at $54,456. There were 861 Indians enrolled, but in two years only 283 bushels of grain had been garnered. Two years later most of the Indians were naked.

War came to the Mission in 1837. The buildings were occupied by Juan Bautista Alvarado—later Governor of California, José Castro, and more than two hundred men. Their foe, Provisional Governor Carlos Antonio Carrillo, was at Rancho Las Flores with an equal force. There in an adobe building was the barracks, with three cannon mounted on the adjoining corral; but they were fired only a few times. Battle was fought with tongue and pen. On April

23, 1838, a treaty was signed which gave the government of California to Alvarado.

Only a hundred Indians remained at Pueblo San Juan Capistrano in 1840. Five hundred were on Mission lands. Santiago Argüello became Administrator with a salary of $1,000 to be paid by the Indians. He put his own brand on the best horses, and supported twenty-two children and numerous relatives at the expense of the Mission. Caterpillars at the same time defoliated the vineyard.

Some old Indians asked to be shot rather than endure life, but seventy liked the republic. Those who wished to keep San Juan Capistrano as a Mission numbered thirty. Alvarado decreed in July, 1841, that houses, fields, cattle, agricultural implements, and other property should be allotted the Indians. One-third of the buildings were to be reserved for the *Comisionado* and accommodation of travelers, one-third should be used by the priest. Proceeds of orchards should maintain divine worship. One-third of the blankets should be given to poor and aged Indians. Sheeps' wool was to be reserved for weaving establishments with Indian weavers. Owners who did not obey regulations should lose their land.

In 1843 Indians were scattered; the Mission was reported as a brothel. Juan Bandini, who had been in charge for a year, left. The buildings sheltered thirty-eight families and four gentiles. The Mission had only five yoke of oxen, and no cattle or food. Father Zalvidéa, who had developed viticulture in California, still tottered to his feet and celebrated Mass.

San Juan Capistrano had a faint flutter of hope when Governor Manuel Micheltorena restored the management of twelve Missions to the Franciscans, but he was banished from California in March, 1845.

Three months after becoming Governor, Pio Pico, third native son to rule California, declared all Missions for rent or sale. Pico, usually overhung with gold chains and jewels, his pockets filled with $50 gold pieces, sold the Mission at auction to his brother-in-law, John Forster, and James McKinley for $710. Two days later the purchasers received a title deed from Pico to a portion of the principal buildings, the furniture, and three gardens. Most of the payment was made in hides and tallow. Forster was in charge of the Mission until 1855. He had a flock of peacocks that preened themselves in the corridors. When Pico fled to Mexico after American occupation, Forster concealed him at his Rancho Santa Margarita.

Before San Juan Capistrano was transferred to the jurisdiction of San Gabriel Franciscans in January, 1848, Father Vicente Pascual Oliva came to a sudden death during a storm. He was buried by Father Ordáz in the presbytery of the church. His resting place was unknown until Father St. John O'Sullivan, in December, 1912, found his remains, still richly vested, under the tile floor.

In February, 1850, Father José Maria Rosales came and remained three years. He was paid with 262 head of cattle, 12 horses, and $12 in cash.

Governor Pico's sale of the Mission was declared fraudulent by the United States Land Commission. On March 18, 1865, President Lincoln returned Mission San Juan Capistrano, including 44.40 acres of land, to the Catholic Church.

In the early 'sixties an effort was made to restore the ruined chapel. The remaining domes were blown down by gunpowder. Walls were rebuilt with adobe. Before the structure could be re-roofed it was melted by a severe storm. This misfortune ended the last effort to bring back the great chapel of San Juan Capistrano.

From 1859 to 1886 the Mission was ministered by Fathers Vicente Llover, Miguel Durán, Joseph Mut, and others. They also attended Indian stations San Luis Rey, Pala, Temecula, Cañada Verde, San Pascual, Agua Caliente, and La Puerta de San Felipe. Father Mut taught school in one of the Mission rooms and lived in the attic reached by a rickety ladder. For twenty-four years after he left, the Mission was attended by visiting priests.

The Mission patio became a recreation ground for Indians and village folk. A bull game was often organized. Through the Puerta Chiquita, or Little Gate, on the north side the bull came, a purse of silver tied on his head. The object was to pull the money off the bull, but his life was spared. Spectators crowded the corridor roof cheering daring contestants.

Smallpox and the saloons helped decimate San Juan Capistrano

Indians, but services were held in Serra's church until the roof became unsafe in 1891. Dust would have claimed the building but for the coming of a dying man on July 5, 1910—Father St. John O'Sullivan of Louisville, Kentucky. Carried off the train on a stretcher, he was taken to his lodgings in a bungalow. The spell of the poplar-lined streets and the blue atmosphere fell upon Father O'Sullivan. In a few days he walked a little. Soon he tottered up the cow path to the Mission.

The Landmarks Club of Los Angeles had preserved some of the walls in 1895 and re-roofed several hundred feet of the cloisters. But vandals had carted away stone and tile. The church was used as a lumber warehouse. Garbage was dumped in the patio, to the disgust of the gaudy strutting peacock, last of the Forster flock. The priest walked over the worn stones and looked at the dismantled olive-crushing mill. He was touched by the broken walls of the cloisters in which cliff swallows nested. The varying widths of the elliptical arches only added to the picturesqueness of the corridor. He sat in the interesting seats with brick bases. His hand rested on the four ancient bells. The swallows and the swifts greeted him joyously, and he felt at home. He passed through the beautiful carved doorway into the chapel. How intensely life had been lived here!

One afternoon late in November, when the sun was touching the arches and pilasters with soft color, he had his tent transported to the Mission ground. Goats were nosing straw and chaff in the garden. He took up his abode here with the peacock, buff-colored owls, gypsy cats, and wild dogs.

The priest prepared his supper and went to bed. Coyote scavengers in the quadrangle yapped at night. Linnets pulling his hair for nesting material told him when dawn broke.

In the morning Father O'Sullivan talked with *rebote* players in the street. He watched Indian women grinding corn on their *metates*. From the leather worker Acú—José Cruz was his baptismal name—Father O'Sullivan heard old tales. Acú was the son of a neophyte, a violin player in Franciscan days. He himself played the flute. He thought no one could ring the bells like him. *San Vicente* should ring first. As the echoes died *San Juan* should chime in with a steady clang-clang. Indians returned to San Juan Capistrano to die. All would be well if Acú tolled the great bells; they seemed eternal.

Acú told Father O'Sullivan of the Virgin's statue once taken to Mission San Gabriel. There it would not stand up.

"Take it back to San Juan Capistrano," said the Father.

On the return journey the statue was light to carry. When taken away, it had been heavy. Nine miles up the Camino Real the people met the Virgin. From that time the statue always stood quite erect at San Juan Capistrano.

Acú gave Father O'Sullivan some phrases in correct Acágcheme, the language of San Juan Capistrano Indians: *O-yósh shé-o-cu-let.* God will punish you. *Toó-she me-rúp.* Don't forget. *Me-wai' no-nah?* How are you, father? *No ló-veck.* I am well. *No ha-ke-le-chel.* I am hungry. *Sepúl á-uck Dios a wúluv.* There is only one great God. Numerals were: *Sepúl*, one; *queh*, two; *páhai*, three; *queh-sáh*, four; *mahár*, five. Acú said that when Indians counted more than five they showed fingers of both hands, and they also counted on the toes.

His strength returning, Father O'Sullivan moved into the Mission, cooking for himself. With Acú Father O'Sullivan often sat before the brick tile fireplace built by Father Mut in the 'sixties and read old books bound in sheepskin with heavy Mission-made clasps. With Acú Father O'Sullivan traced the aqueduct, reservoirs, cisterns, and irrigating systems made by missionaries and Indians.

One morning after Father O'Sullivan had lived several weeks at the Mission, he found a tramp in the room next his own. The rover wished to pay for his breakfast with work. Father O'Sullivan and the tramp began putting the building in order. A few weeks later, when the wanderer went his way, San Juan Capistrano looked like another place. Townspeople began to help the priest, and the bishop gave him charge of the Mission.

One volunteer worker was Don Ramón Yorba, a descendant of Don Tomás Yorba, grantee of eight square leagues of the Paraje de Santiago de Santa Ana. Don Tomás' velvet knee breeches, silver shoe buckles, hat trimmed with silver lace and gold ornaments, his silver-bedecked saddle and spurs were still remembered at the Mission. The Yorbas always rang the bells, cared for vestments, and cooked for visiting priests.

San Juan Capistrano was still beglamoured with the romance of Doña Raimunda Yorba, daughter of Don Bernardo of the reigning family. She fell in love with an Indian boy, son of her father's major-domo. Exiled to Monterey by her family until she agreed to marry one of the Alvarados, she consented on condition that they be married at San Juan Capistrano with festivities at the Santa Ana Rancho. After the ceremony Alvarado's bride sat in the *sala* at the *rancho*, playing her guitar and singing for lost love. All understood.

Father O'Sullivan began collecting money to restore the Mission. Santa Ana Native Sons and Daughters, the Landmarks Club, and the Bishop of Los Angeles helped. Sunday afternoons a pageant was presented. Receipts were used to reconstruct and reinforce the crumbling walls. Insecure pilasters were buttressed. Tiles were brought back from neighboring *ranchos* to roof the building. Serra's church began to live again.

Two large silver torches, the processional Cross, the bookstand for the missal, six bronze candlesticks, statues of Saint Dominic, St. Ignatius, and the Virgin Mary were replaced. But the twelfth Station of the Cross was missing. In the vacant space Father O'Sullivan placed a painting rescued by Doña Magdalena Murillo, the Crucifixion signed "José Francisco Zervas, 1800." It had hung unframed in Serra's church, rains beating upon it. Doña Magdalena kept the painting in her modest adobe dwelling and proudly saw it once more in the church. She also brought back the baptismal font with its crude cover and broken hinges.

San Juan Capistrano's original altar had vanished. In 1906 Bishop John J. Cantwell of Los Angeles obtained in Spain an early Franciscan altar richly carved and covered with gold leaf. In the central niche is the image of San Juan Capistrano holding a Crusader's banner. The Bishop sent the altar to the Mission.

Two hundred years after Serra's birth Father O'Sullivan erected in the garden on August 13, 1914, a monument in memory of

Father Junípero Serra. Ten years later he raised a shaft to the Franciscan and neophyte builders of the Mission.

On Easter Sunday, April 20, 1924, for the first time in several decades Mass was said in Serra's church. A few weeks later San Juan Capistrano was surprised to see Acú in Father O'Sullivan's cast-off tail coat. "Just one month more for old Acú," he predicted. "Bury me in the Father's coat." The bells tolled for him the last of July; San Juan Capistrano villagers hoped that the bell ringer was pleased with the tolling.

Father O'Sullivan flung himself into re-creating the garden. There remained aged pear trees, pomegranates with fiery blossoms, velvety gray olive trees, and Serra's beloved Castilian roses. Tons of debris were removed from the Plaza. Common flowers were planted: roses, geraniums, violets, marguerites, lilies. For fragrance there was rosemary, heliotrope, lilac, magnolias. Brilliancy was brought into the garden with cannas, dahlias, streptosolen, agapanthus, amaryllis, plumbago, and statice. Magenta Bougainvillea and orange trumpet vine entwined themselves in the dove-haunted tiles. San Juan Capistrano's garden became the beauty spot among California Missions and drew thousands of visitors, who watched the pigeons dipping their wings into the peaceful pool. In this shining mirror the peacock liked to gaze upon his iridescent beauty, but he was crushed under the wheels of a train.

For his work of a quarter of a century at the Mission Father O'Sullivan became a Monsignor. At last he could do no more. July 22, 1933, he was placed in the garden he had created. A monument marks his earth-home.

On March 19, St. Joseph's Day, San Juan Capistrano has thousands of visitors to welcome the swallows. Each autumn they leave for the winter, October 23, the day of San Juan Capistrano for whom the Mission was named. Townsfolk are in gala costume. Brown and gold birds come skimming through the air to be saluted by great birds of men that rise to meet them. With unerring instinct the swallows dip down to San Juan Capistrano. Linnets piping excitedly move from branch to branch in gray olive trees and acacias dripping gold. Mockingbirds repeat the swallows' rejoicing notes. Bells ring in gladness. Don Ramón Yorba chants a hymn. Children sing, "Good Morning, Mr. Swallow!" In Serra's church voices are lifted in prayer. The spirit of Saint Francis, who called all birds his brothers, goes out on the air over the radio; San Juan Capistrano becomes the nation's Mission.

VIII

Santa Clara de Asis

SANTA CLARA is my neighbor Mission, a few minutes' drive from the ranch. At one time it led all Missions in neophytes. Within its walls, often fire-swept, developed the University of Santa Clara. In Franciscan times tests were made here revealing the world's richest quicksilver mine, the New Almaden. And here lived Father Magin Catalá, the Holy Man of Santa Clara.

At Mission Santa Clara, for the first time a woman appears in Alta California as patron saint. Clara of Asis at seventeen was touched by the fervent spirit of Francis of her own city. Skeptical of the faith of the lovely woman of the knightly class, Francis gave her the test, "Dress in penitential sackcloth. Beg alms for the poor before your father's door."

Clara proved her faith. "Bewitched!" said her family.

"I will follow the Poor Man of Assisi," she answered.

Doors were barred against her going. She fled by the death portal of the palace. At the foot of the Franciscan altar she sheared off her hair and took the vows of poverty, chastity, and obedience. This was in 1212. For forty years she spread the spirit of Saint Francis. Mission Santa Clara, near that of St. Francis, could hardly have been more happily christened than for her, his most ardent apostle.

In 1769, when Portolá and his company passed this smiling valley where Mission Santa Clara was to be founded, they named it for San Bernardino of Siena. Because of clumps of rugged oaks, later Spaniards called it *El Llano de los Robles,* Plain of the Oaks.

It was not till January 5, 1777, that Lieutenant José Joaquin Moraga led the foundation expedition from the San Francisco Presidio southward. With him were Father Tomás de la Peña and ten soldiers. Winter torrents tore in from the southeast, but the travelers made fifteen leagues in one day.

About forty miles from Mission Dolores, on a bank of the western tributary of the Rio Guadalupe, in a pungent laurel thicket, the new Mission site was fixed. The Indians called it Thamien. Here were three *rancherías*: the Thamiens, the Gergecensens, and the Socoisukas of the Tares tribe. *Socoisuka* was the Indian name for laurel. These natives occupied what is now Laurelwood Ranch near Santa Clara and spoke an idiom similar to that of San Francisco.

A leafy canopy was prepared, a Cross erected. A plot of land two hundred feet square was cleared. On January 12, 1777, Father de la Peña celebrated the first Mass. The probable foundation site was marked with a Cross and plaque in 1921 by Father James A. Colligan.

Nine days after establishment of the Mission, Father José Murguía arrived from Monterey. He spoke the native idiom with slight variations. The Lord's Prayer taught by him to neophytes in the native tongue is still preserved at Santa Clara.

Father Murguía brought Mission property and cattle. The Indians preferred meat to acorns, and stole cattle fattened on luscious wild oats. Chastisement of the thieves engendered bitter feeling among the Indians. They would not cease stealing; three of their number were shot. After Moraga returned to San Francisco hostility continued.

No one was baptized; the Fathers were discouraged. When the new Governor Felipe de Neve came in April to inspect the struggling Mission, he was disappointed in the slight progress. An epidemic changed the situation. Indian children began dying. Missionaries ventured to *rancherías* to baptize infants at the point of death. Peace was established when Father de la Peña made the first baptism on June 6, 1777. At the Ranchería San Francisco he baptized a child six months of age, daughter of Saunin and Tomolinguis. He gave her the name Clara.

Among Spaniards the first baptism was that of a love child, named Antonio, on July 31, 1777, son of María Petra Azeves and José

Antonio González. Before the year was over sixty-seven Indians had been baptized.

The first death was recorded at Santa Clara on June 27, 1777, María Luisa of the Ranchería San Francisco Solano. Her native name was Vignis.

Soon neighbors came to the Mission. Three-quarters of a league distant was founded El Pueblo de San José de Guadalupe, California's first civic settlement, named in honor of the patron saint of the whole California enterprise. On November 29, 1777, fourteen families arrived from San Francisco, sixty-six persons in all.

The locality chosen by Governor Neve for the first pueblo— called for many years, and even today, by Spanish-Californians El Pueblo, was on the eastern bank of the Rio Guadalupe. Each settler was given a yoke of oxen, two cows, a pair of horses, one mule, two lambs, two goats, and all necessary farm implements, with the understanding that animals and goods should be paid for with labor.

On the arrival of the colonists at their destination, Lieutenant Moraga in the name of the King of Spain gave each settler possession of a lot for a dwelling. He next marked out for each pioneer a piece of land sufficiently large to sow a *fanéga* of grain, besides a plot for beans and other vegetables. A large tract of common land near the pueblo colonists were permitted to use for grazing cattle.

In the beginning the pueblo was governed by an *Alcalde* selected by the inhabitants. A corporal and three soldiers served as military guard. Governor Neve asked the Santa Clara Fathers to take charge of the colonists' spiritual wants.

The first settlers cultivated wheat, corn and beans, disposing of the surplus to the troops. From the proceeds they purchased clothing at the government warehouse. Cattle, sheep, and horses were sold to the Presidio.

At Mission Santa Clara in the beginning there were only three men to build church, dwellings, barns, shops, and to dig ditches and plow. Harvests were small. Agriculture did not succeed until irrigation was improved. At the close of the year a church had been built, sixty by eighteen feet, and two dwellings had been erected. Buildings were of timber, plastered and roofed with clay.

When Mission Santa Clara was eight months old the Father President Junípero Serra paid the first of his five visits to the new establishment. He arrived on September 28, 1777, having walked the entire distance of twenty-seven leagues from San Carlos. Serra wrote in the baptismal book that on November 9, 1777, he baptized an eight-year-old boy, son of Fat-laye and Guenchigmis of the Ranchería San Francisco Solano. The boy was christened José Maria. On his way back from San Francisco, Serra again baptized some Indians. Before the close of the year sixty-seven Indians were baptized, eight being adults. Twenty-three were living at the Mission; the others still remained at their *rancherías*.

The first chapel was mired by floods, and a new site was selected —*Gergecensen* or *El Roblar*. Father Junípero came from the north with Father Juan Crespi to assist the two resident missionaries, Fathers de la Peña and Murguía, in laying the cornerstone of the new church November 19, 1781. A Cross now marks the site of the vanished building, southwest from the Southern Pacific station at Santa Clara. The cornerstone of the second church and its contents, several Spanish coins and a Cross, are now in the museum of the University of Santa Clara.

Serra's last visit was May 15, 1784, three months before his death. He came to bless the new adobe church, at that time the most imposing structure in California. He found the Mission in mourning —Father José Murguía was dead, after three years of consuming work in building the new church, and forty years' service in the Missions. The friar had been architect, builder, and laborer in erecting the structure. At his behest Indians had brought great redwood beams and rafters on their shoulders from the Santa Cruz Mountains. They trod the adobe mud and straw for brick. They traveled fifteen miles for rust-red cinnabar rock for paint for artist Davila. They mixed the paint with cactus juice, and decorated the new ceiling. Serra grieved with the neophytes at Santa Clara for the loss of Father Murguía. The Mission was like a tomb.

Father Diego Noboa was appointed to the place of Father

Murguía. For dedication of the church Governor Fages came with a retinue from Monterey. *Comandante* Moraga and Don Ramón de la Vega, secular godfather and official flag-bearer, arrived from San Francisco. Settlers from the new pueblo and Indians looked on while Father Junípero Serra, assisted by Fathers Palóu and de la Peña, sang Mass and dedicated the church. After the ceremony Serra handed the keys of this most august structure in California to the Governor. Proudly His Excellency opened the doors on May 16.

From the beginning Santa Clara Valley was a garden spot, surpassed only by San Gabriel. San José, the new pueblo, in 1790 harvested 1,700 bushels of grain. Hemp also was grown for which the Viceroy promised to pay fourteen cents a pound. In 1804 vessels took away 463 pounds. After American occupation the first nurseries in the state were established here. El Pueblo became known as the Garden City, and in 1849 it was selected as the first state capital. The site of the capitol is marked with a plaque in the Plaza.

In a public granary at San José, California education was cradled. Previously officers had taught their own children. Occasionally a woman had a neighborhood school. The King of Spain ordered the establishment of a school in each pueblo for Indians only. Manuel Vargas, a retired sergeant, in December, 1794, established in a granary the first school in California. Attendance was compulsory. A tax of thirty-seven cents a month was ordered for the education of each child.

At Mission Santa Clara, four miles away, Indians learned weaving, shoemaking, and tanning. Sergeant Joaquin Sanchez was given $15 a month to teach Indians grain growing. They harvested 8,300 bushels. The Mission orchard also made abundant returns: peaches, pears, apricots, apples, figs, and grapes. The first fruits offered by California to the argonauts of '48 and '49 were grapes and pears from the Mission orchards of Santa Clara and San José.

In 1800 Santa Clara had a larger Indian population than any Mission in California—2,228. Each Saturday twenty-four oxen were killed for food. Soon the church was lengthened twenty-six feet to accommodate converts. A new tile roof made the building waterproof.

Twenty-one years after its foundation, tradition says, the Mission received two bells from King Carlos IV of Spain, on condition that they be rung each evening at eight-thirty in remembrance of souls in purgatory. One original bell still exists, inscribed: 1798 AVE MARIA PURISIMA SANTA CLARA. A scroll Cross decorates the side of this bell which weighs about 1,000 pounds. A second bell was made the following year as the lettering shows: AVE MARIA PURISIMA SANTA CLARA RUELAS ME FECIT. 1799. (HAIL MARY MOST PURE. SAINT CLARE. RUELAS MADE ME. 1799.) There was a third bell recast in San Francisco late in the nineteenth century. These three *campanas* were always rung at eight-thirty in the evening.

When Vancouver came to Santa Clara from San Francisco in 1792, he found the cloth woven at the Mission of better quality than that at San Francisco. At the time of his visit 2,000 hides were tanned in one year, but few could be sold for want of a market. There was a master tanner, a shoemaker, also a carpenter and millwright. Natives were working on adobe houses for themselves. Fourteen of these thatched dwellings were completed in 1793, and before 1798 nearly all married neophytes were substantially housed. There was also a corral thirty-six yards square, with walls six feet high built of stout timbers and adobe.

Santa Clara's progress, both spiritually and materially, was heightened with the coming of two missionaries, Father Magin Catalá, who arrived in 1794, and Father José Viader, who followed in 1796, with a large Cross hanging always from the rosary at his girdle.

Father Magin approached Serra in asceticism. When he met a woman, he covered his face with his cowl. He seldom smiled. In conversation he stood with eyes downcast. Abstinence, flagellations —no penance was too severe for his body tortured with rheumatism. He remained on his knees in prayer till sleep overcame him in church or in his narrow cell.

Father Magin's spirit was greatly troubled by pleasure-loving Pueblo San José, the amusement center of northern California. Its inhabitants were seldom at Mass. Father Magin, leading two hundred neophytes, in 1798 cleared a road for four miles through mus-

tard fields between Mission and pueblo. Three rows of black willow
trees were set out. They were watered by the Father and his neophytes. Soon they furnished shade for the beautiful way in which
the friar set up Stations of the Cross. But San Joséans remained
away from the Mission.

Material progress later brought about the massacre of the unique
third row of willows. In 1890 San José felled the aged trees to
make way for the first underground conduit streetcar line. When
there was a storm, however, the cars refused to move. The conduit
was a failure. Old *padres* recalled the legend of Father Magin's super-
natural power. Finally an overhead trolley was installed.

In 1803 San Joséans demanded their own chapel. It did not matter to them that Mission Santa Clara had a new altar from Mexico
consecrated on August 12, 1802. On July 4, 1803, the cornerstone
of St. Joseph's was laid at San José de Guadalupe. Cadet José Maria
Estudillo represented the Governor at laying the cornerstone of the
pueblo church and deposited coins in the stone. Each settler was
obliged to contribute three-quarters of a bushel of grain. Women
helped make adobe bricks. Nine years passed before the church
was completed. Although it had a grass roof, it stood until 1835.

Soon after the turning of the century, Santa Clara's most remarkable Indian neophyte, Marcelo, came to the Mission in a dramatic
manner. He attacked Father Viader, who was taking a walk. The
missionary, six feet tall, captured the Indian and bumped his head
against that of another wrongdoer. After Marcelo was Christianized
he helped carry huge redwood logs to the Mission where he was
made an *Alcalde*. With Indians Cristobal and Pio he was given the
Ulistac grant of 2,401 acres near Alviso. He is recalled for his famous duel with his rival, *Alcalde* Inygo, who ran off with Marcelo's
wife. Marcelo, although ninety, bit off his ear. His death was recorded by the Fathers at Santa Clara, "Marcellus, Indian, aged one
hundred." His photograph in the museum at the University of
Santa Clara shows a head of unusual character and power.

In 1812 Santa Clara Mission Church was so greatly damaged by
earthquakes that it was decided to move the building to the present site. The cornerstone of the third church was laid in 1818, the

year of the second great earthquake. Much material of the second Mission went into building the third. Father José Viader supervised construction. Don Ignacio Alviso, a formidable Indian fighter for whom the town of Alviso was named, was foreman. He was buried beneath the chancel.

The church was simple in its exterior. A baptistry led from the right side, a few feet from the front of the building. An arched doorway in a sloping wall from the right side opened into the cemetery. There was a large square window over the arched doorway of the church, and higher up a niche contained a statue of the Virgin. Under the tile roof was a large painting representing the all-seeing eye of God. Columns on either side of the church ascended to within a few feet of the top of the building. A saint's niche was in the center of each partition. The tower at the left front of the church was not unlike that at Santa Cruz. It sloped upward to the third story and was finished with a glass lantern and crowned with a Cross. At the top of the second story, above the apertures for the bells, was a wooden railing, probably a later addition.

The third church was dedicated on August 11, 1822, eve of the feast of Santa Clara. The saint's image, habited in brown brocade, a monstrance in one hand, a long staff in the other, looked out from the altar over the nave.

Father Magin Catalá never wholly subdued either San José or his own Mission Santa Clara. In 1805 a neophyte and a pagan of the Sennenes were discovered on the convent roof trying to burn the building and kill the missionaries. Troops were hurried to Santa Clara from San José and Monterey.

Mission gardeners produced choice fruits, melons, beans, corn, wheat; but often Indians fled, longing for the wild bumblebee honey, acorns, and hazelnuts of the western foothills. Twenty neophytes were sent to capture the renegades. One Christian was killed, and the rest came running to the Mission. San Francisco had no jail, but in 1822 the Governor ordered a jail built at San José and taxed settlers one-third of all the tallow produced to erect the building.

Father Magin was buried at Santa Clara November 22, 1830, where he had served for thirty-seven years. No Franciscan missionary before secularization was so long at one establishment. Few were so consistent in their lives as he. When he died, his habit was cut into pieces to serve as scapulars. His sandals, crucifix, and girdle of penance were preserved by his followers, some of whose descendants still possess them.

Father Magin Catalá was spared not only secularization of the Mission which came to Santa Clara in 1836, but the misdeeds of Yoscolo, a favorite neophyte and *Alcalde* turned renegade. He armed a thousand Indians with bows and arrows, burst into the nunnery, captured 500 Indian women, seized supplies, and drove 3,000 head of cattle and 500 horses to the mountains near Mariposa. Estanislao, for whom Stanislaus County was later named—a renegade from Mission San José—joined Yoscolo at Mariposa. They assembled a large force.

General Vallejo pursued the rebels with 300 soldiers. The Indians escaped to the mountains. Back on another raid to Mission Santa Clara came Yoscolo. Then he fortified himself in a wildcat lair in the Santa Cruz Mountains, *La Rinconada de los Gatos*, the Little Corner of the Cats—today called Los Gatos. From his stronghold Yoscolo and his warriors made a third raid upon Mission Santa Clara.

Indian fighter Juan Prado Mesa was sent after him. Armed with flintlocks, his men attacked the mountain fortress. Yoscolo and his braves formed a square and fought lying down. Flintlocks conquered bows and arrows. The bleeding head of intrepid Yoscolo was brought back to the Pueblo San José suspended by his long coarse black hair from the pommel of Don Anastasio Mendoza's saddle. A death procession with the gruesome trophy was formed. Round and round the Plaza they went shouting *Vivas!* Yoscolo's head was carried out the beautiful way of faith and prayer, the Alameda of Father Magin Catalá. Surmounted on a pole before Mission Santa Clara, for three days Yoscolo's head warned other Indian rebels against insurrection.

Father José Viader had other trouble besides Yoscolo: taxes. The San Francisco Presidio expected nearly $2,000 annually from the Mission. The Father refused to acknowledge the Federal constitution of Mexico. His exile was impending, he knew. In 1833, the year before Governor Figueroa secularized the Missions, the Father left for Spain.

Viader was succeeded by Father García Diego, Prefect of the Zacatecan Franciscans in California. He remained here three years and later was appointed first Bishop of California. Before he left Santa Clara two-thirds of the cattle and sheep disappeared, movable property vanished, and population declined.

In 1839 Mission Santa Clara was the scene of a great social event: the marriage of Governor Don Juan Bautista Alvarado and Doña Martina Castro, Star of the North. The Governor had fallen in love with her portrait, but he had never seen the *señorita*. He was said to have more ability than any three men in California and was popular, but reckless and dissolute. Alvarado always stirred interest by his energy, individuality, and scandalous life. He tore himself away from the mother of his illegitimate children at Monterey and was to marry the daughter of Don Francisco Castro of San Pablo. All San José and Santa Clara waited on that hot August day for the Governor and his bride.

Doña Martina came, dark and lovely, crowned with roses, on a white horse, her foot resting in a gay sash, her godfather riding behind. General Mariano Guadalupe Vallejo, Alvarado's uncle, arrived from Sonoma in the north.

But His Excellency failed to appear. Don José Antonio Estrada, the Governor's brother-in-law, represented him at the wedding. He also brought the first wedding rings of California gold. Some said that the Governor was ill, some that he had imbibed too freely. Others declared that the Monterey *señora* would not permit his appearance. Alvarado's official excuse was that he was obliged to remain at Monterey for a political conference with La Place, the French traveler.

For eight days the wedding party visited hospitable ranches on the way to Monterey. His Excellency rode out to welcome his bride. Together they entered the capital where festivities lasted several days.

Perhaps the Alvarado wedding was one of the reasons why Father Jesus Maria Vasquez del Mercado, who came to Santa Clara in 1839, declaimed against the Governor. Alvarado ordered General Castro to remove the Father by force from Santa Clara, and place him on a ship at San Francisco sailing for Mexico.

Father José Maria del Real, the last Franciscan, arrived to preside at the Mission. Although 8,475 Indians had been baptized at Santa Clara, only 130 remained. There were 809 sheep, 430 cattle, 215 horses. In 1845 the Mission was valued at $16,179. Father Real ministered not only at Santa Clara but at San José, Dolores, and Sonoma.

When the Mission was most desolate, it became the scene of a great mining discovery, the largest quicksilver mine the world has ever seen, New Almaden. For centuries the Indians had fought wars over red paint, *mohetka*, their cosmetic, dug by them out of a cavern in high black Loma Prieta. Even from far Oregon, Indians had come for red paint. In 1824 Don Antonio Suñol had tried to work the rock as a silver mine, but without success. Father Real's cousin, Don Secundino Robles, brought some of the ore to the Mission in 1845 to show Captain Andrés Castillero, a guest. The captain, who understood mining, had been in the north to buy Sutter's Fort for the Mexican Government. At sight of the ore Castillero's eyes opened wide. He pulverized a small quantity and sifted it upon live coals in a small container. After the ore was heated he sprinkled it with water, covering it with an empty tumbler. Then he held the tumbler to the light.

"Quicksilver! Our fortune is made!" said Castillero to Father Real, who watched the experiment. "The Mexican Government offers $100,000 for discovery of quicksilver."

Castillero filed his claim before *Alcalde* Pedro Chaboya of Pueblo San José. He formed a partnership with General José Castro, Father José del Real, and the priest's two daredevil cousins, Don Secundino and Don Teodoro Robles.

After the American occupation, the New Almaden was sold to Messrs. Barron, Forbes, and Walkinshaw of Tepic, Mexico. As gold and silver mining developed, the New Almaden became one of America's foremost enterprises, a valuable aid in the great new western mines. From 1850 to 1930 it produced 1,039,675 flasks of quicksilver. Today the mine is abandoned.

Governor Pio Pico declared all California Missions for sale, and on June 30, 1846, the orchard and vineyard of Mission Santa Clara were purchased by Juan Castañeda, Luis Arenas, and Benito Diaz for $1,200. The deed was proved to have been antedated, and in 1864 President Lincoln signed the patent giving the buildings and orchard to Santa Clara College, a new institution of learning.

With American occupation of California in 1846, events crowded into Mission Santa Clara. Immigrants seeking Spanish grants arrived from the East. They had no shelter, and so they took possession of Mission buildings. At this time *Alcalde* Bartlett of San Francisco and his men went toward San José making requisition of horses from *rancheros*. Don Francisco Sanchez took prisoner Americans who came to his ranch. One hundred Spanish-Californians joined Sanchez.

Captain Ward Marston of the United States Marines went to rescue *Alcalde* Bartlett. Mission Santa Clara was fortified by American immigrants headed by Captain Joseph Aram. Sanchez led the Californians, and Marston the Americans as they advanced along the road in sight of the Mission. Aram aided Marston. American fieldpieces fired grape-shot. Sanchez replied with muskets. Two Americans were wounded. The Californians disappeared toward the Santa Cruz Mountains. The Americans became entangled in the mustard forest and made no attempt to pursue the foe. They took possession of Mission Santa Clara.

Sanchez sent a flag of truce offering to submit on condition that the United States guarantee protection of property. Armistice was agreed upon. Sanchez gave up his prisoners; his men returned to their ranches. So ended the last conflict of the Mexican War.

On May 31, 1846, Governor Richard B. Mason ordered all persons occupying Mission buildings at Santa Clara and San José to leave immediately. Father Real had permitted immigrants to occupy Mission Santa Clara as well as Mission San José, and they were allowed to remain another year to harvest crops.

For several years genial Father Real made Mission Santa Clara festive. His cousin, Don Secundino Robles of the Santa Rita Rancho, now a part of Stanford University property, was major-domo. Robles arranged bullfights in the Plaza, and sometimes the Father entered the arena. Jesusita, fifteen-year-old daughter of Don Secundino and favorite of his twenty-nine children, imitated her bullfighting father. In scarlet dress with low neck, short sleeves and skirt, Santa Clara saw her thrust *banderias* into the bull's neck. Roistering San Francisco asked, Would the *señorita* perform in the Mission Dolores bull ring? The crowd of San Francisco miners frightened her. The matador of the day, however, was Miguel Espinosa of Monterey. She married him, and became the mother of twenty-four children.

Father José Maria del Real was called to the Mother House at Zacatecas, Mexico. The days of the Franciscans ended. The Jesuits entered.

Mission Santa Clara was never abandoned. Here March 19, 1851, was founded the first college in California to endure. It was established by Father John Nobili, author of a work on physics. From Italy by way of Cape Horn he had come to Oregon in 1844. Arriving at San Francisco in 1849, he had only $150 when he reached Santa Clara. But he established the college in an adobe building. The Plaza was transformed into a campus.

After ridding the building of squatters, Father Nobili housed twelve students. Seated on tree trunks in the garden, professors held classes. Pupils occupied rustic benches under olive trees or grape arbors. The boys' food—soup, vegetables and meat—was boiled in one kettle. Their wash basins were filled with water at the old Mission well. Funds came slowly. Bishop Alemany gave $100. The Sisters of Notre Dame, who in 1851 had established a convent at San José, cheered Father Nobili by saying, "God is rich." In 1855 Father Nobili died from blood poisoning caused by stepping on a nail.

Many alterations were made in the church. The belfry was replaced in 1862 by two towers. Although five feet thick, the walls were removed in 1885 and thrown out upon the Plaza behind the Cross. Some original tiles were used to roof outhouses. The altar railing of the restored church was made of the redwood beams of the old Mission brought from the Santa Cruz Mountains by Indians. The unused old octagonal pulpit was restored and mounted upon a pedestal. Interior decorations and furnishings were kept almost intact, as also were the frescoed ceiling and chancel. Some frescoes were on wood, others on canvas. When possible, these were employed in the new building, retouched by an Italian artist from San Francisco. The Mission still had the original holy-water font and background of the altar. The life-sized crucifix used by Father Magin was treasured. There were also statues of Saints Joachim, Anne, San Juan Capistrano, a portrait of Our Lady, and a copy of the historic painting of *Nuestra Señora de Guadalupe*.

Fires have afflicted Santa Clara. In 1913 valued relics were burned. On the morning of October 25, 1926, a fire destroyed the Mission building erected in 1822 and the students' chapel, built in 1887. Fire bucket crews rushed into the church and saved Father Magin's large crucifix and the statues of Saints Anthony and Francis; but the image of Santa Clara, for a hundred years guardian of the Mission, went into the flames.

Down plunged the tower with its bells. One *campana* was melted. Cold water thrown upon the bell of 1799 cracked it. Later it was recast in San Francisco. The large Mexican bell of 1798 came safely through. Engineering students quickly built a standard in which they hung the bell that the tradition of 128 years might remain unbroken. At the usual hour, eight-thirty, the faithful bell voice thrilled Santa Clara.

On being informed of the destruction of his ancestor's gift to Mission Santa Clara, King Alphonso of Spain ordered a new bell cast at the royal arsenal. It reached San Francisco August 30, 1929. About two and a half feet high, it weighs six hundred pounds. The bell bears the seal of the King and has the inscription: ALPHONSUS XIII REX HISPANIAE HOS AES CAMPANUM CUJUS AD PULSUM B. VIRGO COTIDIE COLERETUR IN LOCUM ILLIUS QUOD A CAROLO IV DONATUM IGNE ABSUNTUM EST LYCAEO S. I. CLARAE MUNIFICE D. D. S. (ALFONSO XIII, KING OF SPAIN, HAS REPLACED THE ANGELUS BELL GIVEN BY CHARLES IV AND DESTROYED BY FIRE, WITH HIS GENEROUS GIFT TO THE UNIVERSITY OF SANTA CLARA IN THE YEAR 1929.) As a part of the dedication of the new church, the royal bell was suspended on October 12, 1929, in the presence of Bishop John McGinley of Fresno, Consul-General Sebastian de Romero of Spain, and many pioneers.

The design of the old building is followed by the new. Its roof is of original tiles which were on a Mission barn. The south wall of the original quadrangle is still in use as part of the Adobe Lodge, but the oldest complete building at Mission Santa Clara is the adobe storeroom, sixty feet by twenty, which will probably be converted into a museum. A spacious adobe building near the university, once the property of the Mission, has been restored and is owned by the Santa Clara Woman's Club.

In spite of fires, the Santa Clara museum has Mission treasures—ancient registers and books, keys to the original buildings, carved Paschal candlesticks nearly six feet tall, old chairs, and a superb choral having 139 pages of black lettering and a wooden case covered with bronze and leather of Franciscan days.

Here in this valley of gardens remains more of the original planting than at any Mission in California. Father Bayma laid out the modern garden in 1862, but there are olive trees at the side of the pergola adjoining the storehouse that were probably set out in 1822. Eight feet in circumference at the base, once they supplied the college with olive oil. There is also an original Castilian rosebush, the largest in the Mission gardens. The oldest Banksia rose in California, planted about a hundred years ago, with a spread of fifty-five feet, once covered the Franciscan colonnade. When new buildings were erected, a pergola was built for the Banksia. The colonnade floor, with coarse creek sand visible in it, is part of the quadrangle walk. Climbing the south wall is an historic La Marque rosebush. On a portion of the cruciform grape arbor is the oldest grapevine in northern California. Near by is the first bignonia vine planted in a Mission garden. The storehouse is almost covered by the oldest English ivy in California. In the quadrangle is an ancient lemon tree, nearly sixty years ago grafted to an orange. For decades on Friday, "fish day," this tree supplied the Fathers with lemons. At the entrance to the quadrangle are three Washingtonia palms of great size, the only variety native to California. They date from 1822, when the third Mission was moved to the present site. In the Alameda connecting Santa Clara and San José, still remain three battered black willows of the original three rows of trees planted in 1798 by Father Magin Catalá and his neophytes.

Cruelly tried by flame and tumult has been this Mission in the garden valley of the oaks. But its symbol still stands before the church, high and unperishing—the original redwood Cross, encased in pine as a protection against vandals, the Cross raised in 1777 by Peña on the banks of the Guadalupe, has persisted through all the Mission's story, valiant as the spirit of Clara of Assisi.

IX

San Buenaventura

In 1768 Don José de Galvez, Visitador-General of Mexico, planned the ninth Mission, San Buenaventura. "My Mission," he called it. He himself packed church goods for the establishment. Jovially he remarked to Father Junípero Serra while they worked, "I am a better sacristan than Your Reverence."

Precisely fifty years to a day after Christopher Columbus discovered the island of San Salvádor on the Atlantic coast, Cabrillo landed opposite the site of San Buenaventura. On October 12, 1542, he took possession in the name of the King of Spain.

Already natives had heard of Christians, *Taquimine*. The Indians lived in large houses near the sea and dressed in skins of animals. They ate fish and *maguey*. So swift and large were the Indian canoes that Cabrillo christened the spot *El Pueblo de las Canóas*. The Indians called it Xucu.

Vizcaíno, arriving sixty years later, wrote that since Noah's Ark no finer vessels had been seen than those made by natives of pine boards bound together with cord. Portolá followed in 167 years, August 13, 1769, and bartered red beads with the Indians for woven reed bowls, polished pebbles, wooden trays and plates. Father Crespi in his diary described the large houses resembling oval haystacks. At a wedding being celebrated, the bride was painted and bedecked with strings of shells. Women wore buckskin skirts and the rest of the body was covered with rabbit skins. Dressed better than elsewhere in California, the men made unusual wood carvings with flint tools. Often ten of these natives went in a canoe far out to sea to fish.

Two years later Father Junípero Serra, walking from San Diego to San Carlos, was struck with the admirable location of this Indian village, *La Asumpta*. To his companions he remarked, "The site of Mission San Buenaventura is found."

Establishment of the Mission was to have been made in October, 1771. Serra had appointed Fathers Antonio Paterna and Antonio Cruzado missionaries. They were at San Gabriel when suddenly San Gabriel Indians rose. The new founding was postponed.

Don Felipe de Neve, the first Governor of Alta California, in a conference with Serra at San Gabriel in March, 1782, agreed to establish not only Mission San Buenaventura but the Presidio and the Mission at Santa Barbara. His Excellency himself, guarded by Monterey soldiers, led the imposing procession that set out in Holy Week for the new site. The day was Tuesday, March 26, 1782. Lieutenant José Francisco de Ortega, discoverer of San Francisco Bay, was in military command. With him were Father Junípero Serra and Father Pedro Cambón. There were also three sergeants, several corporals, one ensign, seventy soldiers and their families, and a number of muleteers and servants.

Only a few miles from San Gabriel furious hoofs came pounding over the trail. A courier bore a message from *Comandante*-General de Croix. War against the Yumas was on. Neve must join forces with Fages. Indians must be punished for the massacre of missionaries and colonists. The Governor turned back to San Gabriel.

Serra went on. He selected a site for the Mission in the center of eighty-four *rancherías*. The natives called it *Zuzu*. It was Cabrillo's *Pueblo de las Canóas*—Portolá's *La Asunción de Nuestra Señora*. On Easter Sunday, March 31, 1782, Serra planted the Cross. He celebrated the first High Mass in a brushwood shelter. Father Pedro Cambón formed the choir. Serra drew up registers of baptism, marriage, and death. He rejoiced that at last Galvez's Mission was established.

This ninth Mission was named San Buenaventura for John Fidanza, who was born in 1221 at Bagnarea, Etruria, Italy. He was supposed to be dying when Saint Francis restored him, a child, to health by prayer. When the boy rose to his feet cured, the saint exclaimed, "*O buona ventura!*"

Thereafter the child was known as Buonaventure. He entered the Order of Saint Francis. When he was told that he was to receive the cardinal's hat, he was washing dishes in the kitchen. While Superior General of the Friars Minor, Buonaventure introduced the Angelus. The Pope directed that morning, noon, and evening the Church recite the Angelus.

Father Serra remained at San Buenaventura for three weeks. He spoke with Indians through interpreters. Natives helped build the first chapel, but they declined baptism. Serra left Father Cambón with a small guard in a little building near the chapel protected by a stockade.

Soon, on April 27, 1782, Father Cambón made the first baptism— a sick child two days old, José Crescencio, son of soldier Eugenio Valdez and a *mulata*, Sebastiana Josepha Quintexa. After Father Cambón retired in the following June, Serra named Fathers Francisco Dumétz of San Carlos, and Vicente de Santa Maria as missionaries. Nine months passed before Father Dumétz baptized an Indian—on December 28, Domingo Joseph, ten years of age, of the Ranchería de Valesque is recorded. Nine months more passed, and only two entries of Indian baptisms were made.

Indians did not accept the new faith, but for a few baubles they hewed timbers in the mountains and brought them on their shoulders for building the new church. They constructed a stone irrigation ditch six miles long. Seventeen acres were enclosed with an adobe wall and planted with fruit trees and grain.

Serra saw few converts at San Buenaventura. When he came to the Mission to administer confirmation on November 21, 1783, he found twenty-two. He died the following year at San Carlos. Even at the end of 1785 there were only 133 baptisms.

The first marriage was recorded on August 30, 1782. Father Dumétz united Alejandro de la Cruz, *Alcalde* at Fuerto, Mexico, and María Concepción Monteil. The first burial was that of José Leon Rodríguez, three days old, by Father Cambón, on April 15, 1782.

Four years after the Mission was founded, Indians thronged San Buenaventura. Fourteen years after the establishment, 1,100 had been baptized. Governor Fages declared them different from other Indians —civil and polite. In 1800 San Buenaventura raised more cattle and grain than any Mission in California, but had the smallest population.

Captain George Vancouver, California's first foreign visitor, in 1793 was delighted with San Buenaventura's apples, peaches, pears, plums, pomegranates, figs, oranges, grapes, bananas, coconuts, sugar cane, indigo, and useful kitchen herbs. Father Vicente de Santa Maria, with a pack train of twenty mules laden with produce, journeyed to Santa Barbara to supply Vancouver's ship, the *Discovery*, with meat, vegetables, and fruit. The Father was Vancouver's guest on the *Discovery* returning to San Buenaventura. The Englishman wrote that buildings and gardens here excelled those at other establishments. He described Father Vicente being welcomed by the Indians, who kissed his hand while he spoke with them in the native idiom.

In 1795 San Buenaventura had war: pagans fought converts. Two native chiefs were killed, and six or seven Indians taken prisoner. One neophyte was placed in chains. The Christians had only a few wounded. Leaders were punished, and peace came.

In this period much building was done. The church was fireswept in 1791, and a temporary structure was erected. Services were held in the Indians' chapel, Santa Gertrudis, near Casitas. The new church was fifteen years in building. Forests of Ojai, Santa Ana, and San Emidio supplied timbers. Clay for brick and tile was found near the Mission, lime came from the Cañada de San Buenaventura. The usual quadrangle was completed with large granaries, tannery, pottery, flour mill, soap factories, weaving rooms, and sixty-five adobe houses for Indians.

The Mission's famous artisans carved the raised pulpit of the church. An altar was brought from Mexico City; its pillars in the Romanesque style were finished in imitation marble with gilded decorations. Vestments, silver vessels, pictures of the Stations of the Cross, and a crucifix with the body of Christ life-size were acquired.

On September 10, 1809, the first High Mass was celebrated by Father José Ignacio Argüello, with Father Marcos Antonio de Vitoria as assistant. On the day following the celebration, the remains of Father Vicente de Santa Maria, who had died July 16, 1806, were removed from the old to the new church. María del Rosario, an Indian girl, was the first to be baptized in the new building, September 30, 1809.

The earthquake of 1812 left the upper part of the new edifice nearly nine feet out of plumb. Fear of a tidal wave drove the community to San Joaquin and Santa Ana a mile distant, where they remained a day. All movable property was transported by Father José Señan, neophytes, and guards several leagues to the Cañada de Purísima Nueva, where a temporary church was erected. There several baptisms and burials took place.

In this turbulent year Father Señan was appointed President of the Franciscans in California and Vicar-General to the Bishop of Sonora, but he continued living at the Mission. Openings in the church were repaired, and an immense buttress was added to the north side and reinforced with stone and mortar.

After the revolution in Mexico in 1810, no stipends came to San Buenaventura, but resourceful Father Señan acquired chalices, gold cloth vestments, and a silver-plated altar bell. New woodwork was placed in the church. An aqueduct brought water from the mountains to be stored in the reservoir known as the *caballo,* because water gushed from a stone horse's head. Fountains were made for the gardens developed in the quadrangle.

Natives were attracted, and in 1816 more than 3,300 had been baptized. Like the soldiers, however, many were half naked. In spite of this condition, San Buenaventura from abundant harvests made gifts to other Missions. Father Señan sent pears, apples, and apricots to his friend Captain de la Guerra at Santa Barbara. Once he included two barrels of grape brandy, and the captain responded with a barrel of wine.

In the bountiful year of 1818, when 13,483 bushels of grain were harvested and 35,274 cattle ranged over the Mission lands, swift couriers arrived from Governor Solá.

"Pirate Bouchard has captured and pillaged Monterey. Flee!"

Nine miles the missionaries carried paintings of Stations of the Cross, altar vessels, images of saints, and a life-sized picture of Jesus. Finally they reached Purísima Nueva.

Bouchard and his motley followers, dressed in Spanish uniforms from Monterey pillage, swaggered into San Buenaventura, but found a deserted Mission. When snow fell in the mountains, Father Señan and his flock returned.

Bouchard's visit was followed by a tragic year. Mojave Indians appeared and asked to see the Father, who was at his devotions. A corporal took them to the guardhouse. On the following day, May 31, 1819, just as Father Señan intoned the *Credo*, sudden cries and lamentations rose. All ran from the church, except the white women and a few neophytes. An Indian insisted upon forcing his way to the priest. A corporal and a soldier were killed. Battle began. Ten Mojaves fell, but only one neophyte. The whites fled. Father Señan buried all the Indians in the habit of Saint Francis.

Father Señan reported to the Spanish Goverment his observations concerning San Buenaventura Indians. Beads and seeds served as money. They made music on a bone whistle, at the same time contorting the body. Their weird songs aroused sadness rather than joy. Indians were eager to sing in the European way and play the Spaniards' instruments. In their native state the Indians did not use fermented grapes but a concoction of wild tobacco, lime, and water. They warred over food and women. Each *rancheria* had a captain who led in war and presided at feasts. There was no distinction among the Indians except that borne by *Alcaldes*, annually elected.

Old men told long tales regarding the creation of the world. Boys paid them to recite such stories.

Some Indians buried their dead. Others burned them on pyres, while relatives and friends, wailing, stirred the fire. Beads, otter and rabbit skins, or some article belonging to the deceased, were interred or burned with the body. From a pole on the grave was hung an oar, a bow, a deer's head, or some other mark to show in which exercise the deceased excelled. In grief they cut the hair, covered themselves with ashes, scratched and blackened their faces, and wailed.

The natives had sacred places in the mountains, swept clean and adorned with beautiful plumage on a pole. Pilgrimages were made to the spot. All remained silent save one who prayed, "Grand Captain of Captains, behold us and hear what we say, give us rain." As an offering they brought herbs, acorns, seeds, and wild fruit.

These Indians imagined souls after death were transferred to a place of delight where they would have fish and plenty to eat, dancing away their lives.

After Bouchard came, crops fell off and cattle disappeared, but the gardens on river banks were thriving. Unexpectedly in 1820 Father Señan fell heir to a legacy of $2,000. He imported from Lima, Peru, vestments, cruets, and sacred vessels. Over the main altar was placed a beautiful Calvary group.

About this time Father Señan indulged in a new luxury: rice, the first time it is mentioned as an article of food in Mission history. He had three sacks brought on mule back from Santa Barbara, for which he paid $31.25.

Governor Solá made demands on the Mission: fourteen lances for each Presidio and four dozen sombreros. President Señan had neither iron nor sombreros, but he sent to the Santa Barbara Presidio nearly two tons of tallow drippings, 112 crates of soap, 30 blankets, some beans and corn, and 200 rosaries made at the Mission.

A tremor of earthquake was felt on January 21, 1821, but on May 16, 1822, there came a political earthquake. Missionaries and neophytes were required to take the oath of allegiance to Agustín Iturbide, Emperor of Mexico.

Even during terrestrial and political earthquakes, Father Señan's energy never slackened. He erected an adobe garden wall and buildings for neophytes roofed with tile, and renovated the Indian girls' apartment. Maximiliano and his wife, María Ysabel, neophytes, helped make clothing and care for linen and vestments. One of Father Señan's last acts was to adorn the main altar of the church with ten mirrors in gilded metal frames.

The Father resigned from his office as President of the Missions, but he was re-elected. At the time of his death, August 24, 1823, he was President. The natives formed a procession and, chanting, carried his body around the patio. For him they built a tomb of masonry in the Mission he had served for twenty-nine years.

Father Francisco Suñer, who in 1824 followed Father Señan, was stricken with blindness and was unable to celebrate Mass. But he preached and heard confessions. Worse than blindness was the decree of the Mexican Congress, December 20, 1827, expelling all settlers born in Spain.

Father Suñer's associate now was Father José Altimira, founder of Mission San Francisco Solano. When the decree of banishment came, to the astonishment of missionaries and to the vexation of Governor Echeandia, Father Altimira and Father Ripóll of Santa Barbara secretly sailed on the American ship *Harbinger* for their native land early in 1828. Blind Father Suñer was left alone, glad when he went to rest on January 17, 1831. He was buried in the church.

Soon the population at San Buenaventura had shrunk to 731. Measles carried off adults as well as children. Indians, male and female, died of venereal disease. Harvests had been reduced to 2,000 bushels of barley, 1,750 of wheat, 500 of corn, 400 of beans. There remained only 4,000 cattle, 3,000 sheep, 300 horses, and 60 mules. The San Miguel Chapel was destroyed by floods. Nine orchards of fruit trees, however, were thriving. Olive groves and vineyards were profitable. At no California Mission were there such large vegetable gardens, an excellent source of revenue.

After secularization of the Missions, San Buenaventura became a parish of the second class. The priest had a salary of $1,000 a year. This did not last long. Governor Mariano Chico, philanderer and erratic poet, indignant because President Durán criticized his misdeeds, in 1837 ordered Father Blas Ordáz to turn the management of San Buenaventura over to Don Carlos Carrillo.

Meanwhile Carrillo had been named Governor of California to replace Juan Bautista Alvarado. This appointment caused the Mission to become a battleground. Here met the forces of Governor Carlos Carrillo and the usurper, Juan Bautista Alvarado. Juan Castañeda captained Carrillo's soldiers; José Castro led Alvarado's men. About two hundred were on each side, all in new flashing uniforms. One gun back of the Mission faced the two guns on the shore side.

Castro ordered Castañeda to evacuate San Buenaventura. The guns barked. Much powder was burned, but only one man was killed on the besieging side. At the close of the second day Alvarado's forces fled. Carrillo sent men in pursuit. They were surrounded and their horses captured. For the next two days their valor was sustained by Mission wine.

Alvarado continued in office four years. Looting of Missions went on, but San Buenaventura suffered less than many establishments. In July, 1839, Inspector-General William E. P. Hartnell found at the Mission 2,208 cattle, 1,670 sheep, 799 horses, 35 mules, 65 goats, 322 *fanégas* of wheat, 182 *fanégas* of corn, 35 *fanégas* of peas, 180 hides, 394 *arrobas* of tallow, 15 *arrobas* of lard, 5 barrels of brandy, 13 barrels of wine, 168 *arrobas* of iron, and $219 worth of soap.

When the French traveler, de Mofras, arrived at the Mission in 1841, *rancheros* were occupying the rooms. Services were occasionally held by Santa Barbara Franciscans. Palm, orange, and banana trees were neglected. De Mofras wrote of the San Buenaventura Indians' water-tight baskets woven with bright feathers and soft rushes, even at that time difficult to procure.

In the collection of Indian baskets donated by Mrs. Phebe Hearst to the University of California are two old San Buenaventura baskets found by Mrs. Zelia Nuttall, the archaeologist, in Mexico City in the early part of the twentieth century. One, bowl-shaped and flat, twenty inches in diameter, has the royal arms of Spain woven and intermingled with two Mission Crosses. It shows that it was made by neophyte Juana Basilia for Governor Solá to be given to Field Marshal Señor Don José de la Cruz. The other basket displays the royal arms of Spain and bears the statement that it was made by Ana María, a native of Mission San Buenaventura.

The first secular priest appointed to Mission San Buenaventura was Father José Maria Rosáles, who arrived on April 21, 1843, and remained five years. Father Antonio Jimeno, his associate, took no salary for services as temporal administrator, but he paid the Mission debts.

After Pio Pico became Governor, Narciso Botello and José Arnaz leased Mission San Buenaventura on December 5, 1845, at an annual sum of $1,630 for nine years. All Mission property was soon ordered sold by the government. On June 8, 1846, José Arnaz bought San Buenaventura for $12,000, and this included 1,407 cattle, 150 sheep, 19 oxen, an orchard of 580 fruit trees, 3,800 vines, and 4 square leagues of land. Arnaz was to leave the priest in the apartment occupied by him and pay the expenses of divine worship. The Indians received nothing.

After much litigation, the United States Land Commission decided that Pio Pico had no right to sell the Mission, and President Lincoln, on May 23, 1862, signed the patent turning over San Buenaventura to the Catholic Church. Besides buildings were 46.27 acres of land.

José Arnaz, who bought the property, laid out the town of San Buenaventura with its squat little red tile-roofed structures. Saint Michael's Day, September 29, was a popular holiday. An adobe bull ring, ten feet high, mounted with tile, was constructed against the Mission wall. The south side of the building formed part of the enclosure. An adobe building on the opposite side served as a north wall. Pole fences secured with rawhide were thrown across the street. The bull's horns were sawn, and occasionally a horse was knocked over. Crowds came from Santa Barbara to see the show.

Back of the Mission for many years mariners were greeted by a Cross twenty-four feet high surmounting the hill at an elevation of 800 feet. Legend says it was erected by Serra, but that is doubtful. The Cross fell. Another was raised on the Loma de la Cruz. This was beaten down by storms. A new Cross was erected, to be blown down November 2, 1875. A piece of this Cross bearing the letters INRI is now in the Ventura Pioneer Museum. On September 9, 1912, civic bodies erected another Cross. Every night it is lighted. Its inscription says that it was erected on the two-hundredth anniversary of the birth of Padre Junípero Serra, who founded Mission San Buenaventura.

Bishop Thaddeus Amat of Monterey in 1873 gave part of the Mission orchard as a courthouse site. Eighty-year-old olive trees two feet in diameter were bearing abundantly. At that time in the lower arches of the Mission four old bells were strapped to crossbeams with rawhide. The reservoir, fountain, and old mill were still objects of curiosity to visitors, although the workshops were in ruins. The railroad came in 1887, and in 1888 modern demands clipped San Buenaventura to Ventura.

A disastrous land boom followed. Father Ciprian Rúbio began making supposed improvements. Already his predecessor, Father Juan

Comopla, had covered the church with ceiling. Father Rúbio hid the old floor tile with wood, razed the sacristy, removed interior decorations made by Indians, stenciled the walls, lengthened church windows, and installed stained glass. He intended to erect a parish church, but the boom ended. Father Rúbio never saw the structures built near the Mission. Thirty-four years passed before the school building was completed. On August 21, 1922, it was taken over by the Sisters of the Holy Cross.

Mission San Buenaventura retains features of interest. Church altars are as they were more than a hundred years ago. In the center of the main altar is a statue of the Immaculate Conception brought from the Philippines in 1801, formless save for head and arms, adorned with a velvet and silk robe. To the right is Saint Joseph holding the Infant robed in white silk. On the left is San Buenaventura, patron of the Mission. Pictures of Stations of the Cross remain as they were when placed on the walls in 1809. In the baptistry is the original font. Here also are decorations made by Indians. One of the treasures of San Buenaventura is the east door studded with handmade nails and carved with the curved lines of the River of Life. In the rear of the church is an old reservoir, and in the courtyard Mrs. Canet Garnier has re-erected an olive crusher.

Old bells still ring in the massive tower on the right with its large-hipped buttress showing the influence of Missions Santa Barbara and San Luis Rey. The north bell facing the town is lettered: s. SAN FRANCISCO 1781. (SEÑOR SAINT FRANCIS, 1781.) The east bell facing the mountains has the inscription: SAN PEDRO ALCANTRARA 1781. (SAINT PETER OF ALCANTRARA, 1781.) Both were suspended from beams by rawhide thongs, but their rusty iron clappers are unused. Governor Fages borrowed the bells from Santa Barbara, and the Fathers never returned them because they had no others. A third small swinging bell hangs in the south arch with the lettering: AVE MARIA S. JOSEPH. The only bell used daily at San Buenaventura is Mexican—large, crown-topped, with a Cross on its side inscribed: AVE * MARIA * PURYSYMA * MARIA * D * SAPOYAN * ANO * D * 1825. * (HAIL MARY MOST PURE. MARY OF ZAPOPAN YEAR OF 1825.) This bell was originally cast for the church of Zapopan, but was later sent to San

Buenaventura, together with three bells of the same size which disappeared. Another bell, once the gift of the Spanish Viceroy to the Mission, is in the possession of *Señora* Isabel del Valle Cram, and is inscribed: MARQUEZ de CROIX–MEXICO NOV. 12, 1770.

In the museum are two wooden bells two feet high, shaped like ordinary church bells, carved from oak, and probably made in California. They were used from noon on Holy Thursday till noon on Holy Saturday, when metal bells had to be silent.

Another interesting survivor of the past in the museum is a banner with the face of the Good Shepherd, similar to the banner carried by Father Garcés on his solitary pilgrimages among the Indians. There are also vestments, a baptismal font, a carved pulpit, and a confessional so beautifully carved by neophytes that it was known throughout California.

Famous for its gardens and orchards in Franciscan days, San Buenaventura still has two of the original olive trees of the Mission's seventeen acres. They stand in front of the May Henning School. Two palm trees also remain, walled in and braced with wire ropes. Once Ventura was called the Palm City.

Candalaria, of the Sespe Indians, lived in Sespe Canyon in 1913, made Indian baskets, and taught dyeing and weaving. She cured her rushes on heated ashes, drew them in and out till they turned white, then dried them in the sun and split them into strands for the baskets. They were dyed black by being buried in mud for a month. Another black dye was obtained from acorns pounded to a pulp and soaked in an *olla* filled with water and reeds. Candalaria related a gruesome tale of a chief's treatment of his daughter who was determined to be a spinster. He called the girl's suitor to his house and told him he might kill her. While the girl crushed chiles in a mortar, a monster with the appearance of a snake descended upon her, entered her abdomen, and tore her entrails to pieces. From that time Indian maidens obeyed their fathers.

Ventura's great Indian romance is embodied in the silky white Matilija poppy, with its large yellow stamens, found in the 'seventies in Matilija Canyon by Mrs. Theodosia Shepherd, who named it for Chief Matilija. Amatil, daughter of the chief, was carried off by

Spanish soldiers after they had exterminated the tribes on Sulphur Mountain. Amatil's lover led a force to attack the Mission. At the foot of Matilija Canyon soldiers and Indians met in battle. The lover was gravely wounded. He made his way to the top of the mountain near Matilija Hot Springs. Amatil found him dying, and remained with him till the end. She hollowed out a shallow grave for her beloved, and at his side died of starvation. The spot where the lovers came to their tragic end is marked with a Cross.

X

Santa Barbara

FROM the beginning Santa Barbara had unique charm, beauty, and grace of living. In 1542 its earliest visitor, Juan Rodríguez Cabrillo, wrote of the kind, hospitable Indians. *Delicioso* he called the climate. A botanist accompanying Father Junípero Serra in 1769 described the abundant wild roses, making a delightful Paradise.

Legend gave California Queen Califía as ruler. Here on Santa Barbara Channel a queen was found, but not young and beautiful. She was aged, and her capital was Civcut near what the Spaniards later called Gaviota Pass. The queen also ruled over Anacoat, Maquinanoa, Paltocac, Olesino, Caacat, Tocane, Opia, Opistopia, Nocos, Yutum, Quiman, Micoma, and Garomisopona. No haughty ruler, she gave welcome to the strangers and spent two nights on Cabrillo's vessel.

Santa Barbara Indians, the Quabajays, were California's first artists. They kept the Portolá company awake all night when the Spaniards camped on the site of the Santa Barbara Courthouse in 1769. Five hundred natives came to call, bringing fish, acorns, gruel, reed bowls, featherwork and skins. Painted and bedecked with feather finery, playing on weird flutes and pipes, they entertained the travelers. Because of one native dancer, his village, not far from today's Carpintería, was called El Pueblo del Ballarin.

But Spaniards thought the hospitality overdone. With beads they bribed the guests to depart.

Proudly the Channel Indians displayed California's first picture galleries. Paintings were set up on massive timbers in walled-in enclosures. Artists danced in worship before their pictures. The men had noses and ears beringed. Powdered wild tobacco was carried in tubes of canes suspended from the ears. Each man had a sharp bone to scrape perspiration from his body.

With only rock implements, the Indians made ten passenger canoes —pomegranate red inlaid with shells. They went far out to sea and caught fish with fiber nets, shell hooks, and basket traps.

Women on the Santa Barbara Channel hid in their dry *tule* huts shaped like half-oranges, guarded by men. When a woman ventured out, she looked attractive, hair fringed and hanging over her shoulders, shells glistening in her ears, long strings of beautiful carved shell beads around her neck and in her hair—her money. So women today wear diamond necklaces and tiaras.

These natives played a game with a rounded ball, a species of American baseball. Among these artistic, athletic Indians, sodomy was practiced, the only place in California where the vice was common.

Santa Barbara Indians buried their dead, placing over the graves bones of whales. On poles painted black, red, and white were hung baskets belonging to the dead, pieces of cloth, shells, and arrows, or locks of hair cut from the corpse. Some cemeteries had basins hewn out of stone, similar to a baptismal font.

Father Junípero Serra walked the length of Santa Barbara Channel with *Comandante* Pedro Fages for the first time on September 6, 1772. From Mexico City he returned here on May 1, 1774; and again in December, 1776, he toiled over this enchanting trail winding along the ocean. In his own time the Presidio with its chapel was established, but Serra did not see Mission Santa Barbara.

Governor Neve did not believe Missions should support neophytes. Natives should live in their own *rancherías,* and there be instructed by missionaries in religion, never in agriculture or mechanical arts. Neve, however, compromised by permitting the Santa Barbara establishment.

In April, 1782, he met Serra at Mission San Buenaventura. The Governor, wearing a three-cornered, white-plumed black felt hat with a gold-braided coat, was an impressive figure when he and Serra and their company arrived at Yanonalit, a large native town chosen for the site of the projected Presidio. Chief Yanonalit, who ruled thirteen *rancherías* on a small bay at a place called by Portolá, San Joaquin de la Laguna, made obeisance to Governor Neve.

Timber was cut for the large Cross and for the small chapel. On April 29, 1782, Serra blessed the site and planted the Cross. The Low Mass celebrated by him was the first said here since the coming of three Carmelite friars with Vizcaíno on the evening of December 3, 1602, preceding the feast of Santa Barbara.

Serra preached to the Spaniards and curious Indians. His disappointment was deep when Neve ordered him to defer founding Mission Santa Barbara. Adroitly Serra called the new establishment a Mission-Presidio. Here he remained while oak timbers were cut for a chapel, missionaries' dwellings, barracks, and storehouses.

The Presidio occupied ground now bounded by Cañon Perdido, Garden, Figueroa, and Anacapa Streets. Its stockade sixty *varas* square was later replaced by a stone wall. Lieutenant José Francisco Ortega was first *Comandante*, and he remained till 1795 in charge of the garrison of thirty-six leather-jacket soldiers, with nine Indian attendants. Father Junípero vainly entreated the Viceroy to make Ortega commander of the California troops.

After founding the Mission-Presidio, Serra returned to San Carlos; but, feeling his approaching death, in 1783 he set out to visit all Missions. From Monterey he arrived by boat in August and administered the first confirmation at what is now Santa Barbara, to nineteen neophytes. After Neve was transferred to Mexico, less than a month before Serra died, he had the happiness to learn that Mission Santa Barbara was to be established.

Governor Fages and Father Vicente Santa Maria chose an appropriate site in the hills, three-quarters of a league from the Presidio— Taynayan, Indians called it. *El Pedregoso*, or "Rocky Mound," was the Spanish name, because the soil was imbedded with sandstone.

In December, 1780, Viceroy Martín de Mayorga christened Santa Barbara for the daughter of Dióscoros, a pagan ruler of the early Christian era who locked his daughter in a tower to keep her from suitors. When he heard that she had learned Christianity from Origen, her teacher, he took her life. Lightning is said to have struck him dead. On this account Santa Barbara is invoked against thunderbolts.

Usually she is pictured standing by a castle tower, in one hand the palm of victory, the other resting on her sword. At her feet lie cannon. She is the protector of artillerymen and seafarers.

Governor Pedro Fages went south for the establishment of the Mission, reaching Santa Barbara Presidio December 14, 1786. Two days later the Mission was formally founded, but the church celebrates December 4, the feast of Santa Barbara. On December 16, a green bower was constructed on the site where the Cross was to be erected. President Fermin Lasuén sang the first Mass, assisted by Father Antonio Paterna. Baptismal, marriage, and death registers were drawn up by Lasuén. He assigned to the new establishment Fathers Antonio Paterna and Cristóbal Orámas.

No converts had been made at the Santa Barbara Presidio Chapel in four years, but neophytes soon came to the Mission. On December 31, 1786, Father Paterna baptized three adults in the guardhouse—a building used as a church, because the Presidio Chapel was crumbling. Catayu, from the Ranchería Guainonase, was the first adult baptized, Antonio Maria. Father Paterna performed the first marriage at the Presidio Chapel on December 3, 1786—that of soldier Joseph Calijito and Juana Vitala Féliz. First to marry at the Mission were Indian José Manuel and Catalina María on February 3, 1787. Father Vicente de Santa Maria, December 29, 1782, recorded the first Mission burial: the two-months-old daughter of soldier Vicente Quijada and his wife Juana. Father Lasuén began the Mission burial register on October 28, 1787. One of the first Indian converts, Augustin, was buried by him on August 8, 1787.

Mission buildings were delayed the first year by heavy rainfall, and the Fathers lived at the Presidio. In 1787 a two-room house for the missionaries was completed, 44 feet long by 14 wide. A chapel about the same size was also finished. A house for unmarried women and girls was built; a granary and a carpenter shop were added. Buildings were of poles with thatched roofs; only one was of adobe. Older Missions sent gifts—household utensils, tools, implements for the fields. The King of Spain gave vestments and church goods.

Planting began in 1786. Barley and peas failed, but 265 bushels of grain were harvested. At the end of 1787 Santa Barbara had 87 goats,

80 head of cattle, 32 horses, 27 sheep, and 9 mules. In 1789 a church 108 feet long and 17 wide was erected to accommodate the Indian population of 425. There was also a jail with a tile roof. Ignacio Rochin was executed for having committed murder.

Yearly each Indian received a blanket, every seven months a shirt, and new breeches semi-annually. Girls' chemises and sackcloth skirts were woven at the Mission. Old garments were burned, never washed.

After finishing tasks, Indians were permitted to visit parents at *rancherías*. Men fished and danced or sang in the courtyard. Runaway Indians were brought back and warned. The second time they were lashed or placed in stocks. If this was not sufficient, they were made to wear shackles for three days while at work. The same punishment was given for concubinage. Women delinquents were chastised always by the hand of another woman.

Highly important building began in 1793—the third church, made of adobe, plastered and also tile-roofed. It was 124 feet long by 25 wide, with a spacious sacristy and brick portico. During the following year, March 19, the new church was dedicated. Large paintings were acquired for the six side chapels. This building was used until the earthquake of 1812.

Before the new church was completed, its builder, Father Antonio Paterna, died. He was buried on February 14, 1793. Since 1750 he had labored on this continent, and was one of the founders of San Gabriel. A man of great power and high spiritual worth, he brought even deserting soldiers back to duty when their officers could not persuade them to return.

In 1792 Vancouver called Santa Barbara the best-constructed and kept of the California establishments. Missionaries discountenanced letting out Indians as laborers at nineteen cents a day with less than a peck of corn a week, although money went into the common Mission fund. Carpenters and tanners were engaged to teach trades to neophytes. Sixty converts wove woolen, cotton, and breechcloths. The wine and brandy manufactured might have been profitable, if foreign liquor had been excluded.

During the last decade of the eighteenth century Mission cattle were destroyed by coyotes, cougars, and bears; but converts came from even the Channel Islands. In 1797 missionaries received Stations of the Cross for the church from grateful seamen. Other gifts were a painting of Saint John the Baptist for the baptistry, a statue of Our Lady of Sorrows, one of Saint Michael, and another of Saint Francis. A gold-plated silver chalice was also presented to the church, with two silver crowns—one for the statue of the Immaculate Conception, one for the Infant Jesus, and a halo for Saint Joseph.

In the large Indian village each family had a separate dwelling. The quadrangle enclosed by the buildings was 825 feet square. Here also was the garden, vineyard, and orchard where youths played the violin, viola, and guitar, dancing until the Poor Souls bell rang at eight.

During the pioneer days gardening began to have a vogue at Santa Barbara. Outside of the Presidio were sixty houses, each with a garden. In 1800 a village was laid out in streets and cross streets. An irrigation system begun in 1799 still supplies water for the Mission. A reservoir 110 feet square and 17 feet deep was completed in 1806. Water was brought two miles from Arroyo Pedregoso, Mission Creek.

Two years later Father Antonio Ripóll erected in front of the Mission the most impressive fountain of native construction in California, often used as a model for fountains. Its octagonal standard supports the bowl, sculptured on four sides. Another eight-sided standard sustaining a carved fluted bowl rises from the center of the bowl, and from this emerges a standard enclosing the water pipe. Below this fountain a crouching stone bear spilled water from its mouth into a reservoir 60 feet long by 16 wide, where Indian women laundered, gossiped, scolded, and laughed.

During a pulmonary epidemic in 1801 that lost the Mission many converts, one of the Indian prophets sped through the Channel *rancherías* warning them that unless they bathed their faces in a certain water and made offerings to the pagan god Chupu, deity of the Channel Coast, they would die. The epidemic passed after the Indians cast seeds, venison, and feathers on the wind, and they returned to Christianity.

Many baptisms had been made at Santa Barbara—3,003—and in 1803 Mission population was at its highest—1,792. The Fathers asked aid from other missionaries. At this time an adobe chapel, San Miguel, was erected about five miles from Santa Barbara. This chapel, 61 feet by 25, many years later could still be seen near Daniel Hill's old residence at the Patera.

During this period the Mission owned several stock ranches, including Tecolote and De las Armas, besides San Marcos, San Miguel, San Estévan, and Dos Pueblos. Corn and beans were planted at San José, the Sauzal—today's Hope Ranch—and in the Arroyo del Burro. Late in the eighteenth century only 550 *fanégas* of wheat and a little corn were harvested. Six hundred neophytes went to the mountains and lived on berries and game. San Diego, San Juan Capistrano, La Purísima Concepción, and San Luis Obispo contributed 300 *fanégas* of wheat and corn. By bartering tallow and hides, the Fathers purchased $10,000 worth of clothing for Indians, groceries, tools, and implements.

With returning prosperity, the missionaries enlarged their living quarters. Along the front wing was constructed a corridor with stone arches and massive pillars of brick tile. While the work was unfinished, on December 21, 1812, the sea became troubled and the earth shook. People fled to the beach chanting litanies. For several months shocks were felt. Terrified *Barbareños* lived in the open air. Both Mission and Presidio buildings were damaged, but repairs were soon made. The Presidio Chapel of wood and tile was finished in March, 1813.

During this same year, on October 21, the King of Spain ordered illuminations, salvos of artillery, ringing of bells, and solemn singing of the *Te Deum* in thanksgiving for the triumph of Russian arms over Napoleon. For the moment Santa Barbara seemed close to Madrid.

About this time Father Ripóll decided to build the fourth church—larger, handsomer—around the old edifice. Indian workers made their own tools and erected the building without one *real* from the government, at the same time providing for the troops. The sandstone walls six feet thick had buttresses nine by nine. There were marble-finished columns and altar tables in Roman style. In the ceiling fresco were used designs from Vitruvius, the architect of Julius Caesar. The hard red cement floor was finely finished. With its simple façade, six engaged columns, Grecian entablature, pediment with heavy dentils under the cornice, thirteen semi-circular tiled arches set back from the main façade, massive bell towers thirty feet high and twenty feet square, the building has influenced the architecture of San Luis Rey, San Buenaventura, and the entire United States.

Over the high stone altar in a bracket stood a statue of Santa Barbara with a painting on each side, one of Saint Joachim and one of Saint Anne. There were smaller statues of the Virgin, Saint Joseph, Saint Dominic, and Saint Francis. In the center niche above the entrance was a painted statue of Santa Barbara. The apex and both angles were adorned with statues representing faith, hope, and charity. Paintings placed in the building were brought from Spain in 1793.

Two months before dedication of the church, Governor Solá sent rocket-maker Salvadór Vejár of San Diego to prepare fireworks for the celebration of September 10, 1820. From San Buenaventura arrived President Señan; from San Luis Obispo, Father Luis Martínez; from San Juan Capistrano, Father Gerónimo Boscana. Neophytes came from Santa Inés and San Fernando with musicians and dancers. Housetops were illuminated. Towers and corridors were brilliant with flags. On Sunday bells began to ring. The procession moved. Governor Solá led with Captain José de la Guerra of the Presidio, Lieutenant Narciso Fabregat of Mazatlan, President Señan, and all the priests. Father Boscana celebrated Mass. There was a new gold-plated chalice set with precious stones. Altar boys had new cassocks. Indian servants carried mats and camp stools for the great families. Each *señorita* had embroidered her own prayer rug. Poorer classes used *tule* mats. Neophytes squatted on the floor—men and boys on one side, women and girls on the other.

Fiesta followed Mass. Musicians of three Missions played three days and nights while Indians and soldiers danced. There were rockets, firecrackers, bull-baiting. Mission and barracks kept open house. Father Suñer wrote in the baptismal book that "neither mishap nor quarrel occurred. It was a lively and continuous and pure blessing to the Lord from the Lord."

Even in the midst of rejoicing the friars who had given their lives to the Mission were remembered. The bodies of Father Antonio Paterna and Father José Dulanto of Mission San Juan Bautista were exhumed and placed in the center of the church.

At this time there were 5,235 Indians in the Santa Barbara district, but they were dying from *mal Galico*. Children were usually born dead. Indians wailed and blew smoke over graves in the direction of the four winds. Cattle also were dying for lack of food. Rich *rancheros* were putting their own brand on Mission herds.

Santa Barbara is the only California Mission with twin towers. It has had several bells. In 1797 there were two. In the eastern tower hangs the most interesting bell, inscribed: 1797 IMAYAMO S. BARBARA VIVA LA S. S. MATRE. (1797. I AM CALLED SAINT BARBARA. HAIL THE HOLY MOTHER.) Another cracked bell of the same date in the lower story of the east tower has the inscription: PURISIMA CONCEP-CION. RUELAS ME FECIT. 1797. (IMMACULATE CONCEPTION. RUELAS MADE ME. 1797.) A bell of later date is inscribed: SANTA BARBARA DE PURISIMA CONCEPCION. This small bell has a Latin cross on either side and is lettered: LIMA 1804. Two other bells are in the tower. One reads: ME FECIT ANO DE 1818 MANUEL VARGAS. MISION DE S. BARBARA DE LA NUEBA CALIFORNIA. (I WAS MADE IN THE YEAR 1818 BY MAN-UEL VARGAS. MISSION OF SANTA BARBARA OF NEW CALIFORNIA.) The west tower bell, cracked and uninscribed, completes the sextet. In the lower story of each tower is also a small bell with a blurred, inde-cipherable inscription. Santa Barbara's lost bell is dated 1722, and for many years was at the Presidio. Later it was taken to the Church of Our Lady of Sorrows. Since 1929 it has hung in the chapel tower of the Jesuit Retreat House at Los Altos, California.

When in 1818 the American brig *Clarion* brought news that Bouchard the buccaneer and his men were coming, Santa Barbara had one of its most dramatic moments. Father Ripóll armed several hundred Indians with bows and arrows, chopping knives and lances— *La Compañia de Urbanos Realistas*. Luckily Bouchard and his men approached no nearer than the Ortega Rancho del Refugio, thirty miles northwest of Santa Barbara, where chests of gold were sup-posedly concealed.

Santa Barbara's peace was again broken when at daybreak on Sunday, February 22, 1824, a messenger arrived from Santa Inés.

"Help! Help! The Indians have risen. Father Uría is imprisoned at Purísima, the only man alive. Send soldiers immediately! Santa Inés and Purísima Indians are on the warpath."

Captain de la Guerra was summoned to protect the Mission. Neophyte leaders, Cristobal and Jayme, promised to remain at peace if the troops did not fire. Father Ripóll told the Indians he would celebrate Mass at the Presidio. After Mass he said to neophytes, "Follow me to the Presidio guardhouse!"

The Indians obeyed. Suddenly they seized soldiers' weapons. Indians fought with bows and arrows. Women fled wildly up Mission Creek, while Spaniards and Indians battled three hours. Two hundred Indians remained in possession of the Mission. The rebels retreated to the Sierras and into the Tulare country. Captain de la Guerra sent eighty soldiers in pursuit.

Father Prefect Vicente Sarría asked Father Ripóll to accompany the soldiers, but he replied, "The troops are going after the fugitives, my beloved children. . . . The Indians regard them as enemies. I prefer to die rather than go with the military force."

When Lieutenant Narciso Fabregat returned to Santa Barbara, victorious after having killed several Indians, Father Ripóll wept and said, "My God, they killed my sons, the Indians!"

Father Ripóll went with Captain Portilla to persuade the Indians to return to Santa Barbara from the Tulare plains. They remained obdurate until an *enramada* was erected and Mass was celebrated. Father Ripóll accompanied the Indians to Santa Barbara. Governor Argüello pardoned the fugitives, but after this uprising Indian population at Santa Barbara decreased.

Father Ripóll took the oath of loyalty to independent Mexico, but he declined to swear allegiance to the new constitution. He returned to Spain, and Fathers Juan Moreno and José Antonio Jimeno were stationed at Santa Barbara.

During his last days at this establishment, an Indian neophyte, Valerio, deserted the Mission and lived in a near-by cave. At night he stole back to get food. Four soldiers and four archers found him cooking his meal over a small fire. An arrow went whistling into Valerio's shoulder. Back at the soldiers the outlaw hurled the arrow;

three other arrows whirred through the air. The lifeless Valerio was carried back to the Mission on a soldier's horse.

Learning did not thrive at Santa Barbara, although Governor Borica established a school on February 25, 1796. José Manuel Toca, a sailor, taught thirty-two children for $125 a year. To this sum each soldier contributed a dollar. After one year José Medina took Toca's place. Later Diego Fernandez taught the Presidio school for $15 a month, but parents would not send their children to school. After Father Ripóll left, Governor Echeandia discontinued the school.

In 1830 Joaquin Solis, the ex-convict revolutionist, swept into Santa Barbara from San Francisco with an unpaid band of soldiers. Solis called upon the Presidio force to join him. Women went aboard the *Funchal*, while the government troops took refuge in the Presidio. After three days' firing Solis' ammunition was expended. He went north, accepted the Governor's pardon, and ended the civil war.

In the next year a great forest fire blazed on the hills of San Buenaventura and ravaged all the leagues between the two Missions. Large cinders dropped upon Santa Barbara. Citizens fled to the beach. Crews on harbor vessels worked all night keeping ships' decks wet. At the house of Captain de la Guerra, the mighty of Santa Barbara supplicated the saints. Fire blackened the Mission vineyard and spread northward, where it died. For months Santa Barbara was surrounded with ominous, smoking hills.

Drouth two years later caused Father Antonio Jimeno to carry the statue of Nuestra Señora del Rosario through the streets. Four *señoras* followed, transporting the Virgin's figure adorned with finery and costly jewels. From the church to the beach they proceeded, accompanied by the music of violin and flute, while prayers and supplications for rain were offered. The procession marched until raindrops fell.

Soon after the drouth was broken, came secularization of the Mission on August 9, 1834. The new commissioner, Carrillo, and Father Jimeno relied upon the Indians for support, but neophytes no longer worked. The Mission and its ranches, however, were valued at $112,960. The handsome, spacious buildings became headquarters for

the southern Franciscans. Father President Narciso Durán was transferred from Mission San José to Santa Barbara.

After Father Durán's arrival, occurred the first wedding of importance uniting California and the United States. Richard Henry Dana,
a Harvard student who came as a sailor on the *Pilgrim*, described the
occasion in *Two Years before the Mast*, after he became an eminent
lawyer. Doña Ana María, daughter of Captain José de la Guerra y
Noriega, became the bride of Alfred Robinson, a merchant.

The de la Guerra home was the largest in the province, but a tent
was erected in the garden for the guests, who ranged from grandees
to Indians. For three days the *Pilgrim's* steward was at the great house
making American pastry and cakes in honor of the American bridegroom. When Alfred Robinson and his bride appeared in the Mission
doorway, on the morning of January 24, 1836, the new bell, which
had just been christened, rang joyfully. The military band in red
jackets trimmed with yellow, wearing white trousers and red hats,
accompanied the bridal party in carriages, followed by men and
women on horseback. From the roof of his dwelling Don José de la
Guerra cast silver among the crowd. The *Pilgrim* saluted twenty-
three times. In the tent the guests *fandangoed* to violins and guitars.

One wing of the de la Guerra dwelling that has not been given
over to fashionable shops is still occupied by Doña Delfina de la
Guerra, who lives here surrounded by ancestral portraits and antique
furniture. The de la Guerras have occupied their residence longer than
any California family.

Shortly after the American-California marriage, Santa Barbara had
a scandal occasioned by Governor Mariano Chico. He was not accompanied by his popular wife, Doña Ignacia Alegre, but by his so-called
niece, Señora Cruz. They were interested in poetry and wild flowers.
From the Mission Father Durán charged the Governor with immorality. "Treason!" shouted His Excellency. The Governor declared that
the missionaries at Santa Inés failed to receive him with respect. He
asked the legislature at Monterey to banish President Durán; and
it was so ordered.

Thirty years the President had served California. When he attempted to go aboard the *Leonidas* at Santa Barbara, the people pre-

vented local authorities from executing Chico's order. Soon the
Governor himself was banished.

Santa Barbara was disturbed by another Governor, Don Juan Bautista Alvarado. With a band of Mexicans and foreign riflemen, he
dismounted at the church, assisted at a *Te Deum*, and asked blessing
on the new flag, lettered *Independencia de California*. Blessing was
denied, but on January 6, 1837, Santa Barbara took the oath of allegiance to Alvarado, California's second native Governor.

President Durán lived in a small apartment at the Mission in 1839,
and Father Jimeno occupied another. The 250 neophytes would
neither cut firewood nor supply food for the Fathers. They stole
horses, broke into wine cellars, attacked girls; but Santa Barbara had
imperishable charm. T. J. Farnham, the American, wrote in 1840
of the old vineyard on the hillside, the walled-in orchard where grew
semi-tropical fruits, and the water cascading from the mountain into
the large pool.

Grandeur came to Mission Santa Barbara on January 11, 1842, with
the arrival of California's first bishop, Francisco García Diego y
Moreno. The population knelt and kissed the pontifical ring when
the Bishop came ashore from the *Guipuzcoana*. In his train were his
niece, Doña Josefita González y Diego, her elderly companion, Doña
Concepción Palomares, Father Miguel Muro, and Father Francisco
Sanchez. Under arches formed by ornamental canes held up by *señoras*,
the Bishop passed into the town. Men unfastened the horses and drew
his carriage. Presidio guns thundered welcome.

At the church the Bishop addressed a multitude. He was so pleased
with the welcoming *fiesta* that he requested the Holy See to transfer
his residence from San Diego to Santa Barbara. He planned to erect a
palace for himself, a theological school, and a monastery. With his
own hands he heaped up stones for a cathedral. Owing to lack of
funds, he established only a small seminary, which was later transferred to the ecclesiastical seminary at Santa Inés.

Suddenly the Bishop's income of $6,000 annually was cut off by
President Santa Anna, who confiscated the Pious Fund for the national treasury. In 1844 the Bishop's fees were only $326. Cattle
were killed and grapes were stolen. On April 30, 1846, California's

first bishop died. He left $97. His tomb in the Mission is often visited.

The Bishop's niece, Doña Josefita, who died at Santa Barbara in 1852, left $530 for the proposed college and church of Our Lady of Sorrows in the city of Santa Barbara. Doña Josefita's companion, Doña Concepción, was revered at Santa Barbara for her image of Saint Francis—the last hope of the dying. If it failed to cure, despair and death followed.

President Durán grew fatally ill, in spite of the image of Saint Francis. He wrote that he had always entreated God to grant him the grace of dying among California Indians. To them he bequeathed his annual income of $400. His life closed on June 1, 1846, and he was interred in the church at Santa Barbara.

Already, December 5, 1845, Nicholas Den and Daniel Hill had leased Santa Barbara Mission for $1,200 a year. On June 10, 1846, Dr. Richard S. Den bought the property for $7,500.

Colonel R. F. Stockton, with 316 marines and seamen, arrived from Monterey, and on August 4 or 5, 1846, raised the Stars and Stripes. With much ceremony, on December 27 of the same year, Colonel John C. Frémont caused the American flag to be hoisted by Lieutenant Theodore Talbot and nine men.

Bishop Alemany formally gave Mission Santa Barbara to the Franciscans on April 18, 1853, for an ecclesiastical college for the education of novices; but the buildings seemed unsuitable. Land was purchased in 1854 from Nicholas A. Den and his wife near the intersection of State and Figueroa Streets. Father J. J. Jimeno was authorized to erect a convent for the teaching staff and to build a church. A chapel was arranged in the Den adobe house until a church could be erected. The edifice was dedicated on Sunday, July 23, 1854.

One of Santa Barbara's most unique Franciscans, Father Francisco Sanchez, came with Bishop García Diego in 1842. He was vice-rector of the seminary at Santa Inés until May, 1850, when he returned to Santa Barbara as master of novices. Alone, barefoot in his brown habit, he walked over California preaching to Mexicans and Indians. He said prayers in amusement places. He insisted upon the marriage of people living in concubinage. Alms obtained by the Father on missionary tours often sustained the Santa Barbara community. Taken to jail once for violating a civil ordinance, he said, "This is where I belong."

Less than a month before he was assassinated, President Lincoln signed a patent, on March 18, 1865, granting 283.13 acres, including Santa Barbara Mission, to the Catholic Church. Bishop Thaddeus Amat lived at the Mission, making the church his pro-cathedral.

In 1915 all Franciscan monasteries, convents, and Indian Missions in California, Oregon, Washington, and Southern Arizona were united in a province under the patronage of Santa Barbara. The first provincial was Father Hugolinus Storff.

After 113 years, once more, on June 29, 1925, the Mission walls rocked, swayed, and crunched. The western tower crumbled as if crushed by a sledge hammer. The eastern tower was cut in half by the temblor. The bells jauntily hung in the air suspended by rawhide thongs to the beams. Apertures were in the roof. Buttresses were wrenched from walls. An adobe wall in the upper story of the monastery was cracked and out of plumb. Sandstone walls six feet thick in the lower story bore the earthquake well.

The sanctuary light burned on, and the bells still sounded. A standard was erected in the garden at the western end of the building near which was constructed an altar. Here the bells were suspended.

Father Augustine engaged Architect Ross Montgomery to restore the building. Pala Indians assisted. Indian paintings were retouched by Thorwald Probst. Luis J. Mohr, of Santa Barbara, harmonized the restored portions of the museum so that they retained their unique appearance. On August 10, 1927, dedication of the new-old church took place. As Father Augustine said, in his Restoration Ode, once more "the Queen of Missions held her royal sway."

Today Santa Barbara Mission includes the home of the Fathers, two gardens, and a cemetery. The present sandstone church is the most solid structure of its kind in California—165 feet long, 39 feet wide, 30 feet high, with towers extending 30 feet skyward. The fine Monastery façade is supported by 13 Roman arches above a paved corridor. The Fathers' living quarters join the church on the southwest. Their two-story adobe building is 240 feet long and 50 feet wide. Sixty Franciscans take care of the Mission property.

From the western tower may be seen the Sacred Garden in the rear of the building. Wives of rulers and their attendants are the only women permitted to enter here. Mrs. Benjamin Harrison, wife of the President; Princess Louise, daughter of Queen Victoria and wife of the Marquis of Lorne, Governor-General of Canada; and Queen Elizabeth of Belgium have walked in this Sacred Garden, which has fifty flower beds bordered with boxwood thirty years old.

Here bloom pansies, coral bells, violets, stocks, nemesias, candytuft, asters, snapdragons, zinnias, petunias, delphiniums, breath of heaven, fuchsias, roses, heliotrope, teuchrium, nandina, japonica, fatsia, bauhinia, deutzia, Peruvian daffodils, narcissi, lilies, anemones, callas, amaryllis, agapanthus, cannas, and parkinsonia. Periwinkle, pittosporum, and coprosma are here. There are coleus, ferns, cinerarias, and begonias. Four hundred kinds of cacti and succulents brighten a corner. Jasminoides, bignonias, jacarandas, Bougainvillea, pomegranates, oleanders, strelitzia, streptosolen, flaunt their gay colors. From the tropics are lemons, oranges, bananas, palms, and hibiscus to make up this unique garden among the California Missions.

For more than a century Santa Barbara's altar light has not been extinguished. The past re-awakens as you walk over flagstones rutted by heavy boots of *Conquistadores*, dainty heels of *señoras* and *señoritas*, sandals of Franciscans, and bare feet of Indians. Long-gone days revive when you climb the narrow stairs to the belfry, where doves live with deep-voiced bells hanging from hand-riven beams. You enter the museum. You see Bishop García Diego's writing set and some of his furniture. Here is the first altar at the Mission; the first music that the Indians studied; hand-made parchment volumes of prayers; vestments worn by Serra; the crown piece of an ancient altar tabernacle ornamented with opalescent abalone.

In the east garden is the cemetery with the dust of thousands of Indian neophytes. Here lies the first Ortega, Don José Francisco, Portolá's daring trail maker and discoverer of San Francisco Bay. The granite tomb of Doña Angustias de la Guerra Jimeno Ord says that she wished to rest among those she loved so much.

The guide recounts the strange story of the wild woman of San Nicolas Island who rests in this cemetery. In 1835 Captain Charles

Hubbard, in his ship *Peor es Nada,* sailed for the island to bring Indians to the coast for the *padres.* A child was left behind as the natives hurried into the boat. Its mother desperately jumped overboard and swam through the kelpy water to the island shore. Mother and child were forgotten; they were only Indians.

In 1850 Father Rúbio heard that the woman was alive on the island. He paid a man to go to her rescue. No woman was found. Three years later she was discovered by George Nidever, a strange creature dressed in bird skins and feathers, living on roots, with black and white dogs as companions.

Gladly she came to the Mission. Rare foods were her delight, but the change from a root diet shortened the life of Juana María, the wild woman of San Nicolas Island. As you leave the garden of death, you read the tablet placed by the Daughters of the American Revolution to mark her grave. You turn to look back at the life-sized figure of the Son of Man upon the Cross against a greenery background. Death's darkness becomes light.

XI

La Purísima Concepción

MISSION LA PURÍSIMA CONCEPCIÓN is near Lompoc, southeast of San Luis Obispo, in fields of blossoms rainbowing down to the Pacific. During its days of decay, for several years the building housed bandits. In the 'fifties Salomon Pico, cousin of Governor Pio Pico, sallied forth from its portal to make a "rosary of Yankee ears." Later from this Mission the Yankee daredevil, Jack Powers, with his lawless band of five, preyed upon travelers between San Luis Obispo and Santa Barbara.

These dire deeds failed to sully the Mission of Most Pure Mystery of the Immaculate Conception of the Most Holy Virgin Mary, Mother of God, Queen of Heaven, Queen of Angels, Our Lady. In Spanish its name is *La Misión de la Purísima Concepción de la Santísima Virgen María, Madre de Dios y Nuestra Señora.*

As early as 1779 it was planned to have a third Mission on the thickly populated Santa Barbara Channel. Eight years later Father President Lasuén determined to make the foundation despite threatening storms. Accompanied by a military guard, he set out from Santa Barbara.

Near a stream of water overlooking a wide plain with timbered mountains in the rear, he found a sheltered site—Algsacupi, the Indians called it. Fifty *rancherías* surrounded the place. Father Lasuén blessed the site, raised the Cross, and celebrated Mass on December 8, 1787, feast day of the Immaculate Conception. Torrents descended soon; work was suspended.

In the middle of March, 1788, building was resumed, supervised by Sergeant Pablo Antonio Cota. Early in April Father Lasuén appeared with the first two missionaries, Father Vicente Fuster and Father José de Arroita, a newcomer.

At Purísima they found hungry bears in winter and hissing rattlesnakes in summer. One convert was bitten twice at the same time by two rattlesnakes. Despite bears and rattlesnakes, within four months zealous missionaries made 79 converts.

On April 9, 1788, Father de Arroita baptized twenty-three-year-old Matisaguit of the Ranchería Quajauchu. He also performed the first marriage ceremony at Purísima, May 10, 1788. Two Indians, Mariano Tamolechet and María Concepción, both of whom had been previously married in their pagan state, were remarried at Purísima. Father Fuster interred the first Christian Indian at Purísima on February 14, 1789, Juana de la Cruz, or Parbula.

Toward the end of 1790 the Fathers had converted 301 natives, but Fuster retired from Purísima. He was succeeded by Father Cristóbal Orámas, one of the founders of Santa Barbara. Large crops were produced. Stock increased. During the first decade La Purísima had nearly a thousand neophytes, many of whom excelled in weaving.

Before the end of 1802 the flimsy church of 1795 was replaced by an adobe building with tile roof and brick corridor 200 feet long, 60 wide, and 30 high. The quadrangle was completed and flanked by adobe Indian dwellings. Dining room and workshops were added, 100 feet long and 25 wide.

Father Mariano Payeras, a Majorcan who arrived in 1804, developed Purísima. Understanding Indian dialects, he prepared a catechism and a manual of confessions in both native idiom and Spanish. Suave and kind, the Father became President of the Missions, always living at Purísima. His diary describes his exploration of California north as far as Fort Ross.

Father Payeras was assisted by Father Gregorio Fernandez, the angel, Father Juan Cabot, the sailor, and scholarly Father Gerónimo Boscana. Under Father Payeras converts reached the highest number at Purísima—1,520. Worship of Chupu, the native god, was uprooted. Nearly the entire population within a radius of twenty-five miles had been baptized within two decades.

Grain could not be raised without irrigation at Purísima, but

springs were found. Desirable livestock was bred. From north and
south *rancheros* came to buy Palomino horses, the finest in California.

On December 21, 1812, the earth shook for four minutes. Half an
hour the shocks continued. The earth opened, belching forth black
sand and water. Church walls were thrown out of plumb. Nearly all
adobe buildings fell, injuring neophytes. From crest to valley floor,
the Mission hill was cleft. Even today the opening is visible.

Huts of grass were hastily constructed for shelter and religious
services, but the Indians feared the settlement would be swept into
the river. They thought Chupu must be the true god; they left the
Mission and would not return.

In another year Father Payeras began rebuilding the Mission on a
site four miles northward across the river at Amun, or Los Verros,
the Canyon of Watercress. Las Flores, some called it; here were California's most beautiful wild flowers. Temporary grass and wood huts
were erected. Irrigation ditches were dug to the Santa Inés River,
but sheep perished by the hundreds in the drouth of 1816 and 1817.
Children were born dead. Half the neophytes fled to the Tulares. Fire
destroyed the converts' houses.

Notwithstanding difficulties, in 1818 the new adobe and tile church
was completed. Again rain fell. *Ranchos* now extended fourteen
leagues from north to south, and six leagues from east to west, producing in 1821 wheat, barley, and corn that amounted to 8,000
bushels. One hundred thousand pounds of tallow were sold. Between
1822 and 1827 Purísima furnished Santa Barbara Presidio with nearly
$13,000 worth of supplies, including sixty-four serapes.

Father Payeras did not live to see his Mission completed. At fifty-
four, on April 28, 1823, it is said that he heard the distant bells of
San Gabriel, San Juan Capistrano, San Luis Obispo—eleven bells
from eleven belfries in chorus, joined by bells of Purísima. He
swooned and died, kissing the Cross. He was buried under the pulpit
of the church he built.

Jovial Father Blas Ordáz succeeded Father Payeras. Before a year
passed neophytes at Santa Inés and Purísima rose and seized the
church. Throughout the night Corporal Tiburcio Tápia with five or
six men defended Father Ordáz and the soldiers' families. Three white

men, one woman, and several Indians were killed. When his powder gave out Father Ordáz surrendered. Both he and Father Antonio Rodríguez were Indian prisoners. The rebels erected palisades and mounted two rusty cannon on the church walls. Pacómio, an educated neophyte, and four hundred Indians held the church.

The Governor's troops failed to arrive from Monterey. Captain de la Guerra hurried from Santa Barbara in February with a force and attacked. The Indians yelled, fighting with cannon, swivel guns, and muskets. Weapons in inexperienced hands did little damage. Cavalry prevented the Indians' flight. Sixteen natives lost their lives in the two and a half hour conflict, and there were many casualties. Several Spaniards were killed and wounded.

Father Rodríguez was held prisoner for some time. But he interceded for the neophytes and obtained the best possible terms for their surrender. Seven Indians were executed in spite of his efforts, and eight others were condemned to eight years at the Presidio. Pacómio, Mariano, Benito, and Bernabé were sentenced to ten months at the Presidio, and perpetual exile. General pardon had been promised, and Father Ripóll of Santa Barbara deeply grieved over these punishments. Governor Argüello, however, regretted that his deputies had been so lenient.

Father Ordáz continued building the new church. Timbers were cut in the Santa Inés Mountains, floated down the river to within a mile of the Mission, and hauled with teams up the hill. On October 4, 1825, the new church was dedicated; a long narrow adobe structure with twenty-one rooms facing north, well built and buttressed, with square pillars extending along the front. The sacristy had unusual carved doors. Over the pulpit was a painted canopy. Native musicians played violins, horns, and drums in the gallery reached by a long wide ladder. Near by were twelve smaller buildings.

La Purísima had no *campanario*, or tower. Five bells were suspended from the lower end of the colonnade; the standards supporting them are still visible. One of the bells has disappeared. Two, together with other church goods, were transferred in 1851 to Mission Santa Inés for preservation. They are replicas of bells at Santa Barbara and San Luis Obispo, but both are cracked. One is inscribed: MANUEL

VARGAS ME FECIT ANO E 1818. The other bell says: MANUEL VARGAS
ME FECIT ANO E 1818. MISION DE LA PURISIMA DE LA NUEBA CALI-
FORNIA. (MANUEL VARGAS MADE ME. YEAR OF 1818 MISSION OF
PURISIMA OF NEW CALIFORNIA.) The third La Purísima bell, smaller
than the others, is in the church at Guadalupe, a few miles from
Santa Maria. It is lettered: M. V. LIMA 1817. (MANUEL VARGAS LIMA
1817.) The Guadalupe bell, recast from the Santa Inés bell of 1817,
and Purísima's third missing bell were taken to Guadalupe in 1876
by Father J. B. McNally, who was stationed at Santa Inés. Until
1923 a fourth Purísima bell hung in the Lompoc Catholic Church
tower, but while Father Roure was in Europe the bell was stolen.

Drouth, frosts, flood, fire, earthquakes, and civil war scourged the
Mission. Decay began. At the close of 1831 only 404 Indians remained.

While Father Juan Moreno was at Purísima, in 1834 Domingo
Carrillo became *Comisionado;* but the Mission was not secularized
for a year. The estate was valued at $60,000, including Ranchos Sitio
de Misión Vieja, Sitio de Jalama, Los Alamos, San Antonio, Santa
Lucia, San Pablo, Todos Santos, and Guadalupe.

After 3,245 Indians had been baptized at Purísima, reports ceased.
But as early as 1836 there was no resident missionary for the population of 120. Two hundred cattle were slaughtered to purchase $800
worth of clothing for half-naked Indians. Father Miguel Gómez
walked or rode 20 miles to minister to the Mission. Father Francisco
Sanchez was the last Franciscan here.

A smallpox epidemic reduced the ex-neophytes near the Mission
to fifty in 1845. At this time Governor Pico sold the buildings and
two vineyards, all that was left of the estate besides the church
property, to Don Juan Temple of Los Angeles for $1,110. The Mis-
sion was virtually abandoned.

After the sweet-to-do-nothing 'forties were succeeded by the gold-
seeking 'fifties, Salomon Pico and his men boomed into Purísima,
they said, to avenge the conquest of California by the United States.
Ostensibly Pico was a *ranchero,* but feeling grew bitter over the
travelers who disappeared near the Mission. With his "rosary of

Yankee ears" Pico took refuge in Lower California. There in 1860 he was executed.

Another highwayman came to La Purísima—Jack Powers, originally of Stevenson's regiment. With him was his band of five, including Rafael Monea and Pio Linares. Short, dark-haired, and bearded, Powers resembled a Spanish-Californian. He assumed the manners of a Don, danced and gambled. His lair was the Mission. California's swiftest rider, in twelve hours he sped on his gray mule a hundred miles from the scene of crime. He boldly swaggered over to Mission Santa Inés, took possession of the College Rancho, discharged the major-domo, and established himself and his company as owners. He was later killed by his own men in Mexico.

In the late 'fifties and 'sixties Don José Ramón Malo, who owned the 15,000-acre Purísima Rancho, leased the church building and lived there with his family. He had a large merchandise store at the Mission, the only one in the county outside of Santa Barbara. In recent years his daughter, Doña Josefa Malo de Janssens, of Santa Barbara, recalled parading up and down the church as a child, wearing vestments.

After the Malos moved to Santa Barbara in 1865, the J. W. Rochin family occupied the Mission front rooms. In the rear lived the *vaqueros* who had charge of 3,000 head of cattle. Services were held only on Easter Sunday. Then came the de la Guerras of the San Julian and Los Alamos Ranchos, the Foxens of the Tinaquaic, the Arellanes of the Guadalupe and Laguna, the Danas of Nipomó, the Cotas of the Santa Rosa, and the Valencias of the Nojoqui.

Rochin disposed of the Purísima Rancho to Hill and Commodore Thomas Ap Catesby Jones, who in 1842 commanded the Pacific Squadron of five vessels. On October 19 of that year, he thought he was saving the country from the British, and at Monterey raised the United States flag for the first time over California. Jones was relieved of his command, and he retired to Santa Barbara, where he gave the first Shakespearean performance.

In 1890 all that remained of the Mission were roofless walls and a few arches of the corridor half hidden in a tangle of mustard. Stairs had collapsed. On the wall hung part of the painted pulpit with sounding board awry. Cobwebby rags of the old canvas ceiling sadly fluttered. Inside the broken altar rail was a pile of earth, stone, and rubbish heaped up by shovels of treasure seekers. In one corner of the building lived a badger. Mud swallows hung their nests in broken cornices. The Virgin's image still remained.

The building was often used as a stable and sheepfold. Near by was a round stone irrigation tank overgrown with moss. The pear orchard with scattered trees still bore tough-skinned fruit. Red, yellow, and white *tunas* enlivened the scene. Visitors defaced the church, carrying away massive beams. Tiles from the roof still cover Santa Barbara houses.

In 1903 the Union Oil Company bought the property. The company had the roof tile placed for safety near the church. On condition that it be restored, the company offered Purísima to the county or state. Interest seemed as dead as the abandoned Mission standing in the Indian-summer atmosphere on the brown-coated hills.

About 1910 Father John Raley came to Lompoc and aroused interest in Purísima by inspiring celebration of the one hundred and twenty-fifth anniversary of the Mission. This was followed by the erection of a tall electric Cross on Mission Hill near the site of the first Purísima. It was unveiled on December 12, 1912, in the presence of a large assembly. A few Indians from the Santa Inés Reservation chanted hymns. In November, 1914, Father Raley called a meeting for the restoration of Purísima.

Supervisor-Editor Ronald M. Adam of the *Lompoc Record* assisted much in the campaign. People visited the fallen Mission, its walls marked with insurrection bullets of 1824. The oil company gave Santa Barbara County six parcels of land on which stood various Mission ruins. Later the Catholic Church donated a portion of the cemetery where Father Payeras was buried. In January, 1935, additional land was purchased, and the 507-acre tract, including Mission grounds, became a state park.

The restoration project was taken over by the Civil Conservation Corps, aided by a distinguished advisory committee. Miss Pearl Chase of Santa Barbara supervised the work. Mr. F. C. Hageman was employed as senior foreman architect with Mr. Edwin Rowe to landscape the grounds. On January 6, 1935, an original brick 120 years old was laid in the cornerstone of the missionaries' residence.

This building, with its several uniquely fluted columns, was in the best state of preservation, and was made a basis of restoration. Soon 240 men of the CCC camp were at work. They removed tons of dirt from the building 318 feet long and 65 wide. At first they followed the Indian method in making adobe bricks and tiles for walls and roof. Pits 10 feet long, 8 wide, and 6 deep were filled with clay and straw soaked with water. Brawny barebacked men in rubber boots tramped, tramped till the mud was smooth enough to be molded into brick. Others shoveled clay from pits into forms where it set. The bricks, two feet long, one foot wide, and four inches thick, dried on straw. Adobe mortar served as cement. Handwork gave way to a swift mixing machine.

New walls rose, or old ones were buttressed with concrete. Redwood timbers were brought from another CCC camp 1500 miles distant and hewn into flooring. Fallen colonnade columns were renewed. Tile, hinges, and hardware for doors and windows were reproduced with authenticity. After the Federal Government had spent $250,000 on the project, at last the building was re-dedicated on September 15, 1937. Mr. Joseph Knowland, chairman of the State Park Commission, and Father Agustine Hobrecht, O.F.M., of Santa Barbara Mission, spoke. The Purísima restoration is the best in California and invaluable to students and the public. The building will be used as a museum.

Persons possessing Purísima property have promised to return it. Mission Santa Inés has vestments, bells, registers of marriage, baptism, confirmation, and death, bearing signatures of Padre Presidente Tápis and Padre Prefect Sarría. They have also the census of Purísima Indians for the years from 1824 to 1858. Another early census is at Saint Vibiana's Cathedral, Los Angeles.

Landscape-architect Rowe has restored three large fountains and a cistern. He has planted at the Mission twenty-five old olive trees from a ranch thirty-five miles distant, and four large date palms. He has also assembled historic roses, fruits, and herbs; the *padres'* old garden with diagonal walks has been reproduced. From the one remaining

pear tree he made cuttings and grafted seedlings. Twelve varieties of
Mission pears were brought from San Juan Bautista, San Antonio,
San Miguel, San Luis Rey. Santa Clara Castilian roses were set out,
and San Antonio pomegranates. Mr. Rowe has propagated cuttings
of the pepper tree before the colonnade, supposedly planted by an
Indian maiden and her sweetheart to commemorate their love. The
young trees will be sold to augment Mission revenue.

During the reconstruction of Purísima, each day had its drama:
uncovering foundations of major-domos' quarters, tallow works, barracks, weaving rooms, nunnery, reservoirs, fountains, and the first
church. No scrap of tile or hardware was thrown away.

Schliemann seeking Troy was not more excited than the men excavating for the tomb of Father Payeras. Its location was established
near the sanctuary of the church. Spanish-Californians blessed themselves before they lifted the first shovel of soil. Decomposed redwood
was soon found. Was it Father Payeras' coffin? A few feet below the
surface of the earth a shovel struck something hard; a human bone.
The excavators closed the opening and summoned Santa Barbara
Franciscans.

On August 3, 1936, they came. Reverently once more the workers
opened the earth. A skeleton! The camp surgeon said it was a man
about fifty. Was it Father Payeras?

The Franciscans, Fathers Patrick, Marion, Maynard, and Turibius,
supplied the key; the man in the ground lay with arms folded, as
Franciscans are buried. All agreed that it was Father Mariano Payeras,
builder of Purísima and President of the California Missions, who had
lain in the earth 113 years.

Work on rebuilding the church was begun May 14, 1937. The
corner brick, one of the originals, was laid by Reverend Father Coffey,
Delegate General in Rome of the Franciscan Order, and by Mr. Fred
Johnston, National Park Service, Washington, D. C. Both spoke to
the group and the workers. The church is virtually completed. It is
174 feet long and 46 wide including the colonnade. A bell tower at
the south end extends 21 feet. Beyond the church is a walled cemetery 120 feet by 62. About sixty men are working at Purísima.

It is planned to reconstruct the large workshop building, which will be 323 feet long and 22 wide, bordered on both sides by narrow corridors, all in the form of the letter L. If the government continues its support, the entire community group of buildings will be restored.

Upon all these efforts Father Mariano Payeras seems to smile and give his benediction.

XII

Santa Cruz

SANTA CRUZ, the twelfth Mission, entered California history with the redwood tree. When Portolá and his bewildered men were vainly seeking Monterey, they found near Soquel, a few miles from Santa Cruz, the first redwood—the *Sequoia sempervirens*—later voted the national tree of the United States.

On October 10, 1769, Father Juan Crespi, chronicler of the expedition, wrote that the new tree had a different color from cedar, although the wood resembled cedar... "not the same odor... very brittle... unlike anything we have seen in Spain." It was named *palo colorado* (redwood) from its color. Some of the trees were 350 feet tall, the highest growing things recorded, older than the Christian era. The belt containing them was 450 miles long and 30 or 40 wide. In no other part of the world are redwoods found.

The explorers were pleased, not only with the trees, but with the climate, herbs, and abundant roses of Castile. They idled for a fortnight in the Indian summer when twice they traversed the region. Santa Cruz's first white camper was one of Portolá's soldiers who rode his horse into a burnt-out redwood tree and said, "Now I have a house."

Cabrillo found all very different in 1542. The savage surf at Point Santa Cruz kept him from landing. When Vizcaíno arrived on New Year's Day sixty-one years later, it was so cold that sailors' hands ached while obtaining wood and water.

Portolá had no thought of a Mission at Santa Cruz, although Father Crespi of his company made first mention of Santa Cruz in California on October 18, 1769:

We crossed a good arroyo of running water which descends from some high hill where it rises. It was named Santa Cruz. (Holy Cross.)

Father Francisco Palóu suggested Santa Cruz as a pueblo site. He declared it suitable for a city. "It lacks nothing that is necessary, and in abundance and close to the beach of Monterey." So the historian of the Rivera expedition wrote on December 11, 1774.

Seventeen years passed, however, before the Mission of the Holy Cross among the Costanoan Indians came into existence. Viceroy Conde de Revilla Gigedo sent the order for the establishment. It reached Monterey on August 2, 1790, by the same ship that brought four new missionaries from San Fernando College.

President Lasuén found that everything was ready for the new establishment except sacred vessels. Governor Fages told Lasuén to borrow them and proceed. The missionary led the way over the Sierra from Santa Clara to Santa Cruz. Some neophytes were set to work building a hut for the missionaries a stone's throw from the rushing Rio San Lorenzo, in a canyon overgrown with huckleberry bushes. Here were wild blossoms and maidenhair ferns. Aulinta was the Indian name for the place.

At eight o'clock on the morning of August 28, 1791, the day of San Agustín, Father Lasuén vested himself, blessed the spot, and raised the Cross about 500 yards from the Rio San Lorenzo. Lasuén celebrated Mass, and, leaving Fathers Alonzo Salazar and Baldomero López in charge, returned to Santa Clara by a rougher, more direct route. Lasuén was so occupied with a new foundation, Soledad, that he was not present at the formal ceremony establishing Santa Cruz.

Other Missions were asked by him to contribute to the new foundation. Santa Clara gave 64 cattle, 30 cows, 22 horses, 20 steers, 5 yoke of oxen, 77 *fanégas* of grain, and 27 loaves of bread. San Carlos sent 8 horses and 6 mules. Corporal Luis Peralta and Ensign Hermenegildo Sal of San Francisco came with 70 sheep, 5 yoke of oxen, and 2 bushels of barley.

Ensign Sal, on Sunday, September 25, 1791, made a speech and took formal possession in the name of the Most Holy Trinity, and His Majesty King Carlos IV. Soldiers' muskets barked a salute. Indians were warned not to be alarmed. Fathers López and Salazar said Mass, and a new link was added to the Mission chain. The festival of the Holy Cross is September 14.

Santa Cruz Indians immediately responded. Chief Sugert came with his wife and two daughters, Lucenza and Clara. The women, baptized, created friendliness among others. Chief Sugert promised to be the first native leader.

Winter was approaching, and 25 *fanégas* of wheat were sown by Indians. Blankets and maize paid for their labor. With borrowed tools a timber church 63 feet long and 18 wide was built. The missionaries' dwelling was 75 feet long. Already they had acquired a painting of Our Lady of Sorrows, an image of Saint Francis, and four brass candlesticks. Corrals were enclosed.

Ensign Sal left instructions for the Mission. Soldiers and servants were allowed a weekly amount of maize, beans, tallow, cigars, soap, and chocolate. Indians were to attend prayer, but not associate with guards, enter the church if armed, nor be given meat lest they kill cattle. Fifteen stripes were the punishment for cattle thieves. Armed sentinels picketed the Mission day and night to meet emergencies. Soldiers were forbidden to gamble or communicate with Indians, especially women.

The first baptism at Santa Cruz was October 9, 1791—Moslon, an Indian girl eight years of age, daughter of Ynoc and Frocsen of the Ranchería Achistaca. Fathers López and Salazar gave her the name Micaela. Chief Sugert's daughters aided so greatly that at the end of the year 87 neophytes had been baptized.

On November 6, 1791, Father López performed the first marriage ceremony in the church, uniting Hermenegildo and Josefa, who already had been married according to Indian rites. Soon six Indian marriages were celebrated.

In spite of Mission guards, cattle disappeared at the hands of the Indians. Bears were another menace. Soldiers were ordered to hunt them for target practice. Indians made target practice of soldiers, wounding two. From San Francisco came two companies to punish them.

No sooner were the Indians quieted than the San Lorenzo River rose. The Fathers began erecting a church on higher ground. Timbers were hewn on the mountain slope and dragged by Indians to the Mission. The Fathers tucked their habits in their girdles and taught the Indians to make adobe brick.

On February 27, 1793, the cornerstone of the new church was laid. The building was 112½ feet long, 29 wide, and 25½ feet high, with walls 5 feet thick attractively decorated. Up to three feet foundation walls were of stone, and the remainder were of adobe with a front of masonry. The entrance was formed by two pilasters with a horizontal bar over the arched doorway. A small window under the gable completed the façade. The tower resembled that of San Buenaventura with a vaulted dome; on the summit was a Cross mounted on a small lantern. The monastery with a corridor and a tile roof stretched away from the building.

On May 10, 1794, the church was dedicated. Father Tomás de la Peña arrived from Santa Clara to celebrate Mass. He was assisted by Father Luis Gíl y Taboada and Father Miguel Sanchez. Others present were Ensign Sal of San Francisco, godfather of the church, troops, *rancheros*, neophytes, and servants.

Industry stirred. Stone flour mills were made at San Carlos for Santa Cruz. With the erection of weaving rooms and a two-story granary, two sides of the quadrangle were completed. Twelve hundred bushels of grain, 600 of corn, and 60 of beans were garnered.

Governor Borica came to Monterey in 1794, and difficulties arose. He ordered officers' sons to be educated in manual arts at secular schools. Parents protested; such instruction was against their tradition. The Governor and his cultured wife and daughter felt that Indians should have modified self-government. At each Mission two Indian *Alcaldes* and two councilmen should be trained in self-government. The Fathers and the Governor clashed, each charging mistreatment of the Indians. The missionaries obeyed the letter of Borica's ruling, but evaded its spirit.

The Governor's friendliness to the Indians did not subdue threatening Pajaro natives. Sergeant Pedro Amadór and soldiers were summoned from San Francisco in January, 1795. A few months later Father Sanchez asked protection against threatening Indians.

Neophytes deserted the Mission. Corporal Mesa brought back 90 fugitives. Conditions did not improve. In 1798 Father Manuel Fernandez wrote that 138 neophytes had disappeared; only a few remained to work.

Again in 1797 rains weakened the church. Floods swept over the land when half of the planting was completed. Livestock died. Attracted by a dead whale on the beach, wolves appeared, battling with bears over the carcass.

Despite difficulties, the Viceroy determined not only to civilize the natives but to increase the Spanish population in California. A venture in colonization was made. Villa Branciforte, more ambitious than a pueblo, was named in honor of the Viceroy. It was to be settled with soldiers and fortified, both a military and civil foundation.

Across the river from Mission Santa Cruz a site was selected by Borica. Here were clay, stone, and lime for building. Houses were to cost no more than $200 each. They would be more comfortable than those of Pueblos San José and Los Angeles, where settlers still lived in *tule* huts. Houses and granaries were to be erected at once.

Engineer Alberto de Cordova laid out the Villa to cost $23,000. The Governor asked the Viceroy to send settlers.

Seventeen colonists arrived on the little ship *Concepción*. The Villa was founded by Governor Borica on July 24, 1797. Most of the settlers were bachelors: farmers, tailors, carpenters, merchants, miners, and engravers. Corporal Gabriel Moraga, the Indian fighter, was instructed to erect temporary shelters for the men, watch over their morals, and give them work—the last thing they desired. They were shiftless ne'er-do-wells from Guadalajara, mostly of Spanish origin.

Each settler received outright $25, and was to have annually $116 for two years from the government, and $66 for the next three years. A tile-roofed adobe was to be his and on easy payment: also two horses, mares, sheep, cows, a yoke of oxen, a musket, a plow, and other agricultural implements.

The colonists were obliged to live in redwood shacks while erecting their own adobe dwellings. "Exile from Mexico," they called it. They raised a small crop of maize, wheat, and beans. The establishment seemed a blunder. Soon it was a scandal. Governor Borica tried to regularize life by importing wives from Mexico for the colonists, but no *señoritas* came to the Villa.

Although Mission Santa Cruz possessed nine leagues of land, little was tillable. The rich *ranchos* in Bolsa de Pajaro, were so far away that they could not be protected from lawless Indians and predatory animals. At the foot of Mission Hill lay the best land, a few hundred acres, insufficient to maintain the Indians. Neophytes themselves, afflicted with disease brought by the army, declined to work, preferring to hunt quail and deer, or to fish. Much of the settlers' labor had to be performed a second time.

Mission Santa Cruz was almost as disappointing to its founders as Villa Branciforte. A violent storm in January, 1796, wrecked the water mill and other buildings. Presidio soldiers came to assist the Fathers in repairs. They were nearly as incompetent as Indians. In 1800 only 949 converts had been made, the fewest at any Mission.

Depressed by solitude, sickness, and death among the Indians, and their indifference to Christianity, Fathers Salazar and López retired to their College of San Fernando. Fathers Manuel Fernandez and José de la Cruz Espí succeeded them. Soon they left; in May, 1797, Father Francisco González came. Father Fernandez, in October, 1798, succeeded Father Domingo Carranza. These changes unsettled conditions. The grain yield, however, was encouraging, rising from 650 bushels to 4,300. In ten years livestock multiplied tenfold.

Friction continued between the Mission and the Villa. *Comisionado* Ignacio Vallejo was sent to the Villa in 1799 to improve the community, but the settlers' immorality was not bettered. *Comandante* José de la Guerra wrote the Governor in 1803 that if Branciforte colonists could be banished a million leagues from California for centuries, it would redound to the service of God and the King. "The Mission has all the best land," said the Villa settlers. The Fathers replied, "The Villa outrages neophyte rights."

After President Lasuén's death in 1803, Governor Felipe de Goycoechea of Baja California, suggested that the Mission be suppressed, the neophytes be divided between Santa Clara and San Juan Bautista, and the friars sent to new fields.

In the next decade grain harvests diminished nearly one-half. Large stock decreased, but small stock multiplied one-half. There were 953 horses. Building went forward. In 1810 a nunnery with two wings was erected for unmarried women. The Fathers baptized 135 Indians.

Even struggling Mission Santa Cruz and Branciforte were affected by Napoleon's wars. They sent $500 to aid the Spanish army. With the contribution Lieutenant José Estudillo, *Comandante* at Monterey, wrote Ferdinand VII: "I rely upon your spending it well."

A Santa Cruz street, Quintana, recalls the great Mission tragedy. On October 12, 1812, Father Andrés Quintana was found dead in bed. Long in ill health, his sudden death caused no suspicion. "Natural death," was the verdict.

Two years later an Indian major-domo at New Year's Point overheard Indians discussing Father Quintana's murder. Quickly on a horse he hastened over the Sierra to Mission Santa Clara where he revealed the murder.

The trial disclosed that the missionary had been summoned at night to an Indian supposed to be dying. In order not to break the rest of the soldiers, Father Quintana hastened away with the Indian caller. After visiting the sick person, he was seized by ambushed Indians and told to prepare for death. In spite of begging for mercy, he was hanged from a tree near the tunnel at Felton. His body was brought back to the Mission, placed in bed, and covered with blankets. In the morning it was found by servants, unaware of how he had come to his end.

The murderers pleaded guilty, saying that Father Quintana was oversevere in punishing murder and fornication. Five of the criminals were condemned to receive two hundred lashes each, and to work in chains from two to ten years. Only one survived.

In 1814 tales rose of Santa Cruz's great wealth. The Mission was supposed to have $30,000. In reality it owned a gold chalice valued at $600, another at $380, a vestment at $800, and two copes at $1,200. Santa Cruz ranches extended eleven leagues along the coast and two leagues inland. Twenty-nine hundred cattle at New Year's Point belonged to the Mission, besides 26 horses, 25 mules, and 46 hogs. There were harvested, however, only 500 bushels of wheat, 200 of barley, 200 of horse beans, and 189 of corn. Eight natives were baptized in this year, and there were more deaths than baptisms. In 1816 a new *ranchería* was brought under Mission influence, and the population increased.

Then Monterey's guns thundered—Buccaneer Bouchard! By messenger Governor Solá ordered Father Olbés to abandon Santa Cruz and flee with his valuables and neophytes to Santa Clara. From Santa Clara the Father sent Major-domo Castro and Indians to protect Santa Cruz property.

Bouchard did not reach Santa Cruz, but Branciforte settlers broke down Mission doors, tore curtains, defaced images, and soiled vestments. Whatever could be salvaged was taken to Santa Clara. Father Olbés announced to the Governor that he "would no longer submit to the inhuman outrages of the people of Branciforte."

Matters were worsened by colonists who told neophytes the soldiers would take them prisoner. The following year all Indians but three had fled, although on feast days they received cheese and a barrel of molasses.

Some neophytes returned. Crops were better; sheep and herds increased. Life at Santa Cruz, however, exacted too much; Father Olbés retired in 1821 to the College of San Fernando. He was succeeded by Father Luis Gíl y Taboada, who was continually tormented by Branciforte citizens. In 1823 an effort was made to suppress the Villa and end conflict.

In the following year came floods. Gardens, buildings, and church were threatened with ruin. Neophytes fled, and there were no laborers to repair damages. Ranches, however, prospered. In 1827, 10,000 bushels of grain were harvested, and herds numbered 12,502. Native self-government became a reality in 1831; *Alcalde* and *regidores* were Christianized Indians. Population declined rapidly.

Governor Figueroa, who came to California in 1833, began to emancipate the Indians. Ten thousand dollars was distributed among neophytes at this Mission. On August 9, 1834, Santa Cruz Mission was joined with San Juan Bautista. *Comisionado* Ignacio del Valle directed both establishments. As tribute to the Governor he re-christened the Mission, El Pueblo de Figueroa. Father Antonio del Real, a Zacatecan friar in charge of Santa Cruz, received $1,000 a year. He demanded ten rooms for himself as well as a stable. The Governor gave him only what was necessary.

Mission Santa Cruz was the least prosperous of all California establishments, but at the time of secularization in 1834 it was valued at $79,000. The total number of baptisms was 2,466.

When Santa Cruz ceased being a Mission there were twenty buildings within the Mission Plaza and fifty outside. Workshops supplied necessary articles of mechanism. Still thriving were 1,255 vines and 1,024 fruit trees. Secularization, however, was more complete in 1835 than at any other Mission. Church ornaments, bells, images, and cannon were valued at $23,505. Livestock and implements were appraised at $17,581.

Four years later Inspector William E. P. Hartnell reported seventy Indians at Santa Cruz as clamoring for a final distribution of property. They were given 127 horses, 1,026 sheep, and 36 cattle. The Mission became a smuggling center.

In 1840 an earthquake shook down the church tower, and a tidal wave swept inland 600 feet, carrying away a large quantity of Mission tile.

During this period Governor Alvarado managed the ex-Mission Pueblo. He took possession of the distillery and the houses adjoining the church. Father Antonio del Real was withdrawn by Bishop García Diego to Monterey. There was no missionary at Santa Cruz, nor was there an Indian to ring the bells.

Two years later orchards, land, and buildings of the ex-Mission were valued at less than $1,000. Population of the Mission and Villa was 470. In 1846 Governor Pio Pico placed the Mission on the market, but it was never sold or rented. Between 1844 and 1853 the buildings were only occasionally inhabited.

After Governor Figueroa died at Monterey, his name was detached from the Pueblo. Soon Branciforte was called Santa Cruz. In 1850 Branciforte County became Santa Cruz County. Three years later Archbishop Alemany placed Father Sebastiano Filoteo at the Mission; he was succeeded by Father Benito Capdevilla.

In the 'fifties the Santa Cruz Mission garden extended to what is now the principal business street, where as late as the Civil War grew a row of willow trees. Today Willow Street is known as Pacific Avenue. Like all gardens of the period, the Mission garden was festive with Castilian roses and variegated thistles. Corn was cultivated for *tamales,* beans with chili peppers for seasoning, also pumpkins, melons, and herbs that made famous the cuisine of Spanish-California. Indians ground corn in small stone mills; but after the first flour mill was erected at Santa Cruz, wheat bread became popular. Even at the house of Santa Cruz's great *señora,* Doña Martina Castro, who herself acquired 32,702 acres of land, clay dishes were used. Gourds served as drinking cups for *yerba buena* tea, chocolate, and milk. Cooking was done on adobe ranges with several partitions. Crude four-post beds, strapped together with pieces of hide, had mattresses of sheeps' wool. In the *fandango* room, lighted with tallow candles, weddings, christenings, and feasts took place. At weddings some *señoritas* wore white, but more had bright-colored gowns. Men wore embroidered trousers slashed to the knee and decorated with two rows of buttons.

After the American occupation, Doña Martina's title to her property was attacked, and alone with an Indian servant she rode to the City of Mexico to quiet the title. Within a year she returned, and in 1855 the United States Land Commission confirmed her grant.

In 1850 Ernest de Massey, the French traveler, wrote of the five or six hundred residents in the Mission town: Americans, Mexicans, Californians, Jews, foreigners, and Indians. The church tower had fallen. The bells fastened to rude beams were in the debris. Neophytes had returned to a nomadic life; herds had gone to the wilds. Lands lay idle. Only occasionally were services held. The port, however, was admirable, and the forests were magnificent.

On the morning of January 9, 1857, when ice was half an inch thick, earthquake shook Santa Cruz, crumbling the front walls of the church, which already had lost the tower in 1840. On January 20, another earthquake occurred, leaving Mission buildings weakened. One morning early in February the southwest corner of the church fell with a crash. Later the ruins were used as a storehouse, but even during the days of abandonment a Christmas crib was installed and services were held.

Father Benito Capdevilla razed the adobe church to erect the new edifice on the site near the west end of the Holy Cross Rectory of today. On July 5, 1857, Bishop Thaddeus Amat laid the cornerstone; the new structure was dedicated by him on July 4, 1858.

President Buchanan, on September 2, 1859, restored the Mission and 16.94 acres of land to the Catholic Church.

Of original buildings at Santa Cruz few remains exist. Behind the present church is part of an old patio wall built of great blocks of chalky rock. A little below, there is a portion of the foundation, probably the blacksmith shop. Two trees, survivors of the Mission orchard, thrive north of the hill near the church. Twisted with age, they still bear apples and pears.

In School Street are two well-preserved adobe dwellings formerly belonging to the Mission. The larger one, property of the Neary family, once housed the Mission guard. The smaller building, separated from the larger by a wall five feet thick, belongs to the Rodríguez family.

In the rear of the adobe dwellings is a poetic garden where gnarled fig trees, olives, grapes, and Castilian roses recall the days when Santa Cruz was inhabited by sons and daughters of Spain who believed that the ghost of murdered Father Quintana still walked over the hills.

Santa Cruz is said to have possessed ten bells; they were appraised in 1835 at $3,400, the highest valuation of any Mission church bells. The entire ten have disappeared. For years a large broken bell lay under a rose thicket in the Mission garden. In 1888 two bells, some silver candlesticks, and altar bells were sent to San Francisco and recast into a *campana* by Weed and Kingwell. Another bell was probably taken to St. Francis Church, San Francisco, only to be destroyed in the fire following the earthquake of 1906. One may have found its way to the Church of the Holy Cross, San Francisco. What became of the remaining bells is a matter of conjecture.

In 1931 the late Gladys Sullivan Doyle, whose country home was not far from Mission Santa Cruz, learned that books, vestments, and sacred vessels of the Mission were orphaned and being dispersed. Mission lore was a part of Mrs. Doyle's environment. Her uncle, the late United States Senator James D. Phelan, had aided in the publication of Palóu's biography of Father Junípero Serra, California's first book. About 250 feet from the new church, erected in 1891 in the upper Plaza on Mission Hill, Mrs. Doyle built a replica of the Mission Church almost in its original proportions. The structure bore the plaque: MISSION SANTA CRUZ, FOUNDED SEPTEMBER 25, 1791. DESTROYED JANUARY 9, 1857, RESTORED NOVEMBER 1931.

Lovers of Old California rejoiced in seeing the Mission reappear with its arched doorway, buttresses at the corners, and the tower at the south corner with a circular belfry. Left of the entrance is an arched corridor before the reliquary, which contains vestments worn on solemn occasions. Here are books of baptism, marriage, and death with title pages drawn up by Fathers López and Salazar. Funerals and marriages take place in the reliquary, baptisms in the baptistry.

At the right of the entrance stands the baptismal font from the first Mission. Over the altar in the chapel are three original statues: Saint Joseph, Our Lady of Sorrows, and Saint Michael holding the scales of Justice. Several Spanish paintings, relics of the old Mission, adorn the walls. In the sanctuary is a vivid crucifix. Father John Galvin in 1936 placed in the chapel a statue of Saint Peter acquired from the Rodríguez family, who obtained it from the Mission.

In the circular-shaped dome with its open belfry is an old iron bell which long hung in the Catholic Chapel at Aptos. The bell is not the original one of silver given to the chapel by Don Rafael Castro, but it was brought from San Francisco after early-day bandits made off with the original.

Mrs. Doyle, who built the replica of Mission Santa Cruz, as a child injured her knee, and this incident was the indirect cause of her building activity. Physician after physician vainly tried to cure her. The Francis J. Sullivans, her parents, took her from shrine to shrine in Europe seeking her recovery. Gladys scoffed at miracles, but to please the family she joined the throng at Lourdes. On their return to Paris the girl was astonished to find herself walking without a crutch. Her point of view and her life altered. She became a nurse, and gave not only large means but personal service to others less fortunately placed than herself.

Great Spanish *señoras* aided in building Alta California Missions by contributions to the Pious Fund, but Gladys Sullivan Doyle was the only woman to recreate a California Mission. After the building at Santa Cruz was dedicated, Mrs. Doyle had only one more year of life. By special permission of the city of Santa Cruz she was buried in the baptistry of the chapel erected by her. On the wall of her resting place is inscribed: IN MEMORIAM GLADYS SULLIVAN DOYLE, NATIVE OF SAN FRANCISCO, BORN SEPTEMBER 13, 1889, DIED JULY 2, 1933, DONOR REPLICA MISSION SANTA CRUZ. I HAVE LOVED, O LORD, THE BEAUTY OF THY HOUSE AND THE PLACE WHERE THY GLORY DWELLETH. Ps. 25-8. R·I·P.

XIII

Soledad (Our Lady of Solitude)

FROM the beginning, Soledad, thirteenth California Mission, was unhappy. When the Portolá expedition in 1769 pitched tents on this brown plain of moaning winds and dust storms, they called it *El Campo Real del Chocolate*, Chocolate Camp. They asked an Indian his name. "Soledad," or a native word of similar sound, was his reply. Father Juan Crespi christened the barren region Soledad.

Probably the Mission name, however, came from one of the titles in Spain under which the Virgin Mary was venerated: *María Santísima Nuestra Señora Dolorosísima de la Soledad*. The special devotion to the Virgin's solitude originated with Queen Juana lamenting the death of her husband, Philip I, King of Spain, in the sixteenth century.

Viceroy Revilla Gigedo, on October 31, 1789, suggested to Father Matias Antonio de Noriega, Acting Superior of the Franciscan Missionary Seminary at the City of Mexico, that a Mission be founded between San Antonio and San Carlos. Missionaries arrived at Monterey on August 2, 1790, from Mexico, bringing implements and utensils but no church goods. President Fermin Lasuén requested the Missions to donate vestments and altar vessels for the new establishment.

Purísima gave an altar bread iron and a surplice. San Luis Obispo sent vestments, crystal oil stocks, and a ritual. San Buenaventura offered two bells, vestments, and a missal. From San Gabriel came an altar bread box, bell, altar stone, and two cinctures. San Juan Capistrano contributed an altar bread iron and a manual so aged that Lasuén would not forward it. San Diego gave chalice, vestments, and two sets of cruets.

Before the Mission was founded, at Lasuén's request, the *Coman-*

dante at Monterey on September 29, 1791, sent eleven Indians to erect a shelter for missionaries in Soledad Valley and also a building to protect supplies. Ten days later President Lasuén followed and selected the site; the Indians called it Chuttusgelis. The day was October 9, 1791.

In the presence of Lieutenant José Argüello, the guard, and natives, Father Lasuén sprinkled water on the ground and raised the Cross in honor of *Nuestra Señora de la Soledad*. Surrounded by unclothed Indian men, and women wearing aprons of plaited *tule*, it was for Father Lasuén a day of glory as, looking across the valley toward the Santa Lucia Mountains, he sang Mass. He was aided by Fathers García Diego and Buenaventura Sitjar. Lasuén began the baptismal register with *"Viva Jesus!"*

Father García Diego was in charge of the new Mission. Before the church was erected in a temporary chapel on November 23, 1791, he baptized Clemente, an Indian boy ten months old, son of Iyé and Noipacsi of the Ranchería del Pino. One month later, December 25, the second baptism was administered in the church. In the following year there were 115 neophytes. Few Missions had such success at the beginning.

Unfortunately Father Diego had as associate Father Mariano Rubí, one of the few Franciscan black sheep. A dangerous companion for him came—Father Bartolomé Gilí. Both had been in disgrace in Mexico. They were sent to the California wilds for discipline. Father Rubí had been a professor of Music. In Soledad there were only Indian flutes of elderwood. Indian songs were depressing. Fathers Rubí and Gilí behaved like unruly schoolboys. They robbed storerooms, broke open chocolate jars, stole small kettles and used them for drums. Through dormitories they rolled balls used for games on recreation days. Always restless, they quarreled with Father Diego and each other. "Sons of darkness," they were called by the Guardian of the College of San Fernando. Father Zephyrin Engelhardt, the Franciscan historian, one hundred and fifty years later wrote them down as "hoodlums." Unable to endure his rowdy companions, Father Diego departed for Mission San Antonio.

The unruly missionaries made many converts, but neglected the livestock. They raised no beans. They planted eleven *fanégas* of wheat, two of barley, and two of corn, but they harvested little. The royal surgeon, Pablo Solér, certified that Father Mariano Rubí was suffering from a disease which required a long time to be cured. President Lasuén rejoiced when Father Rubí was sent back to Mexico and Father Gilí disappeared to the Philippines.

Father García Diego returned to Soledad. Converts did not increase, but during his four years at the Mission crops were large.

The burial register shows that the first death of an Indian occurred August 27, 1792. An interesting Indian baptism was made in 1793 by Father Diego, Francisco Miguel, whose parents were natives of Nootka. In 1789 the youth's father had been killed by the American Gret (Gray), Captain of the sloop *Washington*, "belonging to the Congress of Boston."

While Father Diego was at Soledad, he completed in 1794 one-half of the wing of the quadrangle, all of adobe. In 1797 there was an adobe church with a straw roof. In 1800 the baptismal register recorded 704 neophytes.

For nearly four years there was no Christian marriage set down. On May 3, 1795, Father Diego blessed the union of Bernardino Flores and Luisa Isquis. By December 13, 1800, there had been 164 marriages, and 224 deaths were recorded.

One of the builders of Soledad was Indian Gabriel, who had been taught by Father Serra to cut and lay stone at Carmel. He survived till 1890, and was said to be the oldest man in the world—a hundred and fifty years old. His hair was still black, and five teeth remained. During Gabriel's youth in 1802 an epidemic brought five or six deaths daily to Soledad. At the same time several Indians were murdered. Neophytes began to abandon the Mission, but 512 remained to be supported. Fathers Payeras and Jaime were busy burying the dead. Father Payeras departed. In spite of epidemics and tribulations, in 1805 Soledad had its largest population, 688. In the pasture were 3,000 sheep, 1,000 cattle, and 64 horses.

In the depressing time of the epidemic arrived colorful Father Florencio Ibañez, former choirmaster at the College of San Fernando. He never tired of teaching music and reading to the Indians. A musical play written by him was produced at Christmas for many years. He also taught soldiers to read and write. Less friendly to officers, he gave them no better food than the soldiers.

Tall, broad-shouldered Father Ibañez did not mind hot summers with dusty afternoon winds at Soledad, nor chill winters in unheated adobe rooms. He lengthened the church thirty-four feet during 1805, raised the roof nine feet and covered it with tile. Vestments and a silver chalice were obtained. In 1808 a new church was begun to take the place of the old.

Venereal disease brought by soldiers diminished the population, and in 1810 this Mission had the fewest inhabitants in California except San Carlos with 511. The Indians nursed one another tenderly at some springs in the foothills ten miles distant—Paraiso they are called today. Here neophytes baked in the sun and drank soda and sulphur water. Indian mills still visible near these springs are so large that perhaps they were used by an entire tribe.

Father Florencio welcomed his friend, Governor José Joaquin Arrillaga, with vocal and instrumental music. A quatrain is recorded:

> De Sola el nuevo govierno
> Echando a la bigornia
> Convertira en un infierno
> A toda la California.

"Papa Arrillaga," as the Governor was affectionately called, came a second time to Soledad, bent, stricken, to receive the last rites from Father Florencio. Nine days later, on July 24, 1814, the Governor, sixty-four years of age, was shrouded in a Franciscan habit and interred under the floor in the center of the church. Although he was a man of great humanity who remembered even the Indians in his will, after his death large quantities of his silk stockings and handkerchiefs were found in his trunk.

Even during its days of decline Soledad never failed the government's demands for supplies. In 1815, 5,000 pounds of flour and blankets, besides numerous weapons, were sent to Governor Argüello for soldiers and their families at Monterey and San Francisco.

Damp, chill buildings disabled Father Florencio. Mud baths and the sulphur, iron and soda water obtained at springs 1,400 feet above the valley, somewhat alleviated his rheumatic suffering. He could no longer mount a horse, but until the last he said Mass. After serving California's most cheerless Mission for fifteen years, the life of the poet-missionary closed November 26, 1818.

Father Vicente Sarría left Montereyans shivering in fear of Bouchard the buccaneer, at Rancho del Rey on Salinas River, and hastened to Soledad. In the death register he recorded that Father Florencio, although in broken health, at seventy-eight observed all the fasts of Saint Francis and would not use any clothing other than prescribed, except a single stocking which he changed from one foot to the other.

Father Jaime, who succeeded Father Florencio, was resourceful. In 1819 he acquired for the church a red velvet chasuble and gold galloon braid, and also a canopy of embroidered satin.

While visiting Soledad in 1821, President Mariano Payeras in a circular warned friars against luxury: no horseback riding, no vehicle other than an ox cart, and then only while ill. He said, however, that the aged should take care of themselves.

On May 5, 1822, missionaries and Indians were compelled to swear allegiance to the new Republic of Mexico. About this time the church walls were fortified. An aqueduct for irrigating a large acreage was built. Soledad raised 6,075 bushels of grain. Herds numbered 16,351.

Material prosperity was not for Soledad. Floods destroyed the sacristy, and it had to be rebuilt. Father Francisco Uría refused to swear allegiance to the new constitution. Father Vicente de Sarría took his place.

The new missionary was the author of several books. He had been President of the Missions. Of definite character, he was fitted for the highest office inside or outside of the cloister. In 1815 he protested to Governor Solá against the requisition of produce for soldiers. Governor Argüello was warned by him against purchasing a vessel with Mission funds. Sarría combated the plundering of Mission Santa Cruz in 1818. He denounced young intellectual Voltaireans, like Hartnell, Alvarado, and Vallejo. He called upon Governor Argüello to suppress immoral, irreligious books.

President Sarría compromised not even with missionaries. He sold their silver watches in Guadalajara for the benefit of the church treasury. He opposed their wearing shoes and hose instead of sandals. He protested against their traveling in *carretas*—brothers of Saint Francis. Sarría never spared himself in going over the roughest trail to visit the sick and needy. Soledad was a haven for this scholarly Franciscan. Here he could fast and mortify the flesh. But Alfred Robinson wrote in 1830 of the old *padre's* open-handed hospitality at Soledad.

A royalist, Father Sarría in 1825 was ordered suspended by Governor Echeandia. His departure would have left the Missions without a government, and he was permitted to remain at Soledad. He saw the Indians at this Mission hold an election to choose a delegate to the Mexican Congress. The convention was called by chief *Alcalde* Gerónimo on November 19, 1826, in the church. The Indians could not sign their names, but they affixed crosses and sent Juan de Dios as delegate to Monterey. In 1832 Father Sarría saw the church itself collapse when the Salinas River flooded the valley.

His last activity was erecting a new church, a barn-like structure with a sacristy to the right, joined by a large row of adobe monastery buildings. Although only a temporary church, it was roofed with tile and the walls were decorated. No bell-cote was visible, nor was there a beam for bells, although at one time the Mission had two. The Father obtained altar linen, two rugs, and vestments.

When secularization came, November 4, 1834, joining Soledad with San Antonio, the Mission was declared a curacy of the second class. The salary was $1,000 annually, $500 to be paid for the maintenance of divine worship. Missionaries and the administrator were to be supported by ex-neophytes.

The Indians fled to the wilds. Seven years Father Sarría cooked for and preached to the few Indians at the Mission. Food was difficult to obtain from the scant harvests. While celebrating dedication of the Basilica of Assisi, on May 24, 1835, suddenly Father

Sarría sank to the floor and died without receiving the last sacraments, at sixty-eight.

Indians carried the priest's emaciated body to Mission San Antonio, thirty-five miles distant, lighting the trail with pine torches. Father Sarría was interred on the epistle side of the altar at San Antonio.

Soledad was without a priest. Major-domo Nicolas Alviso took charge. The ranch boundaries met those of San Carlos on the west and extended from La Laguna de los Palos in the south, north to Chualar. The Ranchos San Lorenzo, San Vicente, and San Fernando, together with cattle and sheep, were valued at $31,000. Library, sacred vessels, implements, and produce brought the total to $47,000. The church was appraised at $85.

In 1837 only 172 neophytes remained. Cattle ran wild two years later, and the Mission earned only $89. Soon Soledad was in debt. Governor Alvarado ordered Vicente Cantua to sell tiles to buy food for the Indians. Some of Soledad's tiles roofed two buildings on the Alisal Ranch, and others top a wall surrounding the Pedro Zabala house at Salinas.

In 1840 Governor Alvarado wrote Feliciano Soberanes, who was in charge of the Mission, to let Indians shift for themselves. One year later, when de Mofras, the French traveler, visited Soledad, Indians and livestock had vanished. Vineyards were abandoned. Only twenty-one fruit trees were left, and those unpruned.

Governor Pio Pico in his proclamation of 1845 ordered neophytes to re-occupy the Mission. Should they fail to do so, he declared it would be without an owner. The Indians gave no heed. On June 4, 1846, the Governor sold the property to Feliciano Soberanes for $800. Governor Alvarado seized a few cattle left by the despoilers, and took iron and tile from the building for his own house. Soledad was at the mercy of sun and storms.

After American occupation of California, the United States Land Commission, on December 18, 1855, declared that Governor Pico had no right to sell Soledad. In November of 1859, President Buchanan restored the Mission and forty-two acres of land to the Catholic Church.

The last Spanish Franciscan at Soledad was Father José Maria del Real, stationed here in 1839. Father José Maria Gutiérrez, a Zacatecan, served a few months in 1840. Occasionally Father Jesus Maria de Mercado of San Antonio came to celebrate Mass. Devout Indians walked every Sunday to San Antonio. In 1854 Father José Miguel Gómez, first priest ordained in California, was at Soledad for a brief time. Bishop Thaddeus Amat made the last entry in the Mission records at San Antonio on May 30, 1861.

In the 'fifties, Henri Cambuston, a Frenchman from Mexico who married Gabriela Soberanes, had a school and store in the Mission. Alberto Tresconi in the 'sixties used the building as a storehouse for pelts.

Soledad's roof fell in 1874. Melted by rain and sun, the adobe ruins of the church lie in the hayfield owned by Dr. Elmer W. Bingaman. The Soberanes family made some restoration of the second church, which is in the southwest corner of the ruins. Its foundations are of rough rock and flint pebbles mixed with adobe. Little plaster remains on the walls.

Since 1888 part of the Soledad Ranch has been owned by S. J. Kitzmiller. When he came, a niche over the doorway at the entrance enclosed a statue; but this has vanished. In the Kitzmiller pear orchard remain three large tanning vats from Mission days.

In the early 'nineties the Salvation Army colony Roma bought a portion of the land near the ruins and sold it in small tracts to twenty-five Chicago families. The colony holdings were disposed of advantageously. One colonist, a woman, remains.

At the Soledad Parish Church are mementos of the old Mission. On the wall to the right hangs a realistic crucifix. One of the most carefully guarded relics is the monstrance of silver and gold that served the original Mission. In the sacristy are vestments. Others are at San Juan Bautista and Carmel.

Bishop John G. McGinley of the Diocese Monterey-Fresno has charge of the Soledad books of baptisms, patents, the inventory, as well as the census. Marriage and death records have disappeared. At the González Parish Church are thirty Spanish books formerly belonging to the Mission.

More than forty years ago Father Ramón Méstres took the only bell belonging to Soledad known to exist, to Mission Carmel. It was a crude copper bell about a foot high, probably made in California: the *campana de las almas* or Soul Bell. Father Méstres also found the original Stations of the Cross and hung them on the walls at Carmel. Two were stolen, presumably by collectors.

Of all Franciscan planting, there survives only one ancient walnut tree. Soledad, sometimes called the Cowboy's Mission, has been harassed by treasure-seekers excavating for gold supposedly left by the Fathers. They have dug into the walls, blasted the millstone in two, and scattered the bones of the dead.

For years Mass was seldom said at this Mission in which from 1791 to 1841 there were baptized 2,203 neophytes. Winds howled among the ruins. Rains beat down. Fierce sun helped dissolve the buildings where Sarría starved. No one today knows where within these crumbling walls are buried California's Governor Arrillaga and the poet-friar, Father Florencio Ibañez.

In recent years there came to the Soledad Parish Church Father William Stuhlman with a houseful of dogs and canaries. Like Father Sarría, he cooks for himself, his dogs, and the birds. The sunshine of his nature lighted up the Mission ruins. He began planning to reconstruct the chapel. He asked lovers of Old California to assemble on September 16, 1934, in the abandoned Mission ruins. By hundreds they came from distant places. Father Stuhlman raised the American flag, erected an altar, decorated it with flowers and palms, and celebrated Mass. When he returned to his pleasant stucco house at the village of Soledad, it seemed to him, as he approached the door and turned to look at the figure in the niche at the entrance, that he saw a smile in the eyes of Our Lady of Sorrows.

XIV

San José

How daring an undertaking in 1797 was the foundation of Mission San José! The eastern shores of San Francisco Bay were still unexplored. To be sure, Portolá had seen this region in 1769. Three years later Lieutenant Pedro Fages, Father Juan Crespi, and a company had toiled over the hills. During the following twenty years Spaniards seldom visited this pagan land. Now, the first establishment was to be made since unhappy Soledad in 1791.

In 1794 the government ordered the wild district explored. Four natives were sent across the bay from Mission Dolores on two *tule* rafts. One raft was swept out to sea, and two pilots were drowned.

The next year Governor Diego Borica sent Alferez Hermenegildo Sal and Father Antonio Dantí from Monterey to explore the country. Two years later the Santa Clara friars heard that berry and nut crops were scant on the eastern bay shore. The missionaries reasoned that hungry natives might be easily converted. They decided to venture up the shore from Santa Clara. Father Dantí set up a Cross at a place called by him San Francisco Solano.

The San Francisco *Comandante* warned the *padres* that the territory was uncharted, and the Indians were hostile. One bold soldier, Sergeant Pedro Amadór, thirsting for distinction, ventured into the southern part of this heathen land. Unharmed, he came back and reported that he had found a beautiful grove watered by a stream, an *Alameda*. Since that time the word "Alameda" has been applied to the creek and surrounding country.

Father Fermin Lasuén, President of the Missions, although seventy-seven, was eager to make the new foundation. The region he knew well; he had been stationed at Santa Clara for three years. With

Corporal Alejo Miranda, pilot of Vancouver's vessel, and five men, President Lasuén set out to found the, fourteenth Mission in the foothills, fifteen miles east and north of the Pueblo San José de Guadalupe, at the Alameda. *Oroysom* was the Indian name for the site among the Sacalanes that Father Lasuén chose.

There is a tale that the soldiers rolled a stone from Mission Peak to the south; where it stopped, there the Mission was founded. It was named for Joseph, spouse of Mary, and had the imposing appellation of the *Misión del Gloriosísimo Patriarca Señor San José de Guadalupe.*

As temporary church Father Lasuén erected a bowery. On Trinity Sunday, June 11, 1797, the usual foundation ceremonies were held. Father Lasuén blessed the ground, raised the Cross, chanted the Litany of Saints, and preached. The Indians trembled when Corporal Miranda and Sergeant Amadór proudly exploded a pound of gunpowder, and the fourteenth Mission came into being.

Father Lasuén and the soldiers immediately returned to Santa Clara. Only the silent Cross and the vacant bowery remained; but life was never again to be the same at *Oroysom*. Natives looking out on the placid, silvery bay realized that white men would return to the beautiful hills and fertile meadows. They feared strange events.

Five days later Sergeant Amadór and his soldiers were back at *Oroysom* cutting timber. By June 28, water had been brought in an irrigation ditch from springs to the Plaza. The soldiers returned to Mission Dolores. Corporal Miranda returned with five men to complete the work. Missionaries, Fathers Isidóro Barcenilla and Agustín Merino, arrived and took charge of the budding Mission.

The sister Missions San Francisco, Santa Clara and Santa Cruz sent San José de Guadalupe gifts of 12 mules, 12 yoke of oxen, 39 horses, 60 pigs, and 242 sheep.

Soon large, gaudily-dressed natives threatened attack. Governor Borica sent Sergeant Amadór with twenty soldiers to give battle. He brought back many Sacalanes and Cuchillones as prisoners. Ill and irascible, Father Barcenilla wished to abandon the Mission. Corporal Miranda calmed the friar. Soldiers, however, objected to riding after cattle; they were not *vaqueros*. Soldiers and friars clashed.

For nearly two months after the foundation no baptism was made at Mission San José. Father Magin Catalá, known as the Holy Man of Santa Clara, baptized a child, Josefa. About this same time, September 2, 1797, Father Francisco Sanchez performed the first marriage ceremony: Lucas, a Santa Claran neophyte, married Indian Josefa. The first death recorded was on February 18, 1798, when Father Barcenilla buried José Antonio Miranda, son of Alexandro Miranda and María Santos Gutiérrez.

Soon the missionaries were in despair; there were no converts. Legend said the Fathers, trying to make the Indians understand the meaning of the birth in the manger, fashioned a crude cradle and placed therein a doll, behind a screen. When the screen was removed, there was not a wooden doll, but an infant of flesh and blood. A doll in the museum at Mission San José is said to be the original used in the humorous hoax. The close of the second year saw 162 baptisms and 29 marriages.

Hostile Sacalanes again threatened neophytes. Troops were rushed from San Francisco. At the end of 1800, Mission San José had 286 neophytes who worshiped in the wooden church with a grass roof.

Later death cut them down; there were 38 burials. Harvests, however, increased. In three years 3,900 bushels of grain had been raised, and there were 2,000 livestock. Through wild mustard Indians carried hides to the *embarcadero*, whence lighters took them to San Francisco.

So many Indian uprisings occurred that Father Merino was replaced by Father José Antonio Uría. Even Corporal Miranda wearied of the tumultuous Mission and was succeeded by Sergeant Luis Peralta, who rejoiced in peril. He acquired leagues of land in the vicinity, and died about 1850, California's only millionaire.

In spite of Indian attacks, converts came from the far Sacramento and San Joaquin River countries. But rumors of war lowered Father Pedro de la Cueva's gay spirit. In January, 1805, he was summoned to sick neophytes at a *ranchería* of the Luechas. Escorted by Majordomo Ignacio Higuera, two soldiers, and neophytes, he rode a few miles east. Soon the neophytes were struck down by arrows. Father de la Cueva and Higuera were wounded. The survivors dragged their bleeding bodies back to the Mission.

With armed force, Sergeant Peralta rode to the rebellious Luechas, killed eleven, and seized thirty women as hostages. Father de la Cueva was obliged to retire. Before he left in November, 1806, he entertained the German naturalist, Dr. Georg H. von Langsdorff, who arrived in San Francisco with Rezánov on the *Juno*. At Mission Dolores in the spring the Father had entranced the naturalist with descriptions of wild flowers on the southeastern bay shore. While Rezánov was wooing Doña Concepción Argüello, Langsdorff came skimming over the bay in his light *bidarka*. The missionary bade the neophytes prepare a dance for the traveler and his friends.

Langsdorff was enchanted with the Indian girls in scarlet petticoats and white bodices. In his book, *Voyages and Travels*, he pictured finely formed native men and women in *fiesta* costume at Mission San José. He praised the substantial buildings made from brick earth, the kitchen garden watered by a small rivulet, young fruit trees, grape-laden vines which produced fifty barrels of wine a year, sweet and resembling Malaga. The granaries were bursting; even pigeons had daily a *cental* of wheat.

Another church was erected, of brick, long and unadorned, save for admirable mural decorations. Its only external ornaments were pilasters at the doorway and a small niche for an image over the entrance. On April 23, 1809, President Estévan Tápis blessed the new structure and preached. Father Arroyo de la Cuesta, the Indian linguist, celebrated Mass.

Father Narciso Durán carried on the church building. With him was associated Father Buenaventura Fortuni. More converts were made here and a smaller percentage buried than at any Mission save San Luis Rey. Father Narciso was accused of baptizing Indians by force. When punished they protested, "Father, it hurts!"

"Of course," agreed the missionary, "but the pains of hell hurt worse." In 1813 some Indians ran away, but after a fight Mission guards brought them back.

Several acres were enclosed by a high adobe wall; the orchard of fruit and olive trees and the garden were irrigated by pipes from large reservoirs. In front of the Mission was a picturesque fountain with conveniences for washing and bathing. Sheep raising and agriculture throve.

Father Durán was versatile; he passionately converted souls; aided by a neophyte he performed a Caesarean operation; he made the Mission famous for its Indian orchestra. A large parchment music book made by him still exists, written in colors, bound with heavy boards and leather, dated 1813, the preface signed "Fr. N." On feast days throngs came from Mission Santa Clara, Pueblo San José, and by boat from Mission Dolores, to be entertained by thirty Indian musicians performing on violins, flutes, trumpets, and drums. Indians walked all night to take part in the celebration. In 1817 His Excellency Governor Solá was a visitor.

Don Alfred Robinson described a journey he made with Father Viader of Santa Clara to Mission San José in a low-wheeled carriage upholstered in brown cotton and lambs' wool. An Indian boy seated on a mule drove with a green hide rope, assisted by a *vaquero* leading the mule with *reata*. Neophytes with blue and white pennants floating from their hats followed. As Father Viader neared the Mission, bells began to ring and did not cease till the missionaries embraced. Father Viader was later forbidden by President Sarría to use the conveyance.

In the Mission Plaza was the Indian orchestra. Other Indians near by, decorated with feathers and looking like red and black demons, fixed to one spot, beat time to the singing of half a dozen persons seated on the ground. Another set of dancers differently painted and adorned, moving in a quite dissimilar manner, took their places. Dancing Indians were everywhere. Chocolate and cigars were served, but no liquor. A bear and bull fight followed. At sunset bells rang, guns were fired, rockets shot skyward; gaiety continued till midnight.

After Father Buenaventura left in the autumn of 1825, Father Durán served alone. Mission San José became the second establishment in California with its largest population, 1,806. Father Durán refused to take the oath of loyalty to the Mexican Republic, but in nine years he furnished supplies valued at $15,125 to the San Francisco Presidio, from the Mission ranches.

In spite of Father Durán's achievements, Indian rebellions were frequent at Mission San José. Neophytes fled. Sergeant Francisco Soto of San Francisco was sent with 100 Indians and 12 soldiers up the San Joaquin River to capture the fugitives. The Indians escaped by swimming. One native warrior was killed. The Consumnes made an outbreak. An expedition was dispatched against the hostile tribes, destroying a *ranchería* and capturing many natives.

Most formidable of all rebellions was that led by *Alcalde* Estanislao, Father Durán's pride. From him the Father re-learned the vanity of all pride. In 1828 Estanislao fled with Indian Cipriano, gathered a force, and raided ranches. Neophytes of both Missions San José and Santa Clara joined Estanislao, fortifying themselves in a camp near the San Joaquin River. San Francisco troops were called for by Father Durán.

Sergeant Soto and a force of twenty men found Estanislao and his followers in a jungle of brambles and willows. The sergeant exploded fireworks obtained by the English navigator, Captain Beechey, to frighten the Indians. Estanislao challenged the Spaniards to meet him with bows and arrows. Soto received a death-wound. When the Indians heard that their enemy was no more, they danced and feasted at their *ranchería*.

Alferez José Sanchez came from San Francisco with a larger force and swivel guns. The Indians were fortified behind wooden palisades. It was muskets against arrows. Sanchez destroyed the first line, but dared not attack the second. Estanislao retreated to safety.

With soldiers and a fieldpiece Ensign Mariano Vallejo followed up the attack. Estanislao floated down the river grass bundles made to look like soldiers. Vallejo and his men followed the effigies down the stream shooting as they went. Native fortifications were destroyed and the forest where the Indians took refuge was burned. A battle was fought on the edge of the flames.

"We die before we surrender!" shouted the Indians.

And this they did. Prisoners were hung with ropes of wild grapevines to trees. Women and old men were shot. Back at Mission San José, Estanislao surrendered.

Father Durán concealed the Indian and procured pardon for him from Governor Echeandia. He also tried to have Ensign Vallejo prosecuted for killing Indians, but he failed. This battle helped make Vallejo commander-in-chief of the California forces. Estanislao's name has been perpetuated in Stanislaus County and River.

During the twenty-seven years spent by Father Durán at Mission San José, he seldom left save on feast days to visit Santa Clara. Once he went to San Francisco. In 1833, tortured by gout, discouraged by mortality among his neophytes, and by their revolts, he sought the mild climate of Santa Barbara.

Long after Father Durán was succeeded by Father José Maria Rúbio, the Mission prospered, although other establishments declined. Neophytes numbered 6,737 in 1834. With its population of 1,300, San José ranked fourth. There were 18,000 large stock, 15,000 sheep, 1,100 horses. The property was valued at $30,000 with 6,000 thriving grapevines and 600 fruit trees.

After the earthquake of 1838, when José de Jesus Vallejo was administrator, the population fell to 580. Chief Ambrosio of the Moquelumnes marched with a band to avenge Estanislao. Twenty-five Spaniards met them. One white man was killed. Seven others were wounded. Administrator Vallejo at Mission San José asked Father Rúbio to prepare Ambrosio for death. The Indian was shot.

Wild Tulares could not forget Ambrosio. They drove off livestock and horses from Santa Clara Valley to San Joaquin. *Comandante* Juan Prado Mesa set out from San Francisco with a force to discipline the Tulares. Three soldiers fell and three were wounded. An arrow struck Mesa's throat and caused his death.

When secularization was effected in 1836, Mission San José was valued at $155,000, aside from church property and ranches nine leagues by three. Three years later Inspector Hartnell found only 589 half-fed Indians. The women would not show themselves. Administrator Vallejo had carted away clothing. Indians said he kicked them and gave them a hundred lashes. In 1840 he was succeeded by José Maria Amadór.

Father Rúbio left in 1842; but before he departed, he interred in the church, in 1839, Father Rafael de Jesus Moreno, a Zacatecan Franciscan, former President of the Missions, who came from Santa Clara for his health. Father Miguel Muro succeeded Father Rúbio, to be followed in 1843 by Father José Lorenzo Quíjas.

During Father Muro's time there was considerable excitement because he learned from neophytes of the Sacramento Valley of the existence of gold in that region. Mission San José Indians had trouble with Captain Sutter of New Helvetia, later Sacramento. Neophytes on their way to visit the Ochumnes attacked Indians working for Sutter under Pulpule of the Zalesumnes Ranchería. They killed several men and stole women and children. Sutter and Pulpule shot ten San José Indians, delivering to the authorities all neophytes they caught.

Governor Pico, on May 5, 1846, sold Mission San José to his brother, Andrés Pico, and the former Governor Juan Bautista Alvarado for $12,000. The sale did not go into effect. At this time a portion of the Mission was occupied by the family of James Frazier Reed, survivor of the Donner party, some members of which had resorted to cannibalism while starving in 1846 on the Sierra trail. Reed harvested a large crop of pears from the Mission orchard.

Gold-rush days of 1848 and 1849 transformed the establishment into a busy trading post, "Mission Saint Joe." Sensational crops were raised on Mission ranches by John Beard, who one year sold $100,000 worth of potatoes to miners.

Originally Mission San José de Guadalupe had 20,000 acres of land. On March 30, 1858, the United States Courts restored 28.33 acres to the Catholic Church.

One year later came a French priest, Father Julianus Federy. Thinking the buttresses of the church too cumbersome, he had them removed. The old adobe church crumbled under the earthquake shock of October 21, 1868. Father Federy erected the frame church of Norman architecture still serving the parish. Only the tile floor concealed by a wood covering remains of the original church building.

At one time Mission San José probably had four bells. Now it has three. Under the roof on the north was a square opening which contained the 1,000-pound bell bought from Virmond in April, 1826, and lettered with the name of the Mission. An alcove in the southern side of the building later housed the bell which shakes the organ loft when it rings. The name *Señor San José* is on the side of the bell of 1815. Another bell, undated, bears the name *Saint Joseph*. San José de Guadalupe has a legend of a lost sweet-toned silver bell, said to have been stolen at the time of the earthquake of 1868.

Mission San José was a favorite of Archbishop Alemany, who often preached from the little tree pulpit. In 1882 he erected on Mission ground a three-story brick building, Saint Thomas Seminary, later transferred to Menlo Park, California. In 1891 the Dominican Sisters bought the old seminary for a Mother House and orphanage. In the convent garden Sister Justina, a talented sculptress, has erected a shrine to commemorate the Golden Jubilee of the foundation of her Order.

At the right of the present church is the sole survivor of the original structures at San José, a portion of the monastery, one of the most interesting buildings in Northern California. Once it was used as a wine cellar, afterwards as a school. The colonnade ceiling reveals the Mission method of construction, willows bound with rawhide fastened to rough-hewn log rafters. This monastery, a museum, houses historical paintings. At the convent are also several paintings that once belonged to the Mission. In the museum are two admirable statues: an *Ecce Homo* and a figure of San Buenaventura. There are vestments once worn by Serra, the original crucifix, the *Bambino*, the monstrance, processional Cross, ciborium, chalice, wooden candlesticks, silver altar plate, and a bell wheel with one bell missing. In the church is the hammered copper baptismal font surmounted by an iron Cross. Franciscan baptismal, marriage, and death records are in the hands of the Archbishop of San Francisco.

In the rear of the church is an *alameda* of aged but robust olive trees. More have survived here than at any California Mission. From these trees the Dominican Sisters each spring make olive oil. Until 1899 the original vineyard was cultivated by the Sisters. Once the convent caught fire, and pioneers relate how they put out flames with the Sisters' sacramental wine. The vines became diseased and died.

In 1932 a beautiful shrine to Our Lady of Lourdes was added to the church by Mrs. O. L. Starr to commemorate the twenty-fifth anniversary of the ordination of the pastor, Reverend Father John A. Leal, to the priesthood. During his long residence at Mission San José, Father Leal has tastefully developed the Mission garden. In one corner he has erected a shrine to Saint Anthony.

From this secluded garden one steps into the closed cemetery of 1811, where Franciscan Mission San José is recalled. Higueras lie here in great number. Once they owned leagues of land. Before the days of banks one of the Higueras sold a ranch at Pueblo San José and came riding home with bags of gold. On the trail he met "ghosts." When they made off with his gold, he knew they were bandits. Both ranch and fortune were lost. One of the Higuera *señoras* erected a tomb of mystery for her husband and herself. Don Luis Higuera was placed therein by his wife, but her own resting place is vacant. Why this happened, and where she is buried, is unknown. Another Higuera, Josefa, widow of Señor Molina, married the first English settler of the district, Robert Livermore, who was buried in the cemetery in 1858.

A few feet from the Higuera tomb of mystery is the altar site of the old adobe church. Near by lies Father Rafael Jesus de Moreno, once President of the Missions. He died here in 1839 and was interred near the altar. Although his grave is marked only by a wooden cross, flowers are often brought to brighten his resting place.

On the Mission-Irvington Road, about one-quarter mile from the church, is the Indian Cemetery where the turbulent natives, who often shed blood battling for pagan California and terrorized the Fathers, are at peace. In 1915, Mrs. C. L. Stephens erected a monument to the Indians inscribed:

HERE SLEEP
FOUR THOUSAND OF THE
OLHONE TRIBE
WHO HELPED THE PADRES BUILD THIS
MISSION SAN JOSÉ DE GUADALUPE
SACRED TO THEIR MEMORY

XV

San Juan Bautista

SAN JUAN BAUTISTA—its name recalls lavender, heliotrope, boxwood, and the scarlet passion vine over the weather-worn colonnade in the enclosed garden in the rear of the church, as I first saw it. Thirty years ago Fremont Older and I, motoring to Del Monte, were wrecked at San Juan Bautista. While waiting for the car to be repaired, we met half-blind Father Ricardo Closa at the Mission.

The following year we organized a *fiesta* that began the restoration of San Juan Bautista, the fifteenth Mission.

As early as November 15, 1795, Governor Diego Borica ordered explorations to fix the site of San Juan Bautista. Ensign Hermenegildo Sal, with Father Antonio Dantí, led an expedition from Monterey to the banks of Rio San Benito. Here had camped Captain Pedro Fages' company on March 21, 1772. This was half a league from a trail later called El Camino Real. Trees for timber grew near by: willow, poplar, alder, also *tules* for roofing. One league away was limestone and harder stone for foundations. The future Mission site was marked with a Cross. The Indian name was *Popeloutchom*. Spaniards called it San Benito.

Viceroy Branciforte himself christened the Mission for John the Baptist, one of the most popular saints. Twenty-three *rancherías* surrounded the site. Pagans came to watch Father Lasuén bless the water, the place, and plant the great Cross on Saint John's Day, June 24, 1797. Father Magin Catalá of Santa Clara, and Father Joseph Manuel de Martiarena also assisted. The Indians were charmed by the chants and stirred by Father Lasuén's eloquence.

Fathers Pedro Adriano Martínez and Joseph de Martiarena were the first missionaries. They were well equipped with maize, beans, pots, pans, hides for beds, muskets, cartridges, *machetes*, shackles, padlocks, hoes, axes, flints. For the natives there were indispensable trifles—toys, sweets, ribbons, scarfs, medals, cheap musical instruments, holy pictures.

Barely three weeks passed before Father Martiarena, on July 11, 1797, baptized an Indian boy, Tirachis, from the Ranchería de Absayme—Juan Bautista. An Indian woman, sixty, Taajsim, from Ranchería de Motsum, on August 20, 1797, was the first female baptized; Josefa, she was called by Father Martínez. During the first two years 269 Indians were baptized.

Father Martiarena opened the burial register on September 23, 1797, to record the death of a child of one of the guards, Francisco Ballesteros. The second entry was that of an Indian child baptized in *articulo mortis* and buried at the Ranchería Ausaima. María Trinidad, a child, was the first Indian buried in the cemetery, April 23, 1798.

During the birth year of the Mission, Father Martínez united in marriage the first couple—Indians Mateo Ammex and Manuela Nocnoc.

Six months after the foundation, an adobe chapel 42 feet long and 17 wide was erected, with a dwelling of equal size for the missionaries. Indian women also had a comfortable house. Before the year ended a large kitchen, a guardhouse, and four dwellings for soldiers were built, all with *tule* roofs. The usual quadrangle was being created.

Indian trouble began. In 1799 the Spaniards needed saltpeter for gunpowder in the country of the Ansaimes. From their fastnesses twenty-five miles to the east, Indians hurled themselves upon the Mission. Neophytes fought bravely, but eight Indians belonging to the adjoining *ranchería* were killed.

Sergeant Macario Castro led the expedition into the mountains, killed a chief, and brought back four captives, with only one soldier wounded. A few months later the Osos attacked the Mission. Again Castro was sent to the mountains. Chief Tatillosti was killed, and Indians were brought prisoners to San Juan Bautista. The next year Ansaimes stormed the Mission, setting fire to a house and a wheat field. With difficulty they were kept from destroying the establishment. Sergeant Gabriel Moraga was summoned from Monterey. Triumphant, he returned with many prisoners, including chieftains of the Ansaimes and Carnadero Rancherías.

Indian peace came, but on October 31, 1800, the earth shook and opened. Salt water poured forth from subterranean caverns. Adobe walls were cracked. Terrified missionaries slept outdoors in *carretas.*

Soon six adobe houses were built, each with a kitchen and garden. An adobe granary 146 feet long made part of one side of the quadrangle. The guardhouse was completed. All buildings had a tile roof.

Fathers José Martiarena and Domingo de Iturrate obtained permission to erect a new church. President Lasuén and Father José Viader came from Santa Barbara on June 13, 1803, to assist at laying the cornerstone. Don José de la Guerra y Noriega, Ensign of the Cavalry at Monterey, was present, as were Captain José Font and Surgeon José Umueta. In the cornerstone cavity were placed several coins of different denominations and a paper sealed with wax containing a description of the event.

Thick walls 58 *varas* long rapidly rose. Vestments and altar plate were acquired. Neophyte girls made linen for the sacristy. Cloth was manufactured. A kitchen, a tannery, and a building for storing implements were erected. Agriculture progressed. Herds increased. With enthusiasm the quadrangle was completed in 1806.

Two side naves were added to the Mission Church, making this the widest in California, the only one with three naves. It was 160 feet long paved with *ladrillos,* large kiln-baked tiles. Brick arches supported the ceiling. Over the lintel were inscribed the words: *Hic domum est Dei et porta coeli.* (This is the home of God and the gateway to heaven.) On June 3, 1809, a life-sized statue of San Juan Bautista was placed on the main altar in the sacristy, which served as a temporary church. Today it is perfectly preserved, save for a missing finger.

President Estévan Tápis, on June 23, 1812, blessed the church in the presence of Fathers Felipe Arroyo de la Cuesta, Roman Ullibarri, and the missionaries of San Francisco, Santa Clara, and San José. *Alcalde* Manuel Gutiérrez of Los Angeles was the patron.

At one time San Juan Bautista's bells numbered nine. An inventory of 1836 speaks of six. In the 'fifties three bells hung on a wooden beam beside the church, and they could be heard as far as Tres Pinos. The only original bell weighs nearly half a ton, and is used Sundays and feast days. It is inscribed: AVE MARIA PURISIMA. S. FERNANDO RUELAS ME FECET 1809. (HAIL MARY MOST PURE. SAINT FERDINAND. RUELAS MADE ME. 1809.) Companion to this bell and recast from two San Juan Bautista bells, is one bearing the name W. T. Garrett & Sons, San Francisco, Cal. 1874.

Even during the building of the new church, Tulare Indians were not forgotten. Ensign Moraga set out with an expedition to select Mission sites. The missionaries felt repaid by the journey of forty-three days into the wilderness: 141 Indians were baptized by Father Pedro Muñóz.

Harvests were not plentiful at San Juan Bautista. Only 2,000 bushels of grain were garnered, but the Fathers had 20,000 livestock for the 1,901 neophytes.

Father de la Cuesta, who came in 1808 and remained twenty-five years, was San Juan Bautista's most scholarly missionary. From old people and children whose idiom was uncorrupted by Spanish, he learned Indian tongues. He called the children Plato, Cicero, Alexander, and Caesar. He finished his literary work on April 2, 1815. The Smithsonian Institution in 1862 published a volume of his studies edited by Dr. John Gilmary Shea containing 2,884 phrases of the Mutsun Indian language.

Father de la Cuesta said that San Juan Indians had many dialects, but all within a radius of one hundred and fifty miles understood each other. If they did not speak with the nose, tongue, mouth, and ears, Indians laughed. "To be" did not exist in their language. Everything was past or future. Instead of "Who is God?" they said, "Who God?" For "I am," like the French, they said, "I find myself." They had nine past tenses and four forms of future. Thirty-two inflections modified many times the meaning of each verb, and there were irregular verbs besides. "The weather rains," said Mutsuns, until they learned of God, then "God rains." When well dressed their expression was, "I am covered with beautiful feathers." "Noson" meant soul or breath of life. "Matshu" was love. In anger they said, "I will make pieces of you with my teeth." They counted only to ten. To use eighty they used the French form "four times twenty." For mama and papa they said, "ana and appa," like babies trying to express themselves. "Skin soft as a leopard," their phrase, indicated that probably Asia cradled their race.

According to Father de la Cuesta, San Juan Bautista Indians believed that a great deluge drove their ancestors into California, and they never went north again. They had songs for war, healing, games, hunting, dancing, and funerals. Many tunes and words were taken from other tribes and languages; some they did not understand. Most dancers painted themselves grotesquely, imitating bears and coyotes. They wore plumage on neck and shoulders and in their hair.

Indians said that when one died his spirit was in a sacred place made by a sorcerer for asking pardon of the devil. Chochon, a pole painted red, white, and black marked the place. Some said that the spirit went west. The Mutsuns had no idea of God, but they thought beings existed above; stars were their refuge.

Before frail Father Ullibarri died in 1814 the Indians attacked him. The Governor ordered them flogged. From 1815 to 1825 Father Estévan Tápis, President of the Missions, was at San Juan Bautista with Father de la Cuesta. Father Tápis wrote music. He rewarded his Indian pupils with fruit and candy. They learned to sing without musical instruments or accompaniment. Father Tápis' square musical notes of the score of the Gregorian chant are still seen at San Juan Bautista. On November 3, 1825, music died out of this Mission; Father Tápis received last rites from Father de la Cuesta. After serving California Missions for thirty-five years, he was placed in the sanctuary near the gospel side of the church.

After the revolution in Mexico in 1810, the Monterey Presidio demanded food, clothing, and weapons without compensation. Flour, wool, and tallow were traded with Monterey vessels for supplies, and vestments were obtained from ships from Mexico and Peru. A tabernacle for the main altar and new Stations of the Cross were acquired; also images of Saint Anthony de Padua and Saint Isídro for two side altars, a chandelier, a gold wood carving, a painting of Saint Michael, and another of Saint Francis.

The Mission's greatest harvest was in 1820: 7,420 bushels of grain.

Major-domo Joaquin Soto's salary was nine pesos, a young bull, seven *fanégas* of corn, four *almudes* of beans, eighteen tallow candles, and four pesos' worth of soap. An Anglo-American blacksmith, Pedro Bruno (Peter Brown), was employed later as major-domo at $8.00 a month. At this time livestock numbered 23,000.

Labor trouble followed material blessings. Painter Chavez, while decorating the main altar, demanded six *reales* daily.

"Seventy-five cents a day!" said the Father. "Impossible!"

Thomas W. Doak, Bostonian, a deserter from the *Albatross*, appeared, the first American settler in California. Doak, a carpenter, finished painting the altar, "with the aid of God and some *muchachos*." San Juan Bautista called him Felipe Santiago Doc. Here he won a wife, María Lugarda Castro, daughter of the great Don Mariano Castro.

Terror shook the Mission when the horse-eating Tulare Indians arrived, murdered neophytes, and drove away horses. Christian Indians brought the animals back to San Juan Bautista. When again the Tulares came, the Mission was saved by a barrel organ that had found its way from Monterey. Lively tunes like *Go to the Devil* and *Lady Campbell's Reel* did not harmonize with stately chants, and the instrument was placed in the organ loft. When the Tulare Indians appeared in the valley pear orchard booming, "War! War!" Father de la Cuesta brought forth the organ and played wildly. For the first time the pagans heard European music. Captivated, they came to San Juan Bautista, which they intended to destroy. The organ is still in the museum.

When Bouchard arrived at Monterey in 1818, fugitives begged refuge at San Juan Bautista. Suddenly thirty-two neophytes, natives of the barbarous Tulare country, fled, leaving only ten Tulareños at the Mission. Santa Cruz and Soledad also lost Tulare neophytes. The Fathers appealed to the Governor, and the Indians were quieted.

Each week fifty head of cattle were slaughtered for food for San Juan Bautista's 1,200 neophytes. The sale of cattle or sheep hides was the Mission's sole income. Monterey vessels paid only a dollar a hide, or that amount in goods. By bartering with sea captains, the Fathers obtained for the Mission a new carpet, vestments, two candlesticks, two glass chandeliers, several sets of paintings for the processional Cross, a statue of Saint Pascal Baylon, and paintings of all the apostles. A fulling mill was erected, and a lime kiln built for making tile and brick to pave the church.

Governor Solá's demands for blankets and cloth kept weavers busy. Father de la Cuesta himself dyed wool, although he was crippled and at times had to be carried to hear confessions and administer extreme unction. For the welfare of the Mission, he took the oath of allegiance to the Republic of Mexico.

Suddenly harvests failed. Indians died alarmingly. Father Buenaventura Fortuni departed. Father de la Cuesta superintended the *ranchos* with their 700 horses, 10,500 sheep, and 65,000 head of cattle. Governor Echeandia, in October, 1825, ordered the Missions to pay ten per cent of their income for the benefit of the "well deserving troops to conserve the peace of the territory." When the Mexican Congress banished all Spaniards residing in New Mexico and California from the country within a month and from the republic within three months, decrepit Father de la Cuesta retired to Mission San Miguel. From there he went to Santa Inés to die.

After the Mexican Government seized the Missions in 1834, San Juan Bautista became a second-class curacy with the Indians paying the missionaries' salary of $1,000. Father Antonio de Anzar, a Zacatecan Franciscan, took charge of the settlement after it was converted into a pueblo. He blessed the new cemetery on October 24, 1838.

Father Anzar had a parish house of sixteen rooms, but he did his own washing and had no horse to ride to hear confessions at a distance. He was paid in meat and grain; funds for wine and altar bread were wanting. Indians arrived unclothed at the Mission; there was not even a breechcloth to give them. And yet the Mission buildings, the church, the library, the vineyard of 12,000 vines, the orchard of 675 fruit trees, and three ranches—San Justo, Todos Santos, and San Felipe—were appraised at $138,722.

Castro, the Mission town was called, in honor of José Castro, son of the major-domo, who later became commander of California troops. A small settlement of Spaniards, Mexicans, Americans, and Indians lingered around the church. Orchards and garden were neglected, cattle disappeared, implements were stolen. The Indians fled to the Tulares.

In 1837 they returned to attack Rancho Llano de Tequesquite, owned by the richest man in the community, Don José Maria Sanchez. They burned his dwelling, wounded him, and killed two neophytes. After he was drowned in the San Benito River, his widow, famed for her brown eyes, long silvery gold hair, and her five husbands, became one of the legends of the community.

In 1839 Mission San Juan Bautista, the *cabecera* of the district, became the headquarters of young Juan Bautista Alvarado, Don José Castro, and other sons of the territory who plotted within the Mission walls revolution that eventually drove Governor Micheltorena back to Mexico.

Governor Pio Pico's decree was, "Let the Mission system end. Land should be owned by private individuals." In 1846 he sold the San Juan Bautista orchard to Olivier Deleisseques for $7,850, reserving the curate's house, the church, and its belongings.

Colonel John C. Frémont of the United States Army brought the war with Mexico to San Juan Bautista when he arrived in January, 1846, with a small expedition of surveyors, trappers, and Delaware Indians. On Gavilán Mountain, overlooking the Mission, they erected fortifications and raised the American flag. General Castro would not go within range of Frémont's rifles. The Americans retired to Sacramento on March 9; in this same month annually the flag-raising on Frémont Peak is still commemorated.

In the year of American occupation, Edwin Bryant found exhumed skeletons about the cemetery at San Juan Bautista. Gorgeous peacocks during the 'fifties strutted through the Mission corridors, while children of the town picked up iridescent feathers shed by the birds. Father José Antonio de Anzar lived here with the peacocks until November 6, 1854. He made his last entry, No. 5606, in the baptismal book; the Franciscans departed. The Anzar family acquired large land grants in the district. The Father's brother married Doña Antonia Castro, who is buried in the church, the famous *Rose of the Rancho* of Richard Walton Tully's play.

For years ownership of the Mission was in litigation, but November 19, 1859, President Buchanan signed the patent conveying the property to the Catholic Church, 55.13 acres.

Father J. Molinier, first resident secular priest, remained for two years, with Father Peter de Vos, S.J., assisting him for a few months in 1855. Father Francis Mora, later Bishop of Los Angeles, lived at San Juan Bautista from 1856 to 1860. It is said that the Bishop was asked by the Indian choir, survivors of Father Tápis' day, to lock them up on Saturday nights because they could not resist liquor. They wished to be prepared to sing hymns and responses in Latin. Regularly the Indians presented themselves Saturday evening to be jailed in a room behind the church.

San Juan Bautista had its bandit worshipers. In the 'fifties Joaquin Murietta, the Mexican, often rode down from his lair near the New Idria Mine, rolled up in his blanket on the floor of the *cantina*, at dawn attended Mass, and then went on to Santa Cruz.

In the late 'sixties and 'seventies Murietta's imitator, Tiburcio Vasquez, the last Spanish-Californian bandit, often came here to visit his mother, who had a shop. Señora Salazar, disguised as a boy, rode away with the Vasquez band, and for a time they lived in a near-by cave. She died of fright while Vasquez and one of his lieutenants dueled for possession of her. Señora Salazar's body was brought back to San Juan Bautista and laid on her husband's doorstep. The combat between Vasquez and Salazar nearly cost the bandit his life, but he rode to temporary safety.

From this Mission town also went Vasquez's lieutenant, Cleodoveo Chavez. After his chief was hanged, Chavez set out to avenge his death. His own head was brought back for the state's reward and exhibited in an adobe building on the Plaza.

San Juan Bautista's first school was opened at the Mission in 1861 by Father Antonio Ubach, who induced Sisters of Charity of Maryland to found an orphanage and day school in the long room back of the sacristy. In 1871 the Sisters and orphans withdrew to Santa Cruz.

During the gold rush, San Juan Bautista was on the main highway; stages changed horses here. The railroad built in 1870 left the

Mission to one side. Smallpox and drouth made San Juan Bautista almost a ghost town.

Father Ciprian Rúbio, who came in 1865, altered the appearance of the Mission by erecting a bell tower for the bells suspended from a beam between the front and the side of the church where the large cactus plant now grows. Two square rooms were built, one upon the other. The bell rope was let down through the ceiling of the priest's study and from there to the ground floor so that, if necessary, the Father might be his own bell ringer.

Father Rúbio's young Spanish assistant, Father Ricardo Valentin Closa, in 1874 took charge of San Juan Bautista, remaining until he died on March 9, 1916. He saw the earthquake damage to the Mission in 1906. The *fiesta* of 1908, donations by Native Sons, and an anonymous benefactor enabled Father Closa to roof the church, fortify the walls, and hold services in the old building.

On the one hundred and tenth anniversary of the Mission, June 24, 1907, a Cross twenty-four feet high was erected about two miles in a direct line from the Mission on Lomita Cruz. It replaced the Cross planted on the mountain by the missionary Fathers, which was chopped down by a Mormon for a gatepost. Indians declared the site of the Cross sacred; there spirits appeared to converse with them.

In August, 1928, San Juan Bautista came under the direction of the Maryknoll Fathers. The garden has been enlarged without losing its quaint character, supplied by lavender, rose geraniums, Castilian roses, and boxwood. The sundial remains, and the new spacious garden has an attractive fountain. The old jail is now a pleasant guest house. In the rear of the garden an appropriate priest's dwelling has been erected. Near by a convent for the Maryknoll Sisters is in building. On St. John's Day in June, Father Francis J. Caffrey, who presides over San Juan Bautista, gives a pageant and barbecue to raise funds for restoring the Mission.

Artists have long made pilgrimages to this Mission with its locust-bordered Plaza overlooking the old pear orchard in the valley. They delight in the church with its arched corridor supported by large square pillars of flat tile and burned brick, simple and unpretentious.

They study its transept and the nave subdivided by seven arches. Over the entrance door is the church loft.

San Juan Bautista has its original baptismal font carved from native sandstone. Among the earliest statues made of redwood in California, are a life-sized figure of Saint John and four smaller ones probably carved at the Mission. Unique is the crude burial bier constructed in two tiers. An important person was placed on the top shelf; ordinary beings were carried to the grave on the second; common people on the lowest.

The church fronts on the Plaza, which more than any other in the state reflects Spanish California. On the south is the old adobe *cantina* for Spanish troops—later a hotel, the oldest in California. Next door is the two-story adobe of Prefect Manuel Castro, later owned by the Patrick Breens of the Donner party. On the east is the Zanetta dwelling with its fountain, built for a courthouse before Hollister became the San Benito county seat. Since September 26, 1935, all these buildings have been the property of the state of California.

Last of the San Juan Bautista Indians, Doña Ascensión Solorzano de Cervantes came back to the Mission on February 1, 1930. Born at San Juan Bautista in 1855, she had lived long at Monterey. There representatives of the Smithsonian Institution learned from her the language and lore of the natives. Finally the tales ended. Doña Ascensión asked to be buried at San Juan Bautista with her 4,100 kinfolk. Pioneers—Americans, Spaniards, Mexicans, Indians—united to pay tribute to the last of the builders of the Mission. Doña Ascención's family placed a natural Cross from a tree at the head of her resting place. She looks out over the aged pear orchard through which the Tulares swooped down upon the Mission to be subdued by Father de la Cuesta and his music.

XVI

San Miguel, Arcángel

SAN MIGUEL, California's sixteenth and saddest Mission, was founded in honor of Saint Michael, foe of Lucifer; but here was committed the state's most frightful murder. Cabrillo bestowed the name San Miguel upon San Diego Bay when he arrived, September 28, 1542, on the eve of the feast of the Arcángel.

Two centuries and a half later Governor Borica determined to found Mission San Miguel, Arcángel. In 1795 he sent an expedition led by Sergeant Macário Castro to survey the territory between San Luis Obispo and San Antonio. With Castro was Father Buenaventura Sitjar, one of the founders of San Antonio and deeply learned in Indian languages. A neophyte from the Ranchería Sagshpileel—the natives called it *Vahca*—told the Father that the numerous Indians in this vicinity desired a Mission. All was in favor of the establishment. On a low mesa facing San Antonio there was an admirable site large enough to hold a church, Mission buildings, and a corral. Drinking and irrigation water could be obtained from the *Parage de las Pozas*, by the poplar, alder, and willow trees. Two and a half leagues distant were pines for heavy timber. Limestone was in the hills. There was also clay for tile. Pasture was abundant.

Father Sitjar engaged a young Christian Indian, who lived near by and who had oxen and a wooden plow, to sow wheat before the Mission was founded. The missionary reported to President Lasuén that a favorable situation for the new establishment had been discovered near pools of water.

When San Juan Bautista was one month old, the aged President Fermin de Lasuén journeyed from that Mission to found San Miguel. On July 25, 1797, he blessed the water and the place. The great Cross

was raised and venerated. Assisted by Father Sitjar, Father Lasuén
sang High Mass and preached in the bowery. As soon as he drew up
the Mission registers on foundation day sixteen baptisms took place.
First was a boy, Miguel Maria. Eleven other males and four females,
mostly over seven years of age, were then baptized.

Generous contributions came to the new foundation. San Luis
Obispo sent 152 cattle and two years' provisions. San Gabriel gave
150 sheep and 2 oxen. San Antonio's offering was 100 sheep, a yoke
of oxen, utensils, and beans for one year. From Purísima came 2 yoke
of oxen, 7 mules and 50 sheep. Santa Barbara sent 2 yoke of oxen
and 50 sheep. San Juan Bautista gave 40 cattle. Starving Soledad
donated 2 yoke of oxen. Santa Clara outdid all others with 614 cattle.

Fathers Buenaventura Sitjar and Antonio Horra were San Miguel's
first missionaries. Father Sitjar's familiarity with the San Antonio
idiom brought rapid conversions. Soon small boys spoke Spanish and
Latin. The Indians learned music and could sing from manuscript,
although before the Spaniards came they had only elderwood flutes.

The Mission was built near the extremity of a small pass through
the hills. The unbearable heat made even flies fall to the ground, but
six months saw the rise of a structure of palisades 71 feet by 17. An
adobe house almost as large was erected, and an adobe chapel 34 feet
long. The following year a more substantial chapel was built with a
flat, earth-covered roof 60 feet long and 24 wide. The next structure
was a large house for girls and unmarried women.

Tribulations began from foundation day. The bell was cracked
and useless. Suddenly Father Horra destroyed crops. He concealed
weapons in his habit. Declared insane, he retired.

Father Juan Martín, a friar of great power, took Father Horra's
place, and for twenty years went on building San Miguel. On January 24, 1798, he recorded the first marriages: Timotheo Sajar with
Timothea, and also José Orra with Josefa. Both had been married in
paganism, but they wished the new Christian ceremony.

After the cemetery was blessed, Father Martín recorded the first
burial on March 17, 1798—Eudosia, an adult of San Luis Obispo. In
pagan days Indian burial ceremony had consisted of tying a ball to
the corpse and burning it.

The quadrangle surrounding the patio grew; in 1799 the missionaries' dwelling was completed; in the following year an adobe building 62 feet long and 25 wide was constructed.

As early as 1800 the Mission harvested 2,166 bushels of grain and had 372 horses and cattle and 1,582 smaller animals. In spite of prosperity, tragedy came. Fathers Juan Martín and Baltasár Carnicer, and their guest, Father Marcelino Ciprés of San Antonio, were stricken with stomach pains. Was it poison?

Father Francisco Pujól of San Carlos hastened to succor the two missionaries, and he fell ill. Father Ciprés had him taken to San Antonio. There Father Pujól died in convulsions on March 15, 1801. Three Indians admitted their crime, but the missionaries pleaded for their release. The only punishment given was flogging.

During this year of violence, 204 converts were gained. Missionaries were obliged to ask assistance. Within seven years 1,169 names were recorded in the baptismal book. Neophytes came from 170 *rancherías*. San Antonio spoke one language, San Simeon another, and the Tulares had their own tongue.

The Tulareños, deeply attached to their birthplace, frequently fled from the Mission. Father Juan Martín, in November, 1804, led a missionary expedition seventy miles into the Tulare country. Two hundred children were baptized, but no Mission was established. With a force of soldiers, Father Martín approached Chief Guchapa of the Cholan Ranchería, to ask if he might Christianize the youth. Guchapa refused: "I do not fear soldiers. They die like other men." Thirteen soldiers were sent to capture the chief. On his arrival at San Miguel he was conciliated with gifts and he promised to permit conversions. When he departed, he left his son as hostage.

If it rained San Miguel harvests were large; cattle throve; sheep were excelled only by those of San Juan Capistrano. In spite of lack of water and intense heat, the death rate was lower than at any Mission except San Luis Rey. Indian healers used the juice of roots and barks. The frothy thermal waters, later called Paso Robles Springs, together with soap root, served to purge, and also to cure skin diseases and rheumatism. Missionaries found it difficult to pre-

Courtesy Society of California Pioneers

Mission Santa Barbara, 1883

Mission Santa Barbara

Ruins of first Mission La Purísima

Courtesy A. E. Henning

Restoration project Mission La Purísima Concepción showing missionaries' house and Father Payeras' church unfinished

Mrs. Gladys Sullivan Doyle

Replica of Mission Santa Cruz erected by Gladys Sullivan Doyle.
Picture shows *fiesta* time

Mission Soledad (Our Lady of Solitude) from a painting at height of its prosperity. Now in ruins

Mission Soledad Ruins

Mission San José, 1797

Mission San José de Guadalupe, scene of many Indian conflicts

Mission San Juan Bautista, 1903

Mission San Juan Bautista

Mission San Miguel, Arcángel, before restoration

Mission San Miguel, Arcángel, with recent restorations

Ruins of Mission San Fernando Rey

Mission San Fernando Rey with Monument to Serra

Ruins San Luis Rey de Francia

Plaza Church, Los Angeles

Courtesy Oakland Tribune

Mission San Luis Rey, 1838

Courtesy San Diego-California Club

Mission San Luis Rey

Asistencia of San Antonio de Pala in days of its prosperity

Asistencia of San Antonio de Pala

Mission Santa Inés from a painting in the days of its glory

Mission Santa Inés, one of the best examples of unrestored California Missions

Mission San Rafael, Arcángel, from a painting by Edwin Deakin.
The building has been obliterated

Mission San Francisco Solano (Sonoma)

San Francisco Solano (Sonoma) while it was being restored

vent the Indians' taking wild tobacco and lime, an intoxicating concoction that rendered them insensible.

San Miguel neophytes quickly learned to weave blankets and cloth; supervised by Fathers Martín and Muñóz, in 1805 they made ten thousand tiles for the guardhouse roof. They also built 47 adobe houses.

Much of this work was undone on August 25, 1806, when a fire broke out about midnight. Fathers and neophytes supplicated Saint Michael to save them from the dragon of flames. Before the fire was extinguished, half the church roof was destroyed, two rows of buildings were in ashes, manufacturing plants were gutted, 6,660 bushels of wheat and much raw material were consumed.

With the valiant spirit of Saint Michael, however, the missionaries began to erect more spacious buildings. President Tápis asked for contributions for the afflicted Mission. San Buenaventura gave 600 head of cattle. Looms and cloth were offered by San Francisco, San Luis Rey, Santa Inés, and La Purísima. Provisions for a year were donated by San Luis Obispo, San Juan Bautista, San Carlos, Santa Cruz, and Soledad. San Gabriel contributed $50. San Juan Capistrano sent six mules and fourteen *reales*.

Fortunately the Fathers' quarters were spared. Soon weaving rooms and workshops were in running order. Industries were housed in a structure 175 feet long. A warehouse and 27 buildings were erected for Indian families, each 18 *varas* square. Before the end of 1808 a sacristy was added. As a precaution against fire, the Indians made 36,000 tiles for roofing the church and other buildings.

Tragedy again cloaked San Miguel. Father Marcelino Ciprés of San Luis Obispo made a journey to Monterey. On his return after, eating food prepared by Christian Indians at San Miguel, he suffered a deadly sickness of the intestines resulting in his death. He was interred on the gospel side of the main altar on February 1, 1810.

In this same year San Miguel harvested its greatest grain crop— 8,122 bushels. A large corral was made. At La Playa Ranch a house and granary 75 feet long were erected. In 1811, 20,000 tiles were made. Soap works, granary, tannery, and corral were erected. At the

Rancho de la Asunción a dwelling was built, as was a long granary and houses for neophytes.

In 1814 San Miguel had its largest population of converts—1,066. All rejoiced when, on December 10, Governor José Argüello granted the missionaries permission to build a new church. Two years later the stone foundation was laid. Timbers came from Cambria's pine-covered mountains forty miles distant. Several pairs of original hinges a foot long made at that time are still in use at San Miguel. There is also a fluted holy-water font fashioned from the bole of a tree.

In 1818 the church was ready for roofing. Three years later Estévan Munras directed neophytes in frescoing the walls. Vegetable colors were sized with glue made from bones. Red came from stones picked up on the beach, blue from nightshade. The interesting Munras decorations are as vivid as they were 117 years ago when copied from a book. The reredos was painted in three panels. In the center stands a wooden statue of San Miguel, patron of the Mission, holding scales in his right hand and a sword in his left.

Greatly admired at this Mission is a large shell in shades of pink and green back of the wall pulpit, probably a tribute to Saint James, on whose day the Mission was founded. His symbol is the sea shell.

Like those seen in some European churches, the arches at San Miguel are asymmetrical; the first arch is small and semi-circular, followed by four large arches; and then one elliptical arch forms the center. On the other side are four larger arches and a small semi-circular one.

With the wild Tulare country in paganism, Father Juan Cabot could not have spiritual peace. He led an expedition into that region. Since he spoke many Indian idioms, it was easy for him to baptize thirty-three natives from different *rancherías*. He was attacked by hostile Sumtaches. Peace ensued only after a woman was killed.

Father Martín urged Father Lasuén to establish a Mission in the Tulare country. If this was not done, he wrote, "Satan, war and venereal disease would leave no one to be converted." Near King's River, at what later became Visalia, Father Cabot found a good Mission site. Funds from Mexico failed, and no establishment was made. Greatly disappointed, Father Martín died at San Miguel on

August 29, 1824, after twenty-seven years of service. He was buried on the gospel side of the altar by Fathers Luis Martínez, Juan Sancho, and Francisco Uría.

The Indians, as well as Father Cabot, realized that secularization was impending. Drunk and shouting, "*Soy libre!*" neophytes attempted to kill him. Two soldiers drove off the Indians while the Father defended himself in his house. San Miguel was losing its neophytes. There remained only 7,904 sheep, 2,130 cattle, 120 oxen, and 60 pigs.

When Governor Echeandia, on January 6, 1831, issued his premature decree confiscating the Missions, he sent José Castro, afterwards commander of California troops, to address the neophytes. Through interpreter Francisco, he requested the Indians to choose between the Fathers and freedom. Nearly all stepped to the left with the Fathers.

Father Cabot asked permission to retire, but no one could be found to take his place. When the Mexican Government seized San Miguel, on December 20, 1834, Governor José Figueroa ordered the payment of $400 to the Father, who returned to Spain after thirty years' service in California.

Alvarado told the administrator to "turn the Mission upside down," and that was what happened. In order not to burden the Indians, Father Juan Moreno refused his salary of $1,000 annually, cooked for himself, and planted his own garden.

Administrator Ignacio Coronel was succeeded in 1836 by Inocente García. The administrator flogged the Indians, and they left carrying away half the grain. The inventory of 1837 appraised the Mission at $82,806. This included Ranchos La Estrella, Cholam, Gueguero, Canamo, de la Asunción, San Bartolomé, Santa Rosa, and San Simeon. Santa Isabel had an excellent vineyard. Wheat was sown at Rancho del Paso de Robles. At this ranch a hot sulphur spring boiled up from the ground, forming a rivulet across El Camino Real. A small house erected over the spring was a hospital for rheumatism.

Violence and death continued to afflict San Miguel. Two Tulare Indians killed a major-domo in August, 1839. Before two years passed, the neophyte population was reduced to 201. The herds numbered only 5,075.

When de Mofras came in 1841, he wrote that he met but one man at San Miguel. Thirty Indians were left of the 1,200 inhabiting the place in 1804. The grand buildings were dilapidated. Lands lay uncultivated. *Rancheros* owned the stock.

Father Ramón Abella, the last Fernandino, remained a few months in 1841. The next year Father Miguel Gómez was in charge of both San Miguel and San Luis Obispo. Mission registers were carried in 1844 to San Luis Obispo—San Miguel was little more than an *asistencia* to that establishment. Until 1851 no baptism took place at San Miguel.

In 1845 the Mission was without lands or cattle. Governor Pico warned the Indians to return, or the property would be sold. They gave no heed. On July 4, 1846, Petronillo Rios and William Reed bought the Mission. There was no resident missionary. Three days later the American flag rose over Monterey. Governor Pico fled.

Almost opposite the Mission, Rios erected a two-story adobe building with a gallery, now called the Caledonia. Reed lived at the Mission with his family. One of the reception rooms was used for a saloon. A sewing machine agency occupied another apartment. Carousers and wanderers frequented the place.

Again tragedy came to San Miguel; in 1848 Reed and his Spanish-Californian wife, María Antonia Vallejo, hospitably entertained for days some former American soldiers. Indiscreetly Reed told the strangers that he had sold sheep and had considerable money. From San Miguel the guests started southward. At Santa Margarita they turned back.

In the room now used as a museum at Mission San Miguel occurred California's most appalling murder. Two days later here were found ten heaped-up corpses: those of Reed; his wife; their three-year-old son; their unborn child; Josefa Olivera, a mid-wife attending Mrs. Reed, and her daughter aged sixteen; a four-year-old nephew; Mrs. Reed's brother, José Ramón Vallejo; an aged Indian servant; his nephew, five years old; and the negro cook. With all the gold and valuables, the five murderers had fled.

Governor Richard B. Mason dispatched Lieutenant Edward Ord with a Santa Barbara force to find the fugitives. Near the Ortega

Ranch on the coast, after being fatally wounded, one of the murderers shot and killed Ramón Rodríguez, who had rashly attacked him. Another of the band, Samuel Brenard, leaped into the sea and was drowned. Joseph Lynch, Peter Remer, and Peter Quin were executed at Santa Barbara, December 28, 1848. After these gruesome events the Mission seemed to take on a sinister air; midnight specters of the slain were said to fill the air with their moans.

On September 2, 1859, Mission San Miguel was returned to the Catholic Church by President Buchanan. The property included church, buildings, cemetery, eleven acres of land, nineteen of vineyard, and four of orchard. During the 'sixties occasionally Father Dorotéo Ambrís came from San Antonio to baptize Indians and settlers, but for thirty-seven years there was no resident priest.

A saloon in the cells led off the south corridor. Over the graves of Father Marcelino Ciprés and Father Juan Martín was a stable. A neophyte, Juan José, became self-appointed caretaker guarding the sacred images and vestments. On holy days he assembled straggling neophytes in the empty church and sang hymns and chants learned in happier days. When a priest came, Juan José brought his treasures out of hiding and decorated the desolate building. He lived with the ghosts of dead *padres*. The Angelus always rang an angelic serenade. So he died, pulling the rope for the Angelus.

San Miguel never had a tower. Its bells hung on a wooden standard before the church or between the corridor arches. The foundation bell was cracked. San Antonio loaned a small Mexican bell. It bears a bullet hole, but is still used. It is inscribed: S. S. GABRIEL A. D. 1800. (SAINT GABRIEL. YEAR OF 1800.) Hanging near the ferny pepper tree is a large bell recast in 1888 at the Globe Bell and Brass Foundry, San Francisco, made up of several Mission bells; probably one is the original bell. Its inscription is: BEATO MICHAELI ARCHANGELO DICATA PRIDIEKAL OCT. S. A. D. 1888. (BLESSED MICHAEL ARCHANGEL DEDICATED THE DAY BEFORE OCTOBER 1888.)

Father Philip Farrelly came to San Miguel in 1879 and rode day and night—south beyond Paso Robles, or north to the Salinas Valley, or east as far as the San Joaquin, or west to the ocean. After "Father Felipe" was transferred to Mission Santa Inés in 1886, Father Joseph

Mut arrived from San Juan Capistrano. With $3,000 collected he repaired the *convento* rafters and the heavy tile roof. After three years' struggle he died; he is the only priest buried in the cemetery adjoining the church.

Father Henry S. O'Reilly, in September, 1897, arranged a festival to obtain restoration funds. He renovated some apartments in the main building and plastered the outside of the church and monastery.

A memorial celebration for Father Marcelino Ciprés of San Antonio and Father Juan Martín, builder of San Miguel, was held by Father William A. Nevin on November 13, 1912. He placed marble slabs over their graves. Fifty-four strokes of the bell sounded for Father Juan, and forty-one for Father Marcelino. A choir of Franciscans sang Gregorian chants. A Camino Real bell decorated with Spanish colors and the Stars and Stripes was unveiled.

In 1928 San Miguel and San Antonio were offered to Santa Barbara Franciscans. After the return of the brown-robed friars, frail Father Modesto fought termites, helped put on a new roof, and straightened and covered the ruins in the south end of the monastery. While living quarters were partitioned off, he camped on the dirt floor in an earthen-walled room. His health failed after the garden was begun.

Father Fidelis followed Father Modesto and continued planting. Father Hubert, now stationed in far China, made some new-old benches of termite-eaten timber that look as if they had been at San Miguel since foundation day.

With the coming of Father Tiburcio Wand, there was an intensification of Franciscan energy. He brought to the Mission many relics from San Lucas, Jolon, and King City, all in harmony with the surroundings. A breviary with handmade clasps is inscribed: *Antwerp 1735* and autographed by Father Castañeda.

Many visitors ask to see the Munras murals. They are also greatly interested in the octagonal pulpit hanging like a bird's nest on the right wall, decorated with blue, green, red, gray, and yellow. It is still in use. Once it had a quaint sounding board and crown-like canopy. Ten blurred paintings have been here since the beginning. Over the altar still stands Saint Michael with images of Saint Joseph, Saint Francis, and Saint Anthony.

Father Wand points out the wishing chair in the sanctuary, said to have been made miraculous by Father Magin Catalá, who blessed it for Concha, an Indian girl. He told her to sit in the chair, make a wish, and it would be granted. Within a week Concha had a husband. María de los Angeles Garfis, last of the San Miguel Indians, believes that she obtained three husbands from Father Magin's wishing chair.

After Father Wand arrived at San Miguel he employed a French-Swiss worker who manufactured 75,000 adobe bricks. Five carloads of lumber, four of cement, and three of roof tile have been used in the south wing. He expects in 1938 to have most of the walls roofed. The hall with the old wine vat has been brought back, and so has the room where the Reed family was murdered.

Father Wand is not building merely a museum. He is establishing a vocational training school for young Franciscan Brothers under the supervision of older Brothers. As California's early Franciscan *padres* taught Indians, so Father Wand will teach Franciscan Brothers to be carpenters, painters, cooks, blacksmiths, tailors, fitting them for work in different houses of the Order on the Pacific coast.

Since coming to the Mission, Father Wand has planted fruit trees, begun a cloistered garden, and erected an adobe wall in front of the building. Plaster in places has been brushed off the wall to make it look authentic. The Father tells of a visitor's remark, "Gee, why didn't you get someone who knew his business to build the walls? They look just like the old ones!"

XVII

San Fernando Rey

EXCITEMENT and drama have always been in the air at Mission San Fernando Rey, first establishment in California to have as patron a king: Ferdinand, who ruled Spain in the thirteenth century. San Fernando, now included in the City of Los Angeles, was the battleground of Juan Bautista Alvarado after he usurped executive power. Not far from this Mission of the Spanish ruler, California's first great gold discovery was made, and the first oil well was drilled.

In 1795 President Lasuén had endeavored to find a suitable place for a Mission between San Buenaventura and San Gabriel. For the purpose he sent Father Vicente de Santa Maria with Ensign Pablo Cota, Sergeant José Maria Ortega, and four soldiers; but they failed to discover well-watered, fertile soil.

Alcalde Francisco de los Reyes of Los Angeles joined the company. Unhappily only one suitable site was found, the Rancho San José, belonging to Mission San Gabriel. The *Alcalde* occupied it, hoping to make the land his own. Here was water, limestone, fertile soil. Not far to the northwest were pine forests and excellent pasture. Above all, there were populous *rancherías*—Taapa, Tacuyama, Tucuenga, Juyunga and Mapipinga—with Indians already trained as horsemen, cowherds, irrigators, bird catchers. This site for the proposed Mission the Indians called *Achois Comihabit* when Portolá and his men camped here on August 5, 1769. Father Juan Crespi had named it *Santa Catalina de Bonónia de los Encinos*. For the first time in Mission-founding, the Fathers selected land claimed by others.

On a blazing August day in 1797, President Fermin Francisco de Lasuén left Santa Barbara with Sergeant Ignacio Olivera and five soldiers to found Mission San Fernando. Already on November 12,

1796, it had been christened by Viceroy Branciforte. September 8th came before Father Lasuén had blessed the water and the site, had planted the Cross and said Mass, assisted by Father Francisco Dumétz.

Immediately Indians, witnessing the impressive ceremony, offered five boys and girls for baptism, all from the Ranchería Achoicominga. Father Lasuén christened four-year-old Coyhuoch, son of Mayso and Chamayo, Fernando Maria. The first girl was called Fernanda Maria. Eight other children were Miguel Maria, Michaela María, Gabriel Maria, Gabriela María, Rafael Maria, Rafaela María, Maria Fernando, and María Fernanda. Their idiom was like that of San Gabriel, of the Shoshone linguistic family.

Books of baptism, marriage, and burial, drawn up by Father Lasuén, exist; but the confirmation book is missing. The burial register had a varied history. Sold by a collector, it finally reached the H. E. Huntington Library and Art Gallery at San Marino near San Gabriel. When Mr. Huntington was informed of the devious method by which the book had been obtained, he returned it in 1925 to the Bishop of Los Angeles.

Father Francisco Dumétz was assigned to Mission San Fernando Rey. On September 13, five days after his coming, he recorded the first baptism made by him. Father Juan Cortés came from San Gabriel to assist.

In the little arbor in which divine services were held, the first marriage took place on October 8, 1797. The names of the bride and groom will never be known, because the marriage register has been mutilated. Two months later mention was made of an adobe church eight *varas* square, probably a building already erected by Reyes.

Seven months after the foundation, Father Dumétz, on April 7, 1798, made the first entry in the burial register: neophyte José Antonio. During the first year dwellings and workshops were provided for 135 neophytes. Indians were taught mechanical arts. Forty-five *fanégas* of grain were sown. Storerooms were built, and an adobe house for the guards was erected. Quarters for the missionaries and soldiers were completed. A temporary church was finished.

Santa Barbara, San Benaventura, San Gabriel, and San Juan

Capistrano sent gifts of livestock to the new Mission—500 sheep, 300 cattle, 46 horses, 18 mules, and 16 yoke of oxen.

The first large structure was a granary 50 by 17 feet. Other buildings were added until the wing extended 90 feet. An adobe church 66 feet by 27 replaced the smaller one. Another granary 91 feet long with a storeroom was built. The Fathers' living quarters and *sala* were impressive, occupying the front of the quadrangle 123 feet long. All these structures were roofed with tile.

The century turned, and San Fernando had 501 converts. The largest building was now erected, 300 feet long. Here were housed girls and single women with a courtyard of their own. Higher officials had a residence with a reception room. Six houses were added for guards.

All Missions aimed to complete the quadrangle and provide an out-of-doors living room and recreation center for neophytes. At San Fernando this was achieved in 1802 by building a wing 300 feet long, containing granary, storehouse and carpenter shop.

Converts increased each year. When, in 1803, Chief Piirubit abandoned paganism and accepted Christianity, 361 were added in the register. Rejoicing, the missionaries erected 70 small adobe houses for the neophytes.

The new church was too small. A third house of worship was begun for the 985 converts. Its walls were 185 feet long, 35 wide, 26 high, and from 4 to 5 feet thick. Brick, rocks, and broken material were used in construction, with a lime finish. The façade was without ornament save a square window over the arched doorway. At the right was a two-story tower with a peaked tile roof. San Fernando's new church was dedicated on December 6, 1806, by Father Pedro Muñóz of San Miguel. Father José Señan journeyed from San Buenaventura to preach. Bringing all the musicians from his own Mission, and some of those of Purísima, came Father José Antonio de Urrestí from Santa Barbara to serve as *padrino*.

Father Nicolas Lázaro, on December 12, 1806, made the first baptism in the new church: a little girl.

Mission San Fernando was harassed by settlers coveting land made productive by neophyte labor. The Fathers successfully protested the

granting of Rancho Camulos to Francisco Avila. There was a dispute
with Pueblo de Los Angeles over irrigation rights. On December 31,
1808, Fathers Landaéta and Muñóz reported that a dam of masonry
had been built. Three years later a reservoir was completed with an
aqueduct a mile and a half long.

San Fernando's greatest grain harvest was 12,868 badly needed
bushels for the 1,081 neophytes housed in 1811 at the Mission. Their
textile, leather, and ironwork was notable in California. A *jabonería*,
or soap factory, with two boilers was built. It still may be seen, partly
concealed by shrubbery, in Brand Park, not far from the house of
the Fathers, San Fernando's great building.

This structure, begun in 1810 by Fathers Pedro Muñóz and Joaquin
Nuez, is still used. Its reception room was the largest in California,
243 feet long, 50 wide, with a colonnade of nineteen arches. The earthquake of 1812 damaged the building. Thirty beams were replaced to
support the walls, but the structure was not completed until 1823.

Before the effects of the Mexican revolt of 1810 were felt in California, San Fernando procured several articles of church goods: two
sculptured statues of the Immaculate Conception, a figure of Saint
Joseph with silver diadem, stock for holy oils, vestments, and a
canopy for the Corpus Christi procession. Forty Indian houses were
built in 1819. Artisans had a spacious dwelling near the Fathers'
residence in 1822 that served as workshop.

In 1813 Fathers Muñóz and Nuez described some characteristics
of the San Fernando Indians for the Spanish Government. For pains
in the side the natives applied externally red ants in water, at the
same time striking themselves with nettles. In order to prevent fatigue
in climbing hills, a stick or stone was carried. They painted themselves with ochre of red and other colors, that they might not be
burned.

In their race courses they made a great circle, in the center of
which they raised a pole covered with bundles of crow feathers
adorned with beads. They walked round the poles, blowing to the
four winds, praying to five gods: Veat, Jaimar, Chuhuit, Pichuret,
and Quichepet, husband of one of the few female ruling powers in
California, Goddess Manisar, who controlled planting. After a funeral

feast the hut was burned with everything possessed by the dead. All were commanded never to mention the departed, lest spirits return.

Already Mission San Fernando Rey was scourged with caterpillars on horse beans and locusts in wheat fields, when Captain José de la Guerra demanded soap, shoes, and food for Santa Barbara soldiers. Father Ibarra suggested that soldiers take better care of their shoes, raise their own vegetables, and not expect to be supported by neophytes who had only a blanket and breechcloth apiece. "A bawdry," he called the Santa Barbara Presidio, but he contributed $200 to the military post and in five years gave supplies valued at $21,203. Friction was especially acute because Father Ibarra, a Spanish loyalist, would not swear allegiance to the Mexican Republic.

Robinson in 1829 criticized Father Ibarra's dining table, which was let down from the wall at mealtime. But today Father Ibarra's table is the modern housewife's novelty and convenience.

In 1831 California had a new governor, Manuel Victoria, but deposed Governor Echeandia helped Pio Pico, Juan Bandini, and their group expel Victoria from the territory. From San Fernando south to San Diego ruled Echeandia, who armed the Mission neophytes and those of San Gabriel, San Juan Capistrano, San Fernando, San Luis Rey, and San Diego. Soon the Indians swaggered instead of working. From San Fernando north to Sonoma, Agustín Zamorano held sway.

Governor Figueroa commissioned Lieutenant Antonio del Valle to secularize San Fernando Rey. With a salary of $800 a year, he began work in June, 1835. Rancho San Francisco was granted del Valle. Neophytes were indignant that their property was taken from them. They seized livestock. Del Valle called upon the Governor for soldiers.

At this time Mission herds were large, but crops small. Only 450 bushels of grain were garnered. Population had increased to 792. Appraisers valued 32,000 grapevines at $16,000; 1,600 fruit trees at $2,400; the library of 190 volumes at $417; the buildings at $15,511.

Like Father Esténaga of San Gabriel, Father Ibarra could not watch San Fernando perish. Without asking permission of their Superior, President Durán, the two missionaries departed. Durán did not reproach them for abandoning their unhappy existence. After remaining a year in Sonora, they returned. Father Ibarra later died at San Luis Rey. Father Esténaga in 1847 closed his life at San Fernando. He is buried near the sanctuary in the church.

Invalids were frequently benefited by San Fernando's hot, dry climate. Among those who came here for their health were Father Martin de Landaéta, who died in 1809, and Father José de Miguel in 1813. Father Pedro Cabot followed in 1836. San Fernando Rey had no resident missionary until Father Blas Ordáz took charge on April 16, 1837, remaining a decade.

At this time Juan Bautista Alvarado, who had seized the governorship at Monterey, marched southward with his troops, commanded by General José Castro, to put down the revolt in Los Angeles. *Alcalde* Sepúlveda, with Juan José Rocha and 270 men, met the Alvarado force at the Mission.

"Citizens," cried Sepúlveda, "defend Los Angeles against the Monterey usurper!"

"If San Fernando is not surrendered," replied Alvarado, "I will take it by force!"

The Los Angeleños seized $2,000 of the Mission funds to carry on the war. Rocha, Sepúlveda, and their men retired to Los Angeles. Peace was restored by a council of opposing forces.

In June, 1838, San Fernando became a parish of the second class, with the priest receiving a salary of $1,000 a year. One year later William E. P. Hartnell, Inspector of the Missions, found 416 Indians at San Fernando. Accounts were hopelessly confused.

"Gold!" was the cry that stirred even the dying Mission. It was uttered on March 9, 1842, the feast of Saint Frances of Rome. Francisco López, who had been *Alcalde* of Los Angeles, made the discovery six years before James W. Marshall found gold in Sutter's millrace near the south branch of the American River.

López wished to have wild onions for his birthday dinner. He pulled up some, shook off the soil, and found yellow particles. This was on the San Francisquito Rancho, once property of the Mission, but at that time belonging to the del Valles.

López forgot his birthday dinner and rode about the country shouting, "Gold, gold, gold!" Mission San Fernando was in commotion. Fortune hunters crowded into the country. Another placer mine was uncovered the following year in the San Feliciano Canyon, about eight miles west of Newhall of today.

From the López discovery, the first parcel of gold dust, 18.34 ounces, was sent East in 1842. Alfred Robinson took it to the United States Mint at Philadelphia, where it was valued at $344.75. About $100,000 was washed out by crude mining methods with bowl-shaped Indian baskets.

On the first anniversary of the discovery of gold, March 9, 1843, Father Blas Ordáz celebrated Mass at San Fernando, surrounded by a great multitude, the neophytes joining in music and song. The Mission gained nothing from the gold discovery, but even in recent years fortune hunters have dug in the ruins for gold.

During the gold excitement in 1842, Governor Manuel Micheltorena stopped at San Fernando on his way to Monterey. Already leaders were conspiring against him. Soon he was back at the Mission. The territory ridiculed him, an invalid, for driving south in a carriage, leading four hundred soldiers. The Governor had three cannon; José Castro and the rebels had two. Near Mission San Fernando, all day at long range firing kept up. One side used ammunition, the other small stones. One lost a horse, and the other a mule. No human blood was shed.

Micheltorena's vagabonds could not defeat Castro. On February 27, 1845, the Governor signed a treaty of peace with the rebels at Mission San Fernando, and marched north with his men to music and flying colors.

Mission San Fernando was leased December 5, 1845, by Governor Pico to his brother, Andrés Pico, and to Juan Manso at an annual rental of $1,120. Governor Pico sold the Mission on June 17, 1846, to Eulogio Celis for $14,000.

Soon war again blackened the Mission. On January 12, 1847, Colonel John C. Frémont and his troops took possession of the buildings, maintaining themselves on the sheep and cattle. Don Andrés Pico retired from his Mission residence to his camp two miles distant, where his forces were. Frémont went to visit Don Andrés and negotiated the Treaty of Cahuenga for the United States. California was conquered.

The American Government ordered squatters to leave Mission buildings. President Lincoln, on May 31, 1862, signed a patent giving Mission San Fernando Rey with 75 acres of land to the Catholic Church.

Father Blas Ordáz, the last Franciscan here, departed on June 30, 1847. Thereafter the Mission was attended from Our Lady of the Angels, Los Angeles. Father Peter Verdaguer of the Plaza Church celebrated the last Mass. No entries were made in the registers from September 3, 1852, till 1902.

Early decay set in. Rats devoured the vestments and linen. Musical instruments disappeared. Chalices and sacred vessels lay forgotten in sacristy drawers and chests, but some ornamental mirrors remained on the altar. The baptismal font was only a copper olla. San Fernando's statue from its solitary bracket surveyed the desolation.

As late as 1853 beauty still lingered in the garden: olive, orange, lemon, fig trees, palms, and a prickly pear hedge covered with partly ripened fruit. Lieutenant R. S. Williamson, who at that time came from Washington to determine a practical railroad route to the Pacific Ocean, wrote of a large fountain with a circular basin before the imposing buildings. Shallow stairs led to the belfry, where still hung one large bell and three smaller bells of the original sextet. All that remains of the adobe tower is a smaller portion of the wall near the last window and a triangular section of the front wall.

In 1888 a small bell was suspended from the arch in the western end of the monastery building. A squat iron bell hung in the first archway left of the entrance to the monastery. A third crudely shaped bell with a heavy clapper has come to light in an eastern college, inscribed: AVE MARIA PURISIMA. 1802. At the del Valles' Camulos Rancho was found in 1902 one of San Fernando's most interesting *campanas*. Its Russian inscription is translated: 1796—IN THE MONTH OF JANUARY THIS BELL WAS CAST ON THE ISLAND OF KODIAK THROUGH THE GENEROSITY OF THE ARCHIMANDRITE JOSEPH AND THE ELECTED CHURCHWARDEN, ALEXANDER BARANOF. It is also lettered: DE SN FERNO. Rezánov brought this bell from Sitka in 1806 and exchanged it for grain with *Comandante* José Darío Argüello at

San Francisco, father of Concepción Argüello. The family gave it to San Fernando, and the del Valles took it from the Mission to save it from vandals. It weighs only a hundred pounds, is badly cracked, but of delightful timbre. A large Mexican bell, one of the original sextet, is daily used for the Angelus. It is lettered: AVE MARIA PURISIMA S JUAN NEPOMUCENO 1809.

Unusual events were in the air at this Mission. When Andrés Pico lived here he burned coal oil without realizing that near by would be developed the beginning of California's oil industry. In Pico Canyon in the year 1860 a sheepherder trailing deer observed a seepage of a thick black fluid. He took a canteen of the substance to the Mission. Nothing was known concerning crude oil, and there was no excitement. In this same canyon, however, fifteen years later D. J. Schofield, first president of Standard Oil in California, bored the state's first important oil well.

In the early 'seventies Tiburcio Vasquez, the bandit, fleeing, came on a strange errand to the Mission. For months he had starved in the mountains with Rosario Leiva, wife of Abdon Leiva, one of his band. They had begotten a child. Rosario was eager to have the dying infant baptized. Vasquez begged the priest to go with him to the mountains. After the child's baptism he brought the priest back to the Mission. In leaving the bandit said, "I am Tiburcio Vasquez. Do not betray me, *padre*." The bandit's confidence was not violated.

Soon Sheriff William R. Rowland captured Vasquez in a house in what has since been called Hollywood. Later he was hanged at San José, where his grandfather had been *Alcalde*.

Henry Chapman Ford in 1888 made etchings of dilapidated San Fernando Rey—roofless, the doors in the front and on the south hanging by a hinge. A curious little baptistry had a quaintly arched ceiling near the choir loft.

A crumbling row of buildings connected the church with the house of the Fathers, still an impressive structure used by a land and water company for storehouses and bunk houses. The rear part of the building served as a stable. A dry old fountain was in front near the road. On the opposite side were weeping willows.

Once there had been seventy acres of olive trees bearing mammoth fruit. A few two feet in diameter remained near the Mission. In the middle of the large orchard towered native palms fifty-five feet high.

In 1896 Charles F. Lummis, editor of *Land and Sunshine*, lamented that Mission San Fernando Rey had become a hog ranch, the garden a slaughtering place. Winter rains were devouring the walls. Part of the church ornamented a San Fernando barber shop. Lummis, founder and president of the Los Angeles Landmarks Club, began to raise funds to preserve San Fernando.

The house of the Fathers was re-roofed, and the centennial of the Mission's founding was celebrated in 1897. Five years later Father James E. Burns became the first permanent pastor since 1852.

Marked improvements came after August 6, 1916; Los Angeles had a candle day. Several thousand candles bearing the name of the purchaser were sold at a dollar each, and in the evening simultaneously lighted. Money was thus collected to re-roof the church and fortify the walls. In 1917 the Landmarks Club began making adobe brick in the old adobe mixing wheel.

Six years later the parish and Mission buildings were placed in charge of the religious Congregation of the Oblates of Mary Immaculate, from Aix, France. They renovated the cloister, renewed the foundation under the rear wall, and established a museum.

Visitors wish to see the wine cellar, the huge copper brandy still, the Moorish windows, the murals and scrollwork in the Governor's room, and the portable altar. Nothing, however, attracts more attention than the aperture in the door through which the lonely friars' cats passed.

In Brand Park near the house of the Fathers is Father Junípero Serra's statue, erected by the Mission Land Company which gave the park on November 4, 1920, to the city of Los Angeles. Here also is a star-shaped fountain thirty feet in diameter. Directed by the *padres*, neophytes copied a fountain at Cordova, Spain. Although it weighs many tons, Mr. L. C. Brand at his own expense removed the fountain from a field to its present location, and on July 4, 1922, incorporated it in his gift.

This splendid fountain, Serra's statue, the missionaries' house, and the Memory Garden in Brand Park have long interested visitors. But not more than a hundred yards distant stood the half-forgotten ruined church in the rear of the house of the Fathers, appealing for the hand of the restorer.

In 1937, after half a century of abandonment, once more the ancient edifice that had withstood earthquakes, storms, and vandals seemed to live again. Young Father John Collins, the parish priest, began work. Wide breaches in the walls were repaired with sun-dried adobe; buttresses were rebuilt with fired brick. A tile roof supported by a steel cradle independent of the walls was installed. A newly developed oil composition was applied to protect the adobe bricks against weather without altering their appearance. After weeks of activity on Sunday, September 9, 1937, benediction services were held commemorating the one hundred and fortieth anniversary of the founding of San Fernando Rey.

Annually in June San Fernando has a *fiesta,* the proceeds of which go toward restoring the Mission. These festivities recall the legend of Hueneme, an Indian maiden of one of the Channel Islands, who lived happily with her husband, a chief, at Point Magu.

A witch woman put a spell on the chief. Hueneme returned to her parents' island home. Soon she swam to the mainland and arrived at San Fernando in *fiesta* time. The witch woman, dancing with the faithless husband, mocked Hueneme, "You have no husband."

Hueneme hastened homeward, but she fainted from grief and weariness. A chilicothe vine grew over her shielding her from the sun. When she revived, she sucked the juice from the chilicothe pods and went on.

Hueneme's husband overtook his wife and tried to recapture their old life at Point Magu. Happiness was lost. Casting herself into the sea, Hueneme was turned to stone. Her husband also hurled himself into the sea.

At times Hueneme was wrathful; the great water tossed, sailors were drowned. In her fury huge stones were thrown upon the beach.

Until the white man came, each year on the anniversary of her death Indians made offerings on the shore to commemorate Hueneme's fury. In good weather her breasts may be seen above the waves off Point Magu, her husband's hair floating on the water.

XVIII

San Luis Rey

IN the two wide-flung Americas, San Luis Rey was the most successful Mission and the most august. Its first missionary, Father Antonio Peyri, was suave, farsighted, energetic, eager for life, a genius among builders. He saw San Luis Rey founded June 13, 1798.

Like President Lasuén, Father Peyri considered the site sacred ground; near here had taken place the first baptism in California. Here, on July 22, 1769, the Portolá expedition, seeking the Bay of Monterey, met befeathered Indians smeared with bright paint, warbent. These natives refused to kiss the Cross. Don Gaspar de Portolá, a realist, said, "Give them red beads." Red beads conquered.

The Indians led the Spaniards to a *ranchería* near Old Capistrano. Two baby girls, apparently dying, were baptized: María Magdalena and Margarita. The Spaniards called the canyon *Los Cristianitos* and named the region San Juan Capistrano. After Mission San Juan Capistrano was founded in 1776, the locality was re-christened San Juan Capistrano el Viejo, or Old Capistrano; here was to be the eighteenth Mission, San Luis Rey.

Viceroy Branciforte himself chose the patron of the new establishment, San Luis, the Crusader, ninth King of France, who reigned from 1236 to 1270. Early in 1798 the Governor ordered the *Comandante* at San Diego to furnish an escort to President Lasuén, Fathers Antonio Peyri and Juan de Santiago, who were to make the new foundation among the large *rancherías* in the north between San Diego and San Juan Capistrano. Soldiers were to erect the necessary buildings. The Governor commanded, "Permit no murmuring against work."

Although President Lasuén was more than seventy, he, accompanied by Fathers Peyri and Santiago, preceded the military party. Two days the soldiers worked making the arbor for Mass in a *cañada* one and a half leagues from the sea—*Tacayme,* the Indians called it. Seated on a bundle of blankets, Father Fermín supervised the foundation.

For the great occasion came Don Antonio Grájera, captain of cavalry, some soldiers, and many San Juan Capistrano neophytes. Father Lasuén blessed the water and the place; the tall Cross was raised and worshiped; High Mass was said.

No sooner had Father Lasuén drawn up the baptismal book, the death and burial registers, the book of confirmations, than natives brought twenty-five male and twenty-nine female infants to be baptized. Nineteen remained for instruction.

President Lasuén lingered several days at San Luis Rey. He supervised the building of two rooms, thirty feet long and fifteen wide, made of poles and branches of trees—the beginning of the Mission. He designated where the Fathers' dwelling should be built, where grain was to be planted, and especially the position of the church.

Fathers Antonio Peyri and José Faura were left to carry on the work. Their tools were pickaxes, crowbars, plowshares. They were given blankets and bolts of cloth to clothe the Indians. The females wore only *tule* aprons, the males nothing save rabbit skins in cold weather.

Father Peyri was at home in *rancherías,* factories, fields, and libraries. Even before he learned the Indian idiom, he rolled up his sleeves and taught the natives how to make bricks, producing 8,000 in six weeks.

Timber for Mission buildings was cut in a pine and fir forest nine leagues distant in the Sierra. Indians carried 175 beams to San Luis Rey and built five rooms 90 feet long.

Three chiefs of neighboring *rancherías* and their wives became converts. Father Peyri gave the Indians prizes to study Spanish, but they quickly tired. Natives liked European music, especially if it was sad like their own plaints. They learned to play easily.

San Luis Rey's registers of baptism, confirmation, marriage and burial have been lost; but government records show that six months after establishing the Mission, Fathers Peyri and Faura had baptized

210 Indians, blessed 34 marriages, and buried 5 persons. The buildings housed 214 neophytes.

San Diego, San Gabriel, San Juan Capistrano, and Santa Barbara sent the new establishment 508 sheep, 310 cattle, 64 horses, and 28 yoke of oxen. At the close of the year the Fathers' rooms were finished and roofed with thatch and earth. Soldiers' quarters, a boys' house, a girls' dwelling, a weaving room, a storeroom, and two other buildings were erected. Roofs were of *tule*. Walls were 27 inches thick. Father Peyri attributed growth at San Luis Rey to the power of his own San Antonio. Father Palóu said Satan would envy the success of the Mission.

Livestock increased rapidly; 2,800 bushels of grain were harvested from 80 sown in 1800. A guardhouse was erected for soldiers, a storeroom for the corporal, and a dwelling for each of the six Mission guards. Half the buildings were roofed with tile. When the nineteenth century began, 337 neophytes had been baptized, and only 56 had died.

Missionaries arrived and departed, but Father Peyri always remained. Chill adobe gave him rheumatism, but he lessened his ailment at the hot baths near San Juan Capistrano and returned to new work. In 1802 he made additions to the church. Now it was 138 feet long, 19 wide, 17 high, with a tile roof. Here 1,000 Indians worshiped; 634 lived in the village. Converts came even from San Juan Capistrano and San Diego. In 1806 the women had a commodious apartment with a courtyard 72 feet long connecting with the grand inner patio of the Mission. Healthy young natives were astir in the court.

Ten years after the foundation, 1,100 Indians lived at the Mission. The church had acquired a new crucifix for the pulpit, a painting of Christ being baptized by Saint John, and a statue of San Luis Rey. Improvements were made even at a remote cattle *rancho,* where an adobe dwelling for cowherds and a large adobe corral were built.

Timber for buildings came from Pala. When San Luis Rey had been twelve years in existence, for the first time the *Rancho de Pala,* the Place of Water, appears in records: the beginning of the *Asistencia* San Antonio de Pala, 20 miles northeast near Mount Palomar in a valley watered by the San Luis Rey River. On this elevation had been planted fruit and olive orchards and a vineyard.

Father Peyri mounted the steep incline at the entry to the Sierra Madre to instruct Indians. One thousand destroyed carved stone gods and accepted baptism. In 1818 the Father completed the chapel of San Antonio de Pala, 140 feet long and 27 wide. Crude statues decorated the altar, and primitive Indian murals were on the walls. Enchanted by new ceremonies and music, in less than two years the neophytes numbered 1,300. They were graceful dancers, swift runners, skilled weavers of sheets and blankets. They also grew cereals, cotton, and vegetables.

Associated with Father Peyri was scholarly Father Gerónimo Boscana, author of the treatise on the god Chinigchinich. In 1811 these two planned the new church at San Luis Rey, the present structure—a cordial, warm building facing southeast. The work was carried out by Antonio Rocha, a Portuguese sailor, who had helped erect Mission Santa Barbara.

In one year adobe walls six and a half feet thick arose cornice-high. The church was 170 feet long and 40 wide. A wing was added to the main row of dwellings the next year, and a corridor built along the front. The church had only one story, but it was 30 feet high, and standing on an elevation, its proud proportions had nobility and grace. Especially impressive was its peristyle with 32 square pillars supporting rounded arches. In an octagonal mortuary chapel dedicated to the Third Order of Saint Francis, women took leave of their dead. Travelers on the mesa-land were grateful to Father Peyri for the candle always kept burning in a small cupola sustained by eight columns. A picturesque outside stairway led to the graceful dome, through which a soft light brightened the sanctuary and nave below.

On October 4, 1815, eight bells in the tower pealed forth the joyous news—San Luis Rey, King of the Missions, was completed.

So efficiently had Father Peyri fought disease that the death rate was the lowest of all California establishments. In the hospital neophytes were treated whose blood had been contaminated by Mexican soldiers. Even this building had a chapel. The Mission population increased to 2,603.

Indians in this vicinity had their own medicine man. Sometimes he took from his mouth pebbles, tiny sticks, bones or hair, pretending that the infirmity was removed. He often danced before the patient, sang and made grimaces. To wounds were applied poultices of *tule* leaves, sage, powder of prickly pear. For bites of poisonous creatures and poisoned arrows they moistened in the mouth a stone similar to chalk called *Xaclul* and applied the spittle to the wound.

In 1814 Fathers Peyri and Suñer reported to the Spanish Government characteristics of Indians in this district where the Tamancus idiom was spoken. When the new moon came, the Indians shouted for joy. They howled and clapped their hands at the eclipse of sun or moon, believing that an animal was trying to eat it.

In order to win at games of chance, the natives fasted several days. The night preceding the game they intoxicated themselves with *Mani,* which is composed of a root of the small *taluache* mixed with water. When they lost, the Indians said it was because their rival fasted and drank more. Every *ranchería* was governed by a leader, Captain Not. Seeds, beads, and deer hides were distributed by him to guests.

Natives worshiped a large young hawk which was presented to the chief at a great feast. After they formed a circle around the hawk, they danced and sang dismally, making strange grimaces while they slowly killed the bird. As soon as it was dead they extinguished the fire, wailed, shouted madly, striking confused blows. Again they started the fire and skinned the bird, singing gently. The feathers were made into a skirt and worn by a boy, who danced during the feast in the center of the circle. The chief kept the skirt for veneration.

The Indians believed they would go down after death to Tolmar, where they were all to be reunited to live happily together.

As early as 1810 California marveled at Father Antonio's San Luis Rey, which harvested 67,116 bushels of grain and had 20,000 cattle. Father Peyri protested when San Diego troops seized the Mission Ranchos Las Flores and Santa Margarita with their fine houses, gardens, and vineyards. *Comandante* Ruiz paid no attention. The missionary appealed to Governor Arrillaga, who in return taxed the establishment $150, a large sum at the time. Although the government owed Father Antonio $1,000, he good-humoredly paid the tax and continued building. Soon granaries and women's buildings were constructed of adobe and roofed with tile.

Mission prosperity was retarded by a drouth in 1820 which killed sheep and caused a clothing shortage. There were 2,600 people at the establishment to be fed and clothed.

Fortune turned, and 1827 saw 65,000 livestock at various Mission *ranchos*. San Luis Rey supplied the San Diego garrison with corn, beans, wheat, *manteca,* soap, blankets, mantles, and shoes.

On June 12, 1827, Auguste Duhaut-Cilly commanding the French vessel *Le Heros*, described San Luis Rey at daybreak: a glittering white palace, its buildings covering more than six acres among gardens and orchards. The wide stairway leading to the orchard recalled the citrus fruit conservatory at Versailles. Two beautiful stucco pools had quaintly carved rock gargoyle heads pouring out water. Here Indians washed linen, the waste water irrigating orchards.

Affable and humorous, Father Antonio served the visitors with chocolate, asking news of the Europe that he never expected to see again. Nearly bald, in his gray habit he moved swiftly about ordering beds to be prepared that the guests might rest till dinner.

In the afternoon travelers watched the cock chase, *la carrera del gallo;* the horseback game, *quattro canti;* and a kind of baseball played by both men and women. Father Antonio decided disputed questions so that all contestants were pleased.

After nightfall by torchlight twelve half-naked Indian men danced, their heads adorned with high tufts of feathers, erect, knees bent a little, bodies inclined forward, beating the earth in time with the music; eyes and arms expressing love, hatred, terror; singing mournful songs that moved the listeners like an Aeolian harp in a tempest. They spat noiselessly into the air, pretending to cast out evil spirits. Father Antonio closed his eyes to their superstitious customs.

Duhaut-Cilly described San Antonio's feast: volleys from the barracks, bonfires in the Plaza, High Mass with music by neophyte singers, playing instruments made at the Mission. From Father Antonio's doorstep the Frenchmen watched a bull worried, teased, and finally returned to the pasture. Two hundred Indian girls in white waists and red serge skirts, their hair floating about their shoulders, begged rings and coins of the Frenchmen, turning somersaults to obtain *reales*. Laughing hilariously, they threw themselves upon the visitors and rummaged in their pockets. Duhaut-Cilly and his friends hurled coins far, and took refuge in Father Antonio's room, barricading the door.

When the travelers departed, Father Antonio provided them with a guide who supplied a lunch of chicken, beef tongue, eggs, bread, and cheese. Duhaut-Cilly also had the "best olives grown in California." Seven years he kept a sample of the wine flavored like Paxaret with the color of *Porto purgato*.

Between 1821 and 1830, Father Antonio was assisted by Doña Apolinaria Lorenzana, a Mexican foundling of 1800 who grew up at the Missions. She taught the women to sew and cared for the sick. She acquired the Ranchos Jamacho and La Cañada de los Coches, but she died a blind centenarian in 1884 at Santa Barbara, as poor as Saint Francis.

When Monterey celebrated the independence of Mexico on April 9, 1822, Father Antonio began signing communications with *Dios y Libertad* instead of *Dios le guarde muchos años*.

After Governor Echeandia in 1826 emancipated from the Missions all Indians qualified to be Mexican citizens in the San Diego, Santa Barbara, and Monterey districts, they refused to work. Harvests at San Luis Rey, however, still excelled those of other Missions. In 1828 this establishment garnered 16,497 bushels of grain; there were 58,765 animals on the ranges. At San Luis Rey 2,736 Indians were living when the order came in 1829 to expel from California all Spaniards under sixty years of age.

Father Antonio was seventy, but he decided to leave the beautiful Mission he had built and at which he had administered nearly 5,000 baptisms. President Durán said that he might go to the College of San Fernando in Mexico City and ask for his passport to Europe.

Father Antonio accepted $3,000 of the $14,000 due from the Mission for his services. He wished to pay the expenses of two Indian youths, Pablo and Agapíto, at the College of Propaganda at Rome. Tears streaming down his cheeks, Father Antonio knelt on the hill and for the last time prayed with his neophytes. He gave his farewell look at the Mission where he had spent thirty-four years.

Five hundred Indians heard that the Father was leaving. Hurriedly they rode to San Diego to intercept and bring him back. They risked their lives swimming toward his ship, the *Pocahontas*, to receive the missionary's blessing as the vessel swung out on the tide.

In Spain Father Antonio found that monasteries had been secularized and the friars driven from the cloisters. Ill health and advanced age kept him from returning to the "abundance of California." In Spain he awaited "until the dove, that is to say, death arrived."

At the College of Propaganda, Rome, Father Antonio's neophytes were registered as Agapitus Amamix and Paul Tac. Agapitus died September 26, 1837, and was buried in the crypt in the monastery church at Rome. Paul survived, an exile from California, only until December 13, 1841. Some say that "the dove" called for Father Antonio at Rome in 1835. His San Luis Rey neophytes said, "No, that *padre* does not die." They placed candles and flowers before his picture, praying for his return.

California best remembers Father Antonio Peyri for the pepper tree, *schinus molle,* which he introduced. Sailors brought pepper seed from Peru in 1830 and planted it at the Mission. Chili pepper they called it, but it proved to be the *schinus molle,* with lacy foliage and rose berries, common in California. Descendants of the San Luis Rey trees beautify the state.

Father Antonio created a Mission valued at $300,000. Each of the Ranchos Pala, Santa Margarita, San Juan, Temecula, San Jacinto, and San Marcos had its own chapel. There were 27,500 cattle. Alone of all California Missions San Luis Rey gained in neophytes and livestock between 1831 and 1834.

Father Antonio Anzar succeeded Father Peyri, and he yielded to Father Vicente Oliva. Soon came Father Buenaventura Fortuni. After secularization, Captain Pablo de la Portilla was made *comisionado.* In emancipating the Indians, he requested soldiers to check disorder arising from the distribution of land. Indians stole horses and mules.

Fields were strewn with the remains of dead cattle killed by natives for hides. Concubinage, gambling, and drunkenness were common.

After San Luis Rey became a parish of the second class on May 3, 1834, *ranchos* were more or less under the control of the local authority. When Inspector William E. P. Hartnell came in 1839 he found Indians making cloth for the feast day of the patron saint. At Pala women wore only *tule* aprons.

When Pio Pico became administrator and major-domo of San Luis Rey, he seized livestock and property for himself. He threatened Indians with stocks and punishment if they did not work briskly. He organized bullfights in the Plaza and often met the infuriated bull in combat. He enjoyed the audience's applauding on the roofs. Father Francisco Ibarra, who came at this time, declared that the Rancho de las Flores was a seraglio for the Pico brothers.

Inspector Hartnell displaced Pio Pico with José Estudillo of San Diego. Pio Pico and his brother Andrés refused to give possession. They yielded only when the government granted them the fertile Rancho Temecula.

Governor Micheltorena reinstated the Franciscans in 1843 and Father José Maria Zalvidéa came. He had planted the great San Gabriel vineyards, but now he mortified his tall strong body with a pointed iron girdle. Frequently he was covered with blood. He gave his stipends for Mass to the Indians, and preached in their idiom. He never offered his hand in salutation to a woman, but before his death, at nearly eighty, he was nursed by Doña Apolinaria Lorenzana. He refused to leave San Luis Rey in 1846. The night before he was to be removed he was found holding a crucifix, his open breviary over his heart, asleep. He was placed on the epistle side of the altar.

After Father Zalvidéa's death, San Luis Rey was attended by priests from San Juan Capistrano. The sacred vessels were scattered. Doña Apolinaria found the chalice in an arroyo. She deposited the marriage and confirmation registers, together with some sculpture and images, at Santa Margarita, the Pico brothers' ranch. The baptismal and burial registers were lost.

Thirty years later the *Libro de Patentes y Ordenes* was discovered by Reverend José Montaner of Saint John's Church, at Milpitas, California, in a bookshop at Barcelona, Spain. For fifteen cents the priest bought the folio that the bookseller had purchased of a stranger for five cents. Most of it had been written by Father Antonio Peyri. Several pages from the baptismal register lay loose in the book. Father Montaner returned the folio to the Mission.

In recent years two similar manuscript volumes were discovered at San Juan Capistrano. They contain lists of Indians belonging to San Luis Rey. The first opens with the year 1798 and includes names of converts down to 1810. The larger volume begins in 1808. The last entry in the baptismal register is No. 7061, and was made forty-six years after the founding of San Luis Rey. Two-fifths of the volume was set apart for Pala neophytes.

After soldiers left San Luis Rey, in 1863 Mrs. John Forster, sister-in-law of Pio Pico, carried all the books she could find to the Santa Margarita Rancho. There they remained until 1883. Two large boxes of books and manuscripts were then brought by Judge Richard Egan of San Juan Capistrano to Father José Mut at the Mission. Employees used the papers for cigarettes. Tourists took what they pleased.

Pio Pico kept a store and liquor shop in the Mission building after the Franciscans left. Indians were found intoxicated by the roadside. After Pico became governor, on May 18, 1846, he sold Mission San Luis Rey, including the Rancho of Pala, to José Cot and José A. Pico for $2,000 in silver and $437.50 in grain. On September 7, 1846, Pico was obliged to flee to Mexico.

Then came the Americans with John Bidwell in charge. Early in 1847 United States troops under Commodore R. F. Stockton halted briefly on their way to San Diego. Soon a Mormon battalion under Daniel Tyler arrived and remained several months. Mormon Elder Tyler preached polygamy in the church.

Another Mormon, Captain James D. Hunter, sub-agent for the Indians, had headquarters at San Luis Rey, raising wheat at Pala. Lieutenant William T. Sherman of the Third Artillery, later General Sherman, ordered him to see that no desecration was done to the church or any of its religious articles.

Decay was rapid at San Luis Rey. In 1852 dams and embankments

of irrigation ditches were overflowed, and the garden was filled with
rushes and weeds, where nested herons and waterfowl. A few hundred Indians lazed about in clothing of the United States soldiers.

American troops protected the Mission, but after they left, timbers and tile were carried away for houses and barns. Much of the
roof fell. The dome sank. The original decorations remained, as did
some of the mural ornamentations over each window, stretching
out to the side and forming a star. On the reredos at the side altar
were also visible distemper ornamentations. Soon lizards, horned
toads, and chickens were the only occupants of the building. Birds
sang on the broken walls. Weeds grew up between the tiles of the
chapel floor. For nearly half a century the King of Missions was
abandoned to winds and wanderers.

Fortunately Doña Isidora Bandini de Couts, who lived at the Guajome Rancho near by, always hoped for the restoration of San Luis
Rey. She took the Stations of the Cross and one of the bells to her
spacious adobe for safekeeping. Doña Isidora's hope began to be
realized when President Lincoln on March 18, 1865, affixed his name
to the title deed and returned the property to the Catholic Church.
The document, signed by Lincoln, is in the museum.

In 1892 two Mexican Franciscans, Commissary-General J. G. Alva
and Father D. Rangel, arrived at San Luis Rey. Their monastery had
been confiscated by the Mexican Government, and they were seeking
a building where young men might be trained for their Order. Bishop
Francis Mora gave them permission to restore the church and erect
a novitiate. The community was also to have charge of the Pala Indians and Spanish-speaking dwellers near the Mission.

Father J. J. O'Keefe acquainted the Fathers with local customs and
language and supervised the restoration. Soon decaying walls were
fortified and the church reroofed. The octagonal mortuary chapel
with its original tile floor was brought back. The old Byzantine pulpit
remained in its original position, sounding board gone. As dilapida-
tion disappeared, the colonnade arches proudly stood forth. The interesting façade again appeared with its extension walls to the right
of the main building, its niches for statues, its imposing pilasters
supporting the cornice of the pediment of the semi-circular door-

way arch, and its octagonal tower with four greater and lesser sides, where hung three bells.

Several illuminated chant books of early days used by neophytes were returned. The copper baptismal font, which had been sold to serve base purposes, was found. The original foundation Cross was brought back. Once more in place were the Stations of the Cross long guarded by Doña Isidora Bandini de Couts. San Luis Rey again seemed King of the Missions.

Three hundred assembled for the rededication of the building at ten o'clock on May 12, 1893. Four wrinkled old Indian women, crouching in the doorway, relived their youth as Commissary-General Alva and the community habited in gray received Bishop Francis Mora, Vicar-General Joaquin Adam, Father Luis J. Meier, and Father W. L. Dye. The Vicar-General celebrated Mass.

In August, 1912, Father O'Keefe retired to Santa Barbara, and Father Peter Wallischeck continued the work of restoration. Father Dominic Gallardo and Father Ferdinand Ortiz brought to light murals on the church walls. Old confessionals long sealed in the rear side walls of the nave were also discovered by Father Ferdinand. In the abandoned garden across from the Mission he uncovered the ancient wash fountains with carved rock gargoyle heads described by Duhaut-Cilly.

During the past two years restoration of the original canopy over the main altar has been made. The site of the military barracks has been excavated, revealing walls, tile, and partitions.

In the beginning San Luis Rey had an octet of bells. The oldest known bell, dating nine years prior to foundation, was preserved by Doña Isidora Couts. It is inscribed: s. SAN JUAN. 1790. She gave it to Father Ubach for the Sisters' school of St. Joseph at San Diego. Another bell was obtained by the school and the San Luis Rey *campana* was consigned to the attic. When the Sisters' school building was wrecked by the Whiting Mead Company, Doña Isidora's bell was hung in the domed entrance hall of the Los Angeles residence of William Mead.

Disaster came to San Luis Rey on July 22, 1926, when the tower crashed, hurling to earth bells that had sounded for a century. The

Indians took two bells to Pala, where they still swing from syca-
more beams in the *campanario*. The larger bell hanging in the lower
story of the tower bears an upper and lower inscription: STUS DS STUS
FTIS IMMORTILIS MICERERE NOBIS ANO DE 1816 J. R. (HOLY FATHER,
HOLY, MOST MIGHTY ONE. PITY US. YEAR OF 1816 JESUS REDEMP-
TOR.) N. P. S. SAN FRANCISCO DE ASIS. SAN LUYS REY. STA CLARA.
EULALIA NTRA LUZ CERVANTES NOS FECIT. (OUR PATRON SAINT,
SAINT FRANCIS OF ASSISI. SAINT LOUIS THE KING. SAINT CLAIRE.
EULALIA OUR LIGHT. CERVANTES MADE US.) The upper bell, smaller
in size, is inscribed: SANCTA MARIA ORA PRO NOBIS. (HOLY MARY
PRAY FOR US.) Three of the old broken San Luis Rey bells were
recast into one of the bells in the tower, lettered: SAN LUIS REY
RECAST 1901 STANDARD IRON WORKS SAN DIEGO. The last of the
octet of bells at San Luis Rey is small and of crude Mexican make
weighing about 125 pounds, with the inscription: S. ANTONIO 1808
AVE MARIA. What became of the remaining bells is unknown, but
there is the usual legend of buried bells.

Pala has shared the stormy life of this Mission. In 1871 white men
were there selling Indian girls. Twenty years later the *asistencia* was
bought by blacksmith Viele, who was also a rancher and had a general store in the building. At first he locked the church, but he later
returned chapel bells and cemetery to the Catholic Church.

Soon vestments were taken away, altar images were broken. One
statue, however, San Luis, brought from the Mission for preservation,
was still venerated. At annual reunions Indians carried the figure,
decorated, at the head of the procession.

Disease killed the natives, who crowded into adobe rooms near
the *asistencia*. White people came only to buy blankets. When Franciscans took charge of San Luis Rey in 1892, Pala's hopes revived.

In December, 1901, the Los Angeles Landmarks Club visited
the *asistencia*, still poetic under ferny pepper trees, and asked to put
the building in order. Nine poles for rafters were hauled from the
slopes of Mount Palomar. Tiles were purchased from distant ranches
whither they had been taken from San Luis Rey. Two women of
the Agua Tibia Rancho donated 800 tiles. Priests' rooms and the
sacristy were re-roofed.

Worshipers greatly increased when in 1903 the United States Government bought in this vicinity 3,438 acres of land and united the Pala, Pauma, Rincon, and Warner's Ranch Reservations. The natives swept the Plaza, built *enramadas* of boughs, erected altars, and on Corpus Christi Day made a picturesque procession with banners and candles. When a priest came, they crowded the church.

Unique among California Mission buildings is Pala's *campanario*, the only detached bell tower among the Missions. It recalls the *campanario* at San Elizario near El Paso, and the one of Mission Guadalupe at Juarez. Apparently it was designed by the builder of San Luis Rey and Santa Barbara. Two stories high, it stands in the cemetery on a pyramidal base of adobe and boulders, each story pierced by a bell aperture. Doubtless it was built at a distance from the church to protect the main structure should the bells fall during an earthquake.

After standing a century, the *campanario* in 1916 plunged to the earth. Father George D. Doyle, resident pastor at that time, rebuilt the bell tower on the original site on a substantial concrete base, so far as possible using old material, even the cobblestone foundation. The same glistening Cross crowned its top, and growing from an aperture was the same cactus at the foot of the Cross, originally planted by a bird.

After restoring the *campanario*, Father Doyle asked friends of Missions to save the chapel. The original floor tiles were taken up, the ground was leveled, and the tiles reset. From Warner's Ranch the Indians brought their old altar. Whitewash was removed from the walls of the interior, and murals were retouched by a Franciscan Brother. Indian women made drawn work for the altar. Once more the ancient candlesticks were in place. Coppery hands filled vases with flowers; Margarita, the basket maker, made the altar her devotion. Indians fashioned an interesting statue of olivewood. In gratitude for restored health, a native woman brought a carved figure of Jesus and Saint Joseph.

At Pala are still visible ruins of workshops, granaries, and corrals. About two hundred and fifty Indians live here in adobe houses and frame huts raising peppers, corn, and watermelons. They hold fairs and *fiestas* in brush houses.

For many years an Indian school was maintained here, but now young people go to the Bonsall Grammar School, Fallbrook High School, and even to Sherman to finish their education.

Father Julian Girardot, a Franciscan from San Luis Rey, comes once a week to celebrate Mass, goes to Pechenga, and then to Pauma, Rincon, La Jolla, and Warner's Hot Springs.

Metropolitan magnificence of a few years ago dazzled Father Antonio Peyri's simple Pala. Frank Simons, who with his wife kept a trading post in one corner of the *asistencia,* was prospecting in the hills. One mile to the left of Pala he saw glistening dirt on a little mound thrown up by ants. "Gold!" he cried.

It was something rarer, the sacred jewels of the Indian god Chinigchinich. Rubbed on the legs, these stones were thought to impart swiftness. One of the jewels was stolen by a native woman. Ravens flew around her house causing her to sicken; she had offended mighty Chinigchinich. After she carried the jewel back and buried it in the sand, it was said that the gratified god restored her health. These sacred jewels were christened kunzite for the geologist, Dr. George F. Kunz.

Tiffany of New York reached into Pala and gained control of the land. Frank Simons' pretty black-eyed widow, who still operates the trading post, has a vault filled with kunzite and tourmaline, arrows of the great god Chinigchinich.

Rarer than sacred jewels is Queen Isabella's Madonna at the Guajome Ranch, owned by Cave J. Couts, who was born in the adobe house where he lives. His father, Lieutenant Cave J. Couts who came with Graham's battalion in 1850 to the Mission, married Doña Isidora Bandini of San Diego. She and her sisters, Doña Josefa Carrillo and Doña Arcadia Stearns, made from their own gowns the American flag raised over San Diego in 1846.

In 1854 the Couts came to this adobe ranch house and it became the social center of Southern California. Here Helen Hunt Jackson gathered some of her material for *Ramona;* and Peter B. Kyne at this house prepared the *Pride of Palomar.* The novel was filmed in the patio. Cave J. Couts, Jr., in the last decade built a chapel near his dwelling and dedicated it to his mother. It houses his treasure: a Madonna painted on wood, brought by his grandfather, Don Juan Bandini, from Peru in 1800. Queen Isabella gave the Madonna to Columbus when he set out on his painted galleon in 1492. From Columbus it came to the princely Bandini family.

For the descendants of neophytes in the vicinity of San Luis Rey and San Antonio de Pala, there is still greater treasure than royal gifts and jeweled mountains. It is the *Pater Noster* taught them by Father Antonio Peyri in their own language:

Niawup tat mai apsu mabo etchmak misihche niama atchipoi koi pai ichihua nia pahicha mulpihi mai. Mihattle nia koshur sauo niniuk ni apsiou pakiennak epohu nieumok meumakle manatle omaho atlich kaumok. Piapehe.

XIX

Santa Inés

SANTA BARBARA COUNTY is blessed with Missions, the only one to have three. Last to be founded was Santa Inés. Simple and pleasing, it is little marred with restoration. It retains something of the innocence of Saint Agnes, who is shown with a lamb in her arms and presides over the Mission. On Saint Agnes Eve, January 20-21, country girls appeal to the saint to reveal their future husbands.

In the last days of Mission founding, wild Tulareños between San Luis Obispo de Tolosa and Santa Barbara dominated the land, menacing settlers. "They must be Christianized," said the Fathers.

Governor Diego Borica followed the counsel and gave the name Santa Inés to the projected Mission. Even in 1795 explorations had been made to find a suitable site. President Fermin Lasuén suggested that the new establishment be placed near the junction of three Passes: San Carlos, El Refugio, and Gaviota. The place was called Alajulapu and was among thirteen *rancherías* in the territory of the warring Chumash tribe. In English the name means corner.

North from Santa Barbara, President Estévan Tápis, Lieutenant-*Comandante* Raimundo Carrillo, Sergeant Felipe de Goycoechea, nine leather-jacket soldiers, and some natives wound in and out among the foothills on the trail trod by Portolá and Serra. On the way neophytes from La Purísima joined the company. At the Ranchería Teguep President Tápis paused to baptize a sick woman. The company lingered at Calahuasa, a *ranchería* of thirty huts.

They marveled at Nojoqui Falls, showering the mossy mountainside with liquid silver. To natives the falls were sacred. Once, when the sun had burned the valley brown and for lack of food animals had fled, Indians went into the canyon depths to placate the Great Spirit.

Legend said a white-clad form led them to the shimmering mountainside. The drouth was broken. Each year thereafter Indians made offerings to the shining spray, in gratitude to the unknown for having saved their ancestors when rains failed.

From the Nojoqui Falls missionaries and soldiers passed on to the sycamore-lined Santa Rosa River, filled with trout—the stream now called Santa Inés. Near by, on a wooded elevation partly enclosed by the oak-covered mountains of San Rafael and Santa Inés, President Tápis and the *comandante* decided to build the nineteenth Mission, last in the south.

In mid-morning, September 17, 1804, a brush *enramada* was prepared. President Tápis blessed the water and the ground, and erected a large Cross. Later he celebrated Mass, assisted by Fathers Marcelino Ciprés of San Luis Obispo, José Antonio Calzada, and José Romualdo Gutiérrez. Later the President preached.

Because the new establishment was among the ferocious Chumash tribe, a larger guard than was usually assigned to protect a Mission was sent to Santa Inés: nine soldiers and a sergeant. Fathers Calzada and Gutiérrez were given charge of the new station.

Twenty-seven native children were baptized the first day. Three chieftains came. At the end of the first year the Mission had 225 neophyte residents. Half of them already had been baptized at neighboring establishments.

The Chumash Indians, who worshiped their god Achup or Chaupa, held three northern islands in Santa Barbara Channel, but their territory extended inland to the Tulare country. Timber for their twenty-five-foot canoes was obtained on remote mountaintops. Spacious Chumash dwellings often had fifty occupants.

The Chumash were California's first moneylenders. Clam shells made into beads were their coins. Vancouver presented to the British Museum their basketry of distinguished coloring, brilliant feather blankets, hot water bottles, flat-bottomed with asphalt lining applied with hot pebbles. Their crude paintings of animals and the sun have been found in caves and on cliffs, but the date of this art is undetermined.

From older Missions neophytes came to Santa Inés to teach the

Chumash converts to make adobe brick. Mountains forty-five miles distant supplied rafter timbers: pine, oak, and sycamore. Nails were scarce, and rafters and beams were bound together with rawhide strips. Sea shells supplied lime. Walls and roofs were protected with a gluey preparation of prickly cactus plant soaked in water, giving a smooth, whitewashed appearance.

At the end of the first year the Fathers had completed a wing of the new Mission, 232 feet long and 19 wide. A granary almost as large was erected. The church with a sacristy was 100 feet long, and had a small house for the Fathers. In 1805 a wing was added with a tile roof 145 feet long. A third wing was erected in 1806, 365 feet long, 19 wide, with a corridor extending 75 feet. The church, the *padres'* quarters, the *sala*, the convent for unmarried women and girls, storerooms, offices, workshops, stable and barns, nearly completed the quadrangle. A pathway led 200 feet from the patio to Indian huts forming a compact village.

Water was flumed underground from the mountains by cement pipe, some of which is still used by ranchers. A large tannery made of huge river boulders covered with cement stood directly in front of the Mission at the end of the orchard, now a wheat field to the right of the church.

On the morning of December 21, 1812, two violent earthquake shocks cracked the walls, bringing down the roof and a corner of the church. Many Indian huts were destroyed.

Father Calzada, in spite of frayed nerves, began rebuilding, aided by neophytes. Meanwhile services were held in a granary. On the foundation of the old, the Fathers began a new church 140 feet long, 27 wide, with a large vestibule on the right. Bricks strengthened the adobe wall and paved the church. The building, ceiled with painted wood and roofed with tile, was dedicated July 4, 1817.

Before the new church was completed, paralysis struck down Father Calzada, December 23, 1814. The first American Franciscan friar to serve in California, he was interred on the gospel side of the church he had begun. He was born in Cuba in 1760; he received the habit at Havana.

Santa Inés had eight deep, arched windows placed high—protection against Tulare attacks. In the beginning there was an adobe altar built out from the wall. Natives painted frames for the Stations of the Cross. Archways over the choir were also painted by them on canvas, ingeniously stretched over a wooden frame and bound with leather strips. The entire interior was decorated in red, yellow, brown, and black; but unfortunately all walls outside the sanctuary and sacristy have been whitewashed.

The church belfry with three openings somewhat resembled the vanished belfry at San Gabriel, and was similar to the one of the Santuario de Guadalupe, Guadalajara, Mexico. The top aperture held a bell inscribed: ANO DE 1804 S. S. JUAN BAUPTISTA. (YEAR OF 1804. SAINT JOHN BAPTIST.) An unlettered bell has since been taken to a dwelling near the Mission. The third of the trio had the inscription: AVE MARIA PURISIMA 1807. It bore a crown-top with the double cross in ornamentation. Probably this bell was a gift of the Bishop of Sonora. The smallest bell had the lettering: M. V. LIMA 1817. (MANUEL VARGAS. LIMA 1817.) The two bells at Santa Inés that once belonged to La Purísima Mission, now hang in the lower story of the tower. They were brought here for safekeeping. One is lettered: MANUEL VARGAS ME FECIT ANO E 1818 MISION DE LA PURISIMA DE LA NUEBA CALIFORNIA. (MANUEL VARGAS MADE ME. YEAR OF 1818 MISSION OF PURISIMA OF NEW CALIFORNIA.) The other bell has the inscription: MANUEL VARGAS ME FECIT ANO E 1818. The only bell in daily use was purchased by Father Alexander Buckler in 1912 and is inscribed: HY. STUCKSTEDE BELL FOUNDRY COMPANY ST. LOUIS, MO. 1912 SAINT AGNES.

Santa Inés' great festival was January 21, the *Dia de Santa Inés*, feast day of the saint, with horse racing and bullfights in the square back of the Indian village. On Holy Saturday, *Sabado de Gloria*, an image of Judas, made of *malva*, wild hollyhock, was tied to the saddle of a wild bronco, causing the horse to rear and caper. The effigy was taken down and burned. On these days the Indian orchestra played: Rafael, the flute; Miguel, the tambour; Felipe, the horn; Benanjio, the triangle.

Music was never gayer, nor did bells peal more merrily than on November 5, 1822, when "Pirate Joe" Chapman took as his bride, at the Mission, Doña María Guadalupe Ortega, with Father Antonio Rodríguez officiating. The reformed pirate of Bouchard's band was baptized José Juan after he won the heart of the descendant of Ortega, discoverer of San Francisco Bay. She first saw him when he was about to be dragged to death at a horse's heels by an Indian, and she saved his life. Governor Solá granted him amnesty for entering California as a pirate, and the Boston buccaneer became a California citizen. He helped build the Plaza Church at Los Angeles and the old gristmill at Santa Inés. Father Sanchez of San Gabriel declared it "a marvel that any one so long in the darkness of the Baptist faith could give such an example of true Catholic piety to older Christians." When Pirate Joe died about 1849, he left a *rancho* of 5,000 acres near Los Angeles.

Jovial Francisco Xavier de la Concepción Uría ably served Santa Inés for sixteen years, and was well liked in spite of his quick temper. During his administration neophytes rose in revolt because the military guard inflicted petty injustices and cruelties. Neophytes had not minded when they saw soldiers dashing about in fine saddles made by them without payment; but when one of the Purísima neophytes was unjustly flogged at Santa Inés, rebellion blazed.

Even in the far Tulare country, Pasquala, an Indian girl, heard that all Christians were to be killed. Often she had stopped with her kinsfolk at the Mission on their annual journey to the coast for shells and fish. Once while at the Mission she fell ill but was cured. Pasquala and her family were so grateful that they became Christians. Her father was working in the vineyard when pagans killed him and carried the girl and her mother back to the Tulares. The mother died. When in 1824 Pasquala heard that the Tulareños were about to attack her beloved Mission, she took a little dried vension and acorn-meal and ran wildly praying to reach Santa Inés. Over the mountains she stumbled, staggering into the Mission.

"*Padre!* War! War!"

Father Uría had been a soldier before he became a missionary. He helped the military guard improvise a fortress and erect cannon.

The rebels set fire to the *padres'* quarters. Wounded Francisco Bermuda carried the war alarm to Santa Barbara. Sergeant Anastasio

Carrillo and his soldiers hastened to Santa Inés and put out the fire in the sacristy.

After saving the Mission, Pasquala died at Santa Inés from exertion caused by running to warn the *padres.* Despite the rule that no Indian may be buried in the church, Father Uría wished to have her placed within its walls.

After the revolt Father Uría departed for Soledad, where little that was exciting transpired, but he had peace. Don William Domingo Foxen, a picturesque Anglo-Californian, took up his residence at the Mission and helped repair the damage caused by the revolt. He married Eduarda Osuna of Santa Barbara, and acquired two leagues of the Tinaquaic Rancho. In 1846 he guided Captain John C. Frémont and his forces over the horse trail of San Marcos Pass. With his aid the Americans eluded Spanish-Californians awaiting them Christmas morning in an ambush at Gaviota Pass.

Several *ranchos* were acquired by the Mission: Alamo Pintado, Alisal, Cañada de los Pinos, San Carlos de Jonata, Corral de Quati, Dos Pueblos, Los Prietos y Najalayegua, Marcelino, Tequepis, La Zaca, San Marcos, Nojogui, Tajiguas, San Lucas, and Las Lomas de la Purificación. The land extended from seven to nine leagues north to south, and from five to thirteen leagues east to west. Large crops of wheat, corn, and barley were raised, and in 1810 six tons of hemp were shipped to Mexico. There was an orchard of 987 fruit trees. At one time in the 1820's the Mission had 12,368 livestock, and accumulated stores of tallow, hides, and wool. Between 1822 and 1827 Santa Barbara Presidio was furnished with supplies valued at $10,767, for which nothing was received.

When 1831 came, only 456 persons were living at the Mission, but there had been 1,372 baptisms. Santa Inés was called Little Santa Barbara.

In the summer of 1836 the Mission story altered: Governor Mariano Chico came, and—was it the Governor's wife? No, Señora Chico was in Mexico. Señora Cruz companioned the Governor. His Excellency was a poet, but Father José Joaquin Jimeno felt that the Governor had taken more than a poet's license. The Padre's hospitality was arctic.

The indignant Governor reported the slight to President Durán. His Excellency was told that since secularization the Governor had no claim on Mission hospitality. Governor Chico carried the matter to the Assembly at Monterey. President Durán and Father Jimeno were rebuked. Straightway Santa Inés was secularized.

Church buildings were appraised at only $4,945, but furniture was valued at $14,527. Ornaments and sacred vessels were set down at $6,251. The library had 166 volumes. Mission and possessions were valued at $59,169.

Don José Ramirez was appointed *Comisionado*, soon to be succeeded by Don Francisco Cota, followed by Don Ramón Malo. Mission lands rapidly depreciated in value. Santa Inés in 1839 had only 315 neophytes.

Scholarly Father Felipe Arroyo de la Cuesta chose to end his days here. Although afflicted with rheumatism, for four years he had himself wheeled about in a chair surrounded by and teaching Indian children. On September 20, 1840, he was buried on the gospel side of the altar.

Four years later President Durán reported that Santa Inés had 215 half-clothed neophytes. As general servants, they received less than a dollar a month; but even missionaries were paid only $7.

Despite lean remuneration, Bishop García Diego determined to build near the Mission California's first ecclesiastical seminary—*El Colegio Seminario de María Santísima de Guadalupe de Santa Inés de Californias*. Governor José Micheltorena granted land within the boundaries of Santa Inés upon which to establish the new seminary: *La Cañada de los Pinos*, four *cañadas* embracing 35,499 acres—the College Rancho. Besides land, the Governor promised the seminary $500 annually on condition that any Californian seeking higher education might be admitted. The Bishop asked contributions for the seminary. Wealthy parents were expected to pay $150 a year for a boy's education.

At seven A.M. on May 4, 1844, the founders assembled in the church. Pontifical Mass was celebrated in honor of Our Lady of Refuge, to whom the college was to be dedicated. Present were: Bishop García Diego, Fathers José and Antonio Jimeno, Francisco

Sanchez, sub-Deacon Doratéo Ambrís, and Father Gómez of San Luis Obispo. In the crowded church Father González Rúbio drew up the constitution of the new college. The first buildings were in the rear of the Mission. Later was erected a college building called San Isídro. Father José Joaquin Jimeno was rector and Father Francisco Sanchez vice-rector. When the Bishop came, seminarians wore a brown mantle and a red sash bordered in yellow silk on a green and black background, with the image of Guadalupe in the center on white satin. Black trousers and jacket were their street costume.

There were thirty-three students at the seminary in 1845. No woman was permitted to enter. A porter took packages from women at the door. Punishment of collegians was somewhat severe. They might be isolated in a room for a month. If they did not improve, their parents were notified.

Soon the Bishop opened a boys' primary school with tuition and board at $150. Indians might be admitted. Father Francisco González woke the boys at four in the morning to swim in the reservoir. For recreation they walked to the seminary for grapes, fished, and learned to shoot with bows and arrows.

The seminary had a precarious existence. In 1848 only $58 in tuition was received; $96 came as gifts, $25 from Americans. Sale of livestock brought $667. The Bishop donated $250; the rector $239; the vice-rector $300. Expenditures were $211 more than receipts.

On April 20, 1850, Franciscans abandoned Mission Santa Inés. Fathers José Joaquin Jimeno and Francisco Sanchez were last to leave for Santa Barbara. Mission and seminary were turned over to the Picpus Fathers.

Thirty years the College of Santa Inés struggled. In the 'sixties the Christian Brothers had charge, Brother Pascual Doran being Superior. About 1883 the college was given up. A few ruins halfway between Mission Santa Inés and the village of Santa Inés, on the road to Rancho Juan y Lolita, mark where California's first ecclesiastical seminary stood.

José Maria Covarrubias and Joaquin Carrillo in 1845 rented Santa Inés for nine years at $580 annually. On June 15, the following year, they bought the Mission and its land for $7,000. The United States Government repudiated the transaction. President Lincoln on May 23, 1862, signed the patent giving Mission Santa Inés to the Catholic Church.

When the Picpus Fathers came from the Sandwich Islands, Father Eugene O'Connell, later Bishop of Marysville, took charge, modernizing the windows and doors. He laid the first asphalt floor in the county, a pit on the Buell Ranch supplying material. Father O'Connell was succeeded by Father Honoratus Lempfrid of the Oblate Society. The secular clergy, who made Santa Inés their headquarters, also ministered La Purísima.

Mass was celebrated only once a month at Santa Inés. Rafael Vasquez, an old Indian, sometimes said prayers, while Indian women squatted around the side altar. He assisted at monthly Mass and took charge of vestments, but would not allow the garments to be touched. In 1882 the Donohue family came to live at the Mission and kept house for Father Michael Lynch, who moved here from the college. Since his time Santa Inés has had a resident priest.

With the coming of Father Alexander Buckler, an Alsatian, the Mission in 1904 entered upon a new era. When he arrived, the south end rooms were being used as a blacksmith shop. Chickens and domestic animals were housed in the *sala* where Governors and high churchmen had been entertained. The Bryan family occupied one of the buildings and refused to move.

Father Buckler appropriated a room for himself and cooked out-of-doors. He intended to remain only a few weeks. In a few months the Bryans departed. Father Buckler remained twenty years. He gave lodgings, a meal, and wine to wanderers. They attended Mass, and frequently lingered for months to aid him in repairing and rearranging Mission rooms, or to hoe and weed the garden. These homeless men were frequently called by the valley folk "Padre Alejandro's tramps," but they aided in bringing order out of confusion.

Father Buckler's niece, Miss Mamie Goulet, kept house for him, assembled vestments, repaired them, and removed dust and grime from paintings and altar vessels. Santa Inés acquired the welcoming atmosphere of a Spanish-Californian *hacienda*.

Father Buckler had a picturesque assistant, old Fernando, a Peruvian Indian, bell ringer, altar boy, sometimes serving as an entire choir. Frequently he was aided by the younger Fernandito or Margarita Bernal, who sang to the music of horse fiddles. When old Fernando's calloused hands no longer had strength to ring the bells, Father Buckler sent him to Santa Barbara, where he died in 1920.

In 1911 a storm destroyed the greater part of the bell tower leaving only a section of the wall nearest the church. Bishop Thomas J. Conaty and Knights of Columbus rebuilt the tower. It is similar to the original, the lower arches having three apertures instead of two. The side and corner buttresses are reinforced with concrete. The church walls also were hollowed out from the base to the rock foundation beneath and filled with concrete. The entire church was covered with waterproof lime and roofed with sheeting and tile. A pumping plant was installed to drain water from the buildings. The reservoir in front of the church was roofed. After Father Buckler's energy was spent, he went to Santa Barbara and there died on March 7, 1930.

Nearly a century ago the Mission orchard ceased to exist. The fountain and mill long remained. One of the nine pillars of the corridor stands in proud isolation on its brick buttress apart from the Mission. In the front cloister are ten of the original arches, and in the colonnade formed by them are three of the old benches. In the back cloister are nine arches, one of which is Gothic. The others are rounded Roman arches, no two having the same measurements. Indian-made bricks form the floor in nave, sanctuary, and sacristy. Some of the best Mission specimens of butterfly hinges are on the sacristy and choir doors, together with old locks. On the walls are Stations of the Cross brought from Santa Barbara rolled up in saddlebags. An interesting statue is that of Saint Agnes over the altar, carved by an Indian after a painting in the museum. Natives are supposed to have done two other paintings showing the martyrdom of Saint Agnes. Saint Francis of Assisi appears in another painting considered original.

Several wooden candlesticks were made by Indians. Others from Mexico have been gilded, silvered, or bronzed. Carved wooden stat-

ues of Saint John the Baptist and a small wooden figure of Our Lady
of Sorrows are in the church. It is said that the Infant held by Saint
Anthony was taken away years ago by a young couple who put another in its place. Saint Anthony's Infant was supposed to bring
good fortune. Saddles inlaid with silver, made by Indians, are in the
museum. There is also a choice collection of old music bound in
leather covers with rawhide thongs, probably written by President
Estévan Tápis. The black, yellow, and white notes are his. Indian
instruments remain: a small harmonium with rosewood cover, portions
of an organ, and two old 'cellos. There is interesting silver-
work: an incense bowl and spoon; a baptismal oil stock and a monstrance; two chalices, both hammered, one of silver and one of gold;
a processional Cross beautifully chased with a figure of Christ on
one side and His Mother on the other. Much admired is a hand-
hammered baptismal bowl made of a composition of copper, brass,
and zinc, and some altar bread-covers and a host press. A heart-
shaped bullet mold and cannon used in the revolt of 1824 recall the
Purísima uprising.

The famous yellow silk umbrella belonging to Father Urbano of
San Diego is in the museum. The missionary sent an Indian to fetch
it from a trading ship. Fascinated by the novel object, the native
carried it to his *ranchería*. The Father found him kneeling before
the umbrella. For many years it was used by the missionary.

Santa Inés has a large collection of vestments, some made by nuns
from brocade garments of Spanish court ladies. New vestments were
held by the older Missions, and those worn were given away. Santa
Inés, among the last Missions founded, had the oldest vestments,
gifts from Missions in Baja California and Mexico. Vestments from
La Purísima are guarded here to protect them against vandals.

At Santa Inés the adventure of uncovering the past still excites.
In recent time a pewter set for holy oils and a leather case from
Mexico were found in the neglected sacristy. In a Mission outhouse
there was discovered in 1934 a large painting of the Nativity several
hundred years old, declared the work of Murillo.

Franciscans returned to slumbering Santa Inés on November 23,
1924. Father Albert Bibby was given charge of the Mission by

Bishop John J. Cantwell of Los Angeles and San Diego. Fresh from Ireland, Father Bibby, a Capuchin Franciscan, planned to restore the Mission; but within three months he was buried in the shadow of the *campanario*.

Father Casimir Butler installed a graceful fountain and planted the enclosed garden—heliotrope, geraniums, plumbago, and roses rioting among orange trees.

Each May since 1930 Santa Barbara's picturesque *Rancheros Visitadores*, a group of men in costumes of fifty years ago, riding horses, or in old stagecoaches, have gone from ranch to ranch for three days living mostly out-of-doors. The members of this company have done much to keep alive Spanish days. Among its members are: John J. Mitchell, Thomas Storke, Samuel Stanwood, Dwight Murphy, Wilson Dibblee, Max Fleischmann, Edgar Stow, Joel Fithian, and Reginald Fernald.

Santa Inés has its festivals. Occasionally descendants of neophytes come from the Indian Reservation near the *Zanja*. In 1934 Chiquito Solario appeared. Arrayed in the costume of his ancestors, he delighted the audience with forgotten Indian dances.

When natives in the Valley of the Rising Sun go to rest, they wish to be buried in sacred ground where a high white Cross extends its arms blessing their thousands of tribe-folk. On All Souls Day, the City of the Dead is lighted with candles. When the wind whistles down from Refugio's oaken heights, they say it does not extinguish the candle of the earth-home of Pasquala, who surrendered her life to save the Mission of Saint Agnes.

XX

San Rafael, Arcángel

THE date was April 6, 1937. The scene was the Sir Francis Drake Hotel, San Francisco. The occasion was the monthly luncheon of the California Historical Society. Important revelations were to be made, members knew.

Trembling with excitement, Dr. Herbert E. Bolton, notable author and head of the History Department at the University of California, rose. Before the audience he held a crude, battered, rectangular brass plate eight inches by five. Ever since Americans came to California they had been seeking this plate. In every detail it tallied with its description written three and a half centuries before by Drake's chaplain, Francis Fletcher.

In a "conuenient and fit harborough" the brass plaque had been nailed to a post. It bore the Queen's name, the date of Drake's arrival, the giving of the province and people to Elizabeth. Her picture and arms on a sixpence of English money were placed under the plate and Drake's name. The coin was missing from the Bolton plate, but the Historical Society read:

BEE IT KNOWNE VNTO ALL MEN BY THESE PRESENTS

IVNE 17 1579

BY THE GRACE OF GOD AND IN THE NAME OF HERR
MAIETY QVEEN ELIZABETH OF ENGLAND AND HERR
SVCCESSORS FOREVER I TAKE POSSESSION OF THIS
KINGDOME WHOSE KING AND PEOPLE FREELY RESIGNE
THEIR RIGHT AND TITTLE IN THE WHOLE LAND VNTO
HERR MAIESTIES KEEPEING NOW NAMED BY ME AN TO
BEE KNOWNE VNTO ALL MEN AS NOVA ALBION.

FRANCIS DRAKE

Dr. Bolton explained how the archaeological treasure, lost more than three hundred and fifty years, had been found within two miles of vanished Mission San Rafael. Apparently it had been undiscovered while seven flags had flown over California. Portolá had come leading the first overland expedition from Mexico: Anza and Serra. Mission Dolores and the San Francisco Presidio had been built. San Rafael's Mission had risen and fallen. At last, in the summer of 1936, accidentally an excursionist, Beryle Shinn of Oakland, had found the plate a mile and a half west-northwest of San Quentin. He came upon it near an outcropping of rocks on a high ridge and picked it up to repair his automobile, about 500 feet from the water's edge. It lay in his tool box several months. At first, he did not notice the lettering. When he wished to use it, he observed the name *Drake*.

Suddenly realizing that the plaque might have value, Shinn took it to Dr. Bolton. The historian deciphered the crudely lettered Old English, carved perhaps with a cold chisel, words unevenly spaced, indentations packed with hard dirt. The phrasing was authentic. A sea captain said the plate might have been cut out of the brass track of a gun-carriage. In one corner of the plaque was a hole for displaying a sixpence bearing Elizabeth's picture. A sixpence fitted the aperture. After testing the plate for two months, Dr. Bolton made the revelation.

Formerly it had been believed that Drake's Bay north of San Francisco was where Francis Drake remained thirty-six days reconditioning his ship, weakened by barnacles on his circumnavigation of the globe. On June 25, 1916, the Sir Francis Drake Association marked a rocky eminence near Point de los Reyes with a plaque. The Bolton plate indicates that Greenbrae, Marin County, California, was the first English camp on the Western Hemisphere. By six years it antedates the Roanoke settlement of Sir Walter Raleigh. There is a possibility that the plaque was brought from Drake's Bay to Marin County by a traveler.

Drake's chaplain, Fletcher, described California. The natives lived in huts by the waterside with a fire in the center of each shack.

Men were nudists sleeping on bulrushes. Women wore deerskins over the shoulder and bulrushes around the waist.

In order to awe the natives, Francis Drake and Francis Fletcher held divine services in one of the tents, California's first revival meeting. The Indians begged the white strangers to continue singing and playing the four violins. Native women were so moved that they shrieked, tore their flesh with nails, and dashed their bodies upon hard stones and thorny bushes. "Prayer Book Cross," donated by George W. Childs of Philadelphia and unveiled January 1, 1894, stands on an elevation commanding a view of the Golden Gate and the Bay of San Francisco to commemorate the event.

Before Drake appeared a numerous company: from them hung chains of bones and two crowns made of colored feathers. The scepter-bearer led. After him came the majestic king, surrounded by tall men escorted by common people painted in many colors. Even children bore gifts.

The king and all his people sang and danced. Removing his feathered crown, the chieftain placed it upon Drake's head, calling him the *Great Hióh*. Drake accepted it in the name of Elizabeth, the Queen. The Indians called the Englishmen "envoys of the Great Spirit."

Drake traveled into the interior exploring New Albion. When he returned to England, he presented Elizabeth not only with millions in loot from South America but the crown of California.

Theoginas, an aged Indian neophyte at Mission San Rafael, declared a century and a half later that Drake presented his tribesmen with a dog, some pigs, biscuits, and seeds of several species of grain. The Indians planted the biscuits, expecting them to grow. Pioneers believed that the Nicassias Indians—commonly called Nicasio—of the Miwok division of aborigines, owed their superiority to a blend of English blood.

After Drake no foreigners came to the country of Tamal, lazing across the Bay of San Francisco, until 1775, when daring young Lieutenant Juan Bautista de Ayala, about August 1, sailed through the Golden Gate—Indians called it the Strait of Yulupa, Sunset

Strait—to explore the Bay of San Francisco. The lieutenant waited forty days for the land expedition, but Anza and his company did not arrive. After exploring San Francisco Bay, Ayala returned to Monterey.

The tribesmen of the balmy Tamal land at the base of purple Mount Tamalpais were warriors: the Tamaleños, Lacatuits, and the Cainameros. They inhabited the oak-dotted valley and groves of redwood and *madroño*. Farther away were the Bolinas, Cotatis, Olompalis, Petalumas, and Sonomas. Some of these natives ventured across San Francisco Bay on *balsas* to Mission Dolores. On their return they told of the Spaniards, who came from the south, across the sea. Natives were disturbed; they thought they owned this northern land with its animals and the bay with its fish.

Spaniards also had fears; Russians had established a colony at a point three days' ride to the north. Three years after Rezánov came in 1806, Ivan Kuskov arrived on the *Kodiak*, bringing 150 Indians, including 20 women. He left the little colony on Bodega Bay and returned in 1811 as its governor.

In alarm Governor Arrillaga sent Lieutenant José Joaquin Moraga from San Francisco to inform Governor Kuskov that he was violating the treaty between Russia and Spain by occupying California.

Kuskov obtained land by bribing native chiefs, installed cannon, and built a fort. Americans called it Fort Ross, "Little Russia." Russians hunted, trapped, harvested grain, planted orchards and vines, even sent produce to exchange with Californians.

Moraga returned with letters from his superior warning the Russians. Fort Ross's cannon had increased to forty.

Again Moraga carried a protest to Governor Kuskov, who gave a contemptuous Cossack shrug. Governor Argüello commanded Kuskov to leave. Smilingly the Russian Governor remained.

When the Kotzebue expedition arrived at San Francisco on October 2, 1816, Governor Pablo Solá complained to the scientist that Kuskov had occupied Spanish territory five years. A conference was held on board the *Rurik* between *Comandante* Argüello, Don José Maria Estudillo, Kotzebue, the naturalist Chamisso, and Governor Kuskov, who came from Fort Ross. Kotzebue maintained that the decision lay with St. Petersburg. Arrogantly Kuskov erected a chapel at Fort Ross, fenced in 2,000 acres, and planted German prunes.

On his journeys of diplomacy to Fort Ross, Lieutenant Moraga traversed the pleasant country of Tamal. Owing to the alarming mortality among San Francisco neophytes, he suggested that a Mission be founded in this sunny region. Some invalid Indians, transferred to the balmy land across the bay, quickly improved in health.

At last it was determined to found an *asistencia*—San Rafael, Arcángel, so-called because the patron saint was said to heal body and soul. Nanaguanui, a delightful spot commanding a view of Mount Tamalpais and the sweep of hills southward, protected in the rear by a high eminence later called San Rafael Hill, was selected as the site.

Comisario-Prefecto Sarría came for foundation day. Accompanied by Father Ramón Abella of Mission San Francisco de Asis, Father Narciso Durán of Mission San José, Father Luis Gíl y Taboada, and some neophytes, he crossed the bay on December 14, 1817, erected the Cross, and said Mass. On foundation day Father Sarría baptized four small Indians, naming them in honor of Arcángels Rafael, Miguel, and Gabriel. The fourth received the missionary's name, Francisco. Twenty-two other children were baptized two hours later. On January 13, 1818, Juana, born near the Mission, was the first adult to receive baptism. The Mission register, in charge of the Archbishop of San Francisco, records the first marriage at San Rafael: José Maria, a widower from the Ranchito Liluangelia, and María Josefa of Ranchito Saconchini. In December, 1817, Father Sarría set down the first death—Indian Rafael, aged twenty-six. Soon 230 ailing neophytes were transferred to the *asistencia*, and 200 converts were under instruction.

Father Gíl not only spoke the Indian idiom, but he was skilled in surgery and medicine. During his two years at San Rafael he performed Caesarean operations. Immediately he erected an adobe structure 87 feet long, 42 wide, with a tile roof. It contained a justice's chamber, the Fathers' house, and a chapel with twin-starred windows, one above the other, unique in Mission buildings. San

Rafael had no tower, bell-cote, or gable. Bells were suspended from a heavy beam on a standard outside the church. As the Mission grew, the building took the shape of the letter L.

Kidnaping neophytes from Mission Dolores preyed upon the new *asistencia*. Father Esténaga of the older establishment permitted single men to cross the bay in a *lancha* seeking sweethearts. The kidnapers captured some San Rafael girls and started back for Mission Dolores. A San Rafael Indian, robbed of his beloved, followed in a swift canoe, overtook the San Francisco boat near Angel Island, rescued the girl, and gave the kidnapers fifty lashes each. This conflict caused hostility between the Mission and the *asistencia*.

"The Cainameros have come!" cried Corporal Rafael García, in 1824. San Rafael was being attacked. There were only three soldiers to meet the Indians. Quickly García placed wife and children on a frail *tule balsa* with Father Juan Amorós. Tearfully he sent the precious cargo out on the tide, trusting that the prayers of Father Juan would carry them to safety.

Back to battle went the corporal. His little band of soldiers and neophytes repulsed the foe. Father Juan, Señora García, and the children arrived safely on the beach before the San Francisco Presidio.

Father Amorós was a scholar and a skilled artisan as well. Forty years after his death there was at San Rafael a water clock he made, an excellent timekeeper. Personal comfort he scorned. Dried corn roasted over coals was his dinner. For Indian children, however, he carried grapes, raisins, and figs in his habit sleeve. He had a thriving garden and a ten-acre orchard that extended to the marsh land.

Father Amorós made conversions as far north as Petaluma. Rosa, an Indian maiden baptized by him on what later became Santa Rosa Creek, gave her name to Santa Rosa. Soon San Rafael had 520 neophytes. Many buildings were erected with living quarters and workshops for neophytes—all scattered over several blocks surrounding the Catholic rectory of today. The Indians raised horses and learned to make harness and saddles.

Father Amorós was deeply troubled when Governor Argüello and Father José Altimira decided to suppress San Rafael. Their plan was defeated by the Canon of the Durango Cathedral, Agustín Fernandez de San Vicente, who came with Father Payeras, rowing from San Francisco into the *Estero* of San Rafael. With them was Governor Argüello. Bells pealed long and loud. Emperor Augustin had sent the Canon to investigate California's loyalty. He went as far north as Fort Ross and reported that Father Amorós and all his neophytes had taken the oath of loyalty to the Mexican Republic in December, 1822. San Rafael, instead of being suppressed, became a Mission in 1823, independent of Mission San Francisco de Asis.

In the following year Otto von Kotzebue, the Russian traveler, returned to San Francisco with the naturalist, Albert von Chamisso, on their way to Fort Ross. In his *New Voyage* Kotzebue wrote that he was greatly pleased with the location of Mission San Rafael among ancient oaks. He regretted that the Russians had not extended their dominion to San Francisco long before San Rafael was founded.

Kotzebue saw the Mission at its best. Suddenly the Arcángel seemed to fail the establishment. There were 70 deaths in 1825. Neophytes were brought from San Francisco, and in 1828 the Mission had its largest population, 1,140. Livestock trebled—unfortunately at the time of the smallest grain crop: 333 bushels. Soon the earth renewed its fertility; 4,713 bushels were garnered. Between 1826 and 1830 the Mission contributed $1,311 to the Presidio.

Father Amorós built a house in the Petaluma district, then called the Plain of Livantonomé, where gentiles were given their first lessons in Christianity. Mission property extended north nine leagues and also covered the Corte de Madera and the Rinconada de Tiburon. Livestock fed northward to the *ranchería* of Olompali, and also in Cañadas Las Gallinas, Arroyo de San José, Novato, Colomache, Echatamal, and Olompali. The horses went as far as San Antonio. The *laguna* of Ocolom belonged to the Mission, but the natives were warlike.

Father Amorós needed a saintly spirit. There was outlaw Pomponio, native of the San Rafael region. He fled from San Francisco murdering and robbing. Not far from the Mission he hid in the Cañada de Novato. Soldiers took him to Monterey in irons. While his guards slept, Pomponio amputated his heel, slipped off his fetters, and fled. His bloody tracks in the forest brought about his capture and his execution at Monterey on September 6, 1823. Later Indians Marin and Quintin terrorized the Mission guard. Chief Marcelo of the Chologones and Bologones on Mount Diablo was their ally. Marin, chief of the Lacatuits, had been captured fighting, but was converted by the Father. Because of the Indian's prowess as a sailor, Spaniards named him Marin. His followers called him the bravest man in the world. When he became a renegade, Father Amorós appealed to the Presidio for protection.

Chief Marin fled to the little island at the entrance to the creek, El Estero de San Rafael de Aguanni. The Spaniards dared not land. They went to Punta de Quintin. Here they met strong resistance from Marin's ally, Quintin. They captured him and held him prisoner at the Presidio for two years. The Spanish-Indian battlefield, afterwards called Quintin's Point, was renamed by Americans San Quentin.

Quintin was almost as good a sailor as Marin. While a prisoner, he was skipper of a lighter on the bay belonging to the missionaries. Later he had charge of General Vallejo's swiftest lighter and made frequent trips between Yerba Buena and Sonoma.

Marin became a ferryman on San Francisco Bay when boats were made of oil barrels from whaling vessels, secured together by beams and planking. His island refuge, the mainland, and the county bear his name. He died at Mission San Rafael in 1834.

Notwithstanding conflicts with Indians, Mission San Rafael prospered. Boats of ancient design, but navigable, were constructed. Supplies were shipped to the Mission of Sonoma. Indian Monica captained the native crew. In 1832 the Mission had its largest number of livestock, 5,508. The wheat crop was 17,905 bushels. Beans returned 1,360 bushels. Barley yielded ninefold, and maize forty.

Impending secularization, however, caused anxiety to Father Amorós. He was spared seeing the Mission pass into the hands of the state, as it did in 1834. On June 14, 1832, the Father was buried in the church. Years later, when a modern building was erected, in moving the cemetery workmen came upon his body attired in full vestments.

At last in 1834 the government seized the Mission. One month later *Comisionado* Ignacio Martínez outlined the pueblo. San Rafael became a parish of the second class, the curate receiving $1,500 annually. In seventeen years there had been 1,873 baptisms at the establishment.

Unfortunately Father Amorós' successor was Father José Maria Vasquez de Mercado, a missionary charged with many offenses. He had so many troubles with the Indians that it is not surprising that he sought to forget them in debauchery and dancing. Chief Torbidio was his guest at the Mission, but the Indian repaid hospitality by robbing the weaving room. Major-domo José Molino fought Torbidio with his neophytes and captured twenty-one Indians, killing others. General Vallejo was summoned to pacify the Indians.

Father Mercado was called by his Superiors to be tried at Santa Clara for misconduct. He was banished to Soledad Mission for four years. Another Zacatecan black sheep, Father José Quíjas, his successor, had charge of both San Rafael and San Francisco Solano. He was an undisciplined Indian, and often under the influence of drink.

Ignacio Martínez continued as administrator. In 1834 the most valuable property of the Mission was the Nicasio Rancho, appraised at $7,256. Livestock was set down at $4,339; Mission buildings and church property were valued at $2,092; and the garden and orchard at $768. After debts were paid there was $15,025. Population soon dwindled to 300; crops fell off. But John Bidwell said that San Rafael produced the best grapes of any Mission in California.

New energy came to San Rafael with John Read, who succeeded Martínez—the first Irishman to settle on the Pacific Coast, a runaway sailor from an English vessel in 1826. Father Quíjas made him major-domo of San Rafael, a position he held nine years. His ferryboat, the first in California, sailed twice a week from Sausalito to San Francisco. Read, stricken with fever, died in 1843 and was buried in the Mission cemetery at San Rafael.

Another Irishman, Don Timotéo Murphy, succeeded him as majordomo. Even energetic Don Timotéo could not arrest the Mission's decay. The Indians demanded emancipation and distribution of property. Each of the 343 Indians received four sheep and twelve horses.

Nicasio Rancho was turned over to an ex-neophyte, Quilaguegui. José Talis, captain of the Tamales, was permitted to dwell at a distance from the establishment with some neophytes on condition that they occasionally attend Mass. Neophyte Camilo had occupied Olampali since 1834, and he asked title to his ranch. In 1840 there were 150 Indians in the vicinity of the Mission.

One year later de Mofras, the French traveler, found San Rafael a sad place. Only twenty Indians remained, all growing tobacco plants for their *cigarritos*. In the same year, however, G. Wilkes and the members of the United States exploring expedition on a tour of the world were highly entertained on October 24, the patron saint's day, by Major-domo Murphy's *fiesta*, which included a bull-fight in the afternoon and a dance in the evening at the Mission. In the 'thirties and 'forties Mission San Rafael was the scene of many *meriendas* for pleasure-seekers from Yerba Buena and Mission Dolores.

Before Governor Pio Pico ordered Mission San Rafael sold, General Vallejo took much of the stock to Sonoma and transplanted 2,000 of the vines to his Petaluma Rancho. In 1845 the Governor gave notice to the Indians to return to Mission San Rafael in a month, or the property would be sold. An inventory appraised buildings, land, and livestock at $17,000.

Antonio Suñol and Antonio Maria Pico bought the Mission in 1846 for $8,000, but did not obtain possession. Later the transaction was declared invalid by the United States Government, and in 1855 the property was returned with 6.48 acres of land to the Catholic Church.

During the Mexican War early in the summer of 1846, Colonel John C. Frémont and his soldiers came clanking into Marin County. They took possession of Mission San Rafael on June 26, 1846. Two days later Frémont, walking in the corridor, saw three men arrive at the mouth of the estuary. They left their saddles at the boat side and approached the Mission.

Frémont sent Kit Carson, J. B. Swift, and a French-Canadian trapper to meet them. On his return Carson reported that the strangers were Spanish-Californians on their way to Sonoma, and they wished to obtain horses. Carson asked Frémont, "Shall I take them prisoners?"

"I have no room for prisoners," replied Frémont.

Carson and his companions probably misunderstood, and shot down the travelers.

Great was the consternation when it was discovered that the dead men were Don José de los Reyes Berreyesa, an important *ranchero*, and his twenty-year-old nephews, Francisco and Ramón de Haro, twin sons of an *Alcalde* at San Francisco. These war-wounds were long in healing.

In the 'fifties services were no longer held at the Mission. Don Timotéo Murphy took the last of the Indians to live at his ranch near Nicasio. In 1855 he established an orphan asylum, St. Vincent's School, four miles north of San Rafael. After the Mission was closed, San Rafael people rode to the orphanage chapel for Mass.

Franciscan records were kept at St. Vincent's until the 'eighties, when they were given to the Archbishop of San Francisco. The second book of baptisms and the second book of burials, both begun in 1840, are at the San Rafael Parish Church. Father Quíjas made the first records in the volumes.

Even in the 'sixties Mission San Rafael, Arcángel, was in ruins; orchard and vineyard were used as a gypsy camping ground. Mission bells disappeared. In recent years they have been traced by Miss Marie T. Walsh, the historical writer. One serves Mrs. James Burdell at the Olompali Ranch as dinner bell. A second is in a school building at Fallon. The third is in the Catholic Church at El Cajón, San Diego County.

The Marin Historical Society plans to assemble the bells and suspend them from a standard near the location of the original altar of the church. The best information is that it is under the pavement in front of the San Rafael Parish Church. Of all California Missions, San Rafael, Arcángel, has been most completely obliterated. Only a fragment of its tile exists, and that belongs to Mrs. Fred Sawyer.

Buildings and orchards have long since been removed to make

room for the modern city of San Rafael. In 1870 a new church was built near the old chapel.

Two blocks from the Mission in the rear of El Rey apartment house is a gallant survivor of the Mission pear orchard, more than a century old. In 1929 two trees remained. Their large trunks had been battered by storms, but an effort was made to save them. Several men transplanted them to the rear of the courtyard. One tree succumbed to the shock; vines half conceal its dead trunk. Intrepidly the other struggled until two or three branches shot forth and produced a crop in 1934 of four pears, six in 1936, and two in 1937. The hurricane of February, 1938, split the aged tree in half. Mrs. Hart, owner of El Rey, summoned a tree surgeon. One brave young branch blossomed, but 1938 will decide whether it is the end of the Mission pear orchard.

Once San Rafael Indians made excellent baskets, but none of their handicraft remains. They planted vines and orchards, raised horses, cattle, and grain. About 1870 their last chieftain, José Calistro, purchased a thirty-acre tract as a home for the remnant of his people. The others had long since gone to the Happy Hunting Ground of their mighty Gitchie Manito. In 1880 only eighty wigwams existed of the once powerful tribe. A few descendants of Mission Indians live near Bolinas.

Legend recalls Chief Cachow, a San Rafael neophyte, rich in trophies of the chase and in loot of battle. To enhance his distinction in the tribe, he brought to his people Mission beads and trinkets, gifts of the *padres*.

Above all, Cachow wished to please Satuka, of the smoldering eyes, of the Sanelaños on the Russian River banks. No one cooked buckeye meal, venison, and grasshoppers like Satuka. One autumn, when garnered wild grain was overflowing the willow baskets and deer and rabbits were fat and fish were plentiful, her father bade their friends to a feast. Gorgeous in Mission trappings, Cachow arrived.

Satuka crushed the fattest acorns for the San Rafael neophyte, who gave her even the beads from his ears. Within two months, so he vowed, he would return with a deerskin for Satuka's father and make the girl his bride.

Cachow came, but at his side was a fairer girl, clothed like a *señorita*. At the base of a great rock he built a campfire and slept near by with his bride.

Dark as the night was Satuka's heart when she peered over the precipice, beholding the faithless one and his bride. Desperately she clasped the largest rock she could move and crashed down upon the sleeping lovers.

The tribes held a long inquiry over the dead. They heaped up great rocks, placed thereon the three mangled bodies, and lighted the funeral pyre. While the flames rose and mourners wailed, the spirits of the departed soared upward in smoke. And this is how the great rock not far from Cloverdale became known as Lover's Leap.

Purple-vested Mount Tamalpais presides over sun-drenched Marin, county of Mission San Rafael. It was flung up in the titanic battle of fire, flood, and ice which created the Golden Gate. It beheld the coming of Drake, the passing of Cabrillo's galleon, the arrival of the red men from the north. *Tule balsas* sped over the bay at its feet. Ayala's little redwood *cayuco* tossed its way through the Golden Gate. Gray-habited men of the Cross came. Loftily Tamalpais watched winged men roar across wide seas around the world. With awe it beheld workers with threads of steel spin a broad span from shore to shore of the Gate of the West.

XXI

San Francisco Solano (Mission Sonoma)

CALIFORNIA's chain of twenty-one Missions begins with San Diego de Alcalá in the south and ends at San Francisco Solano in the north. The patron of Sonoma is Saint Francis, apostle of Peru and the Indies, who died in 1610 in South America.

Father José Altimira, founder of San Francisco Solano, was a native of Barcelona, not long in these Californias. Young and enthusiastic, he was stirred by a vision, a Mission in the Indian fastness on the northern frontier. The newest establishment transported him with its romance and promise.

When Father Altimira arrived in 1820 at Dolores, the Mission was not thriving. *Ranchos* to the south, once the support of the establishment, had been granted private owners. San Francisco soil was sterile and the climate severe. There were only fifty able-bodied laborers. Women did men's work. Measles and communicable diseases brought by Spanish soldiers had caused many deaths among the neophytes. Tuberculosis also was decimating them. Instead of living at San Francisco, they crossed the bay to balmy San Rafael or went to Father Narciso Durán's thriving Mission San José.

Father Altimira reported to Governor Luis Argüello that Dolores could not continue; suppress San Francisco de Asis and abolish the *asistencia* of San Rafael, he suggested. Those establishments should be succeeded by another Mission, New San Francisco, on the far northern frontier where there were thousands of pagans.

Governor Argüello was little concerned with the souls of natives beyond the Strait of Yulupa, but he feared Little Russia in the north. For three blankets, three pairs of breeches, three hoes, two axes, and some beads, the Russians had acquired a large tract of land from the

Indians, on which they had erected Fort Ross. They even boldly laid claim to the entire northern coast of California. These industrious intruders were tilling soil, capturing sea lions, tanning skins, drying beef, making tile, building ships—protected by forty cannon. The Mission in the north could not be built too soon. The Governor urged Father Altimira to petition the Assembly of California to suppress San Francisco de Asis and San Rafael, and to suggest reestablishing San Francisco de Asis in the north. The Assembly—six men—voted the change.

And so it happened that at dawn on June 25, 1823, an Indian helmsman turned the prow of a boat northward from the sandy peninsula on the western shore of San Francisco Bay. Its passengers were Father José Altimira, *Diputado* Francisco Castro, José Sanchez, the Indian fighter, nineteen men, and some neophytes. They were setting out for the country of the Petalumas and the Sotoyomes.

After the company disembarked near Mission San Rafael, they traveled ten days over tawny hills splattered with belated blue and gold spring blossoms and early magenta summer flowers. They made notes of climate, soil, forests, water. They enjoyed feasting on bear meat and catching fish in the creeks.

In his diary Father Altimira described the journey to Chocuay, where Petaluma now stands, and northeast to Lake Tolay. On the creek later named Sonoma they saw a boat from San Francisco. They camped on San Pedro Creek, now named Napa. Here was admirable pasture land, and the hills would probably grow excellent grapes. They discovered 600 springs.

July 3rd saw them on the site of the present Mission of Sonoma. Without awaiting permission from his Superior, Father Altimira selected a site near a spring tumbling from a mountainside. Near by were abundant timber and stone. On Friday, July 4, 1823, he rose at dawn, assembled some slender straight trees and long willow boughs. One limb was trimmed of twigs to form the upright of the Cross. A shorter piece was for the arms. The ground was blessed, the Cross planted. Stakes of tree limbs were driven into the earth to make an oblong frame in front of the Cross. When the altar was completed, the Bible, the crucifix, and sacred vessels were put *in* place. Joyful hymns, fervent prayers, eloquent discourse, booming muskets announced that Mission San Francisco Solano had come into existence; Sonoma, the city-to-be, was founded.

Next day Father Altimira led the company back to Old San Francisco, as the Mission on Dolores Creek was now called. In Sonoma Valley the tall Cross kept vigil.

President Señan was on his deathbed when he received the report from proud Father Altimira that he had founded New San Francisco; Old San Francisco and San Rafael would soon cease to exist. Although dying, Father Señan straightway informed Governor Argüello that neither His Excellency nor Father Altimira had authority to found or suppress Missions. He mollified the Father, however, by appointing him to minister at the new Mission, pending the decision of the College of San Fernando.

Escorted by twelve men, including an artilleryman to manage a two-pound cannon, and a force of neophyte laborers, Father Altimira arrived at New San Francisco on August 25, 1823—usually given as foundation day. But there is no record of any formal ceremony other than that of the Fourth of July.

In the Sonoma Mission register at Bancroft Library at the University of California, is recorded the first death at the Mission—Quitevia, an adult Indian, on December 26, 1823.

In spite of the opposition of President Sarría, Father Altimira carried on the work. Passion Sunday, April 4, 1824, the church had been completed and whitewashed. President Sarría donated a painting of San Francisco Solano over the altar. The new Mission was a rude structure 105 feet long by 24. Russians sent from Fort Ross vases, hammered brass basins, hand-carved missal stands, picture frames, candles, handwoven linens, embroidered silk veils for the tabernacle, and Mass bells.

Missions sent little aid. Only San Francisco gave: 3,000 sheep, 60 horses, 50 cows, 20 yoke of oxen, farm implements.

On dedication day, April 4, 1824, Father Altimira was happy; twenty-six children of neophyte and gentile parents were baptized. María Esperanza was first; twelve days later came thirteen adult Petalumas, and soon twenty-three Ululatos. Thirty-eight tribes supplied neophytes. Gabriel Puttoy, bachelor, wedded Olegaria Zalatanpi, widow, March 2, 1824—the first recorded marriage.

Soon Father Altimira built not only the chapel but the missionaries' house, the granary, and seven dwellings for soldiers and their families—all of wood. He also erected an adobe structure 120 feet long and 30 wide, with a corridor and tiled roof. Two adobe dwellings were ruined by the rain before they could be roofed, but they were rebuilt and whitewashed.

Father Altimira set up a loom and taught natives to weave woolen cloth. A garden fenced with willows had nearly 300 fruit trees, and 3,000 luscious vines purpled in the vineyard. Large wheat and barley crops were gathered. Horses, cattle, sheep, and hogs fattened in the pasture.

At the end of 1824 Father Altimira had 693 neophytes, more than he expected. Three hundred and thirty-two had been transferred from San Francisco, 153 from San José, 92 from San Rafael. Ninety-six had been baptized at Solano. The thirty-eight neighboring tribes worked harmoniously, although they could not understand San Francisco Indians any better than San Gabriel natives understood those at San Juan Capistrano. At this time already the Mission had established Rancho Santa Eulalia at Suisun.

Soon after coming to Sonoma, Father Altimira named the region the Valley of the Moon, a phrase later used by Jack London as a title of a book when he took up his residence a few miles away near Glen Ellen. The natives had long observed that in winter, when the moon rose farthest north, it appeared seven times in succession, as it swung behind seven distinct peaks before floating clear.

The Valley of the Moon was not long for Father Altimira. Soon after the harvest in 1826 Indians fell upon the Mission, sacked and burned it. The Father and some neophytes barely escaped alive from the ruins. Retreating to San Rafael, they rowed to San Francisco. The Father asked to be transferred to San Buenaventura.

San Francisco Solano was later ministered by Father Buenaventura Fortuni, who tried to rebuild the Mission. In 1829 harvests failed. During Father Fortuni's seven years at Sonoma, however, cattle increased to 2,000, horses to 725, and there was a crop yield of 4,000 bushels.

Secularization was imminent, but Father Fortuni refused to take the oath of allegiance. He was glad when the new military commander of the north, General Mariano Guadalupe Vallejo, twenty-five, arrived in 1833 with his eighteen-year-old bride, Francisca Carrillo of San Diego. The General looked, acted, and spoke like "I, the King." He had the anxieties of a king. From his tower with a field glass he scanned the country from the salt marshes of San Pablo Bay northward to the wooded regions where hostile Indians skulked. Vallejo understood how to meet natives. One day a friendly chieftain entirely naked called upon him. "Are you not cold?" reproved the *Comandante*.

"Is your face cold?" replied the Indian.

"Not at all."

The native pointed to his own body. "I am all face."

Vallejo, assisted by William A. Richardson, in 1835 laid out Sonoma, California's largest Plaza, eight acres with a barracks on the north side. It was protected by mounted cannon, and from the flagpole floated the green, red, yellow, and white of Mexico.

Directly opposite was Vallejo's four-acre garden with the most luxurious adobe north of San Francisco Bay. Each member of the family had several Indian servants. Grinding corn for *tortillas* occupied six Indians. Seven or eight cooked, several did laundry, a dozen sewed and spun. Natives were given no wages, but they and their children were cared for in the *rancheria* in the rear of the adobe *palacio*. Friends and relations of the Vallejos dwelt in lesser houses near by, subsisting on the orchards, herds, vegetable garden, and a hedge of edible cacti. The Vallejos had one of the first pianos in California, and the General gave his children's music teacher several thousand acres of land for instructing them five years.

Vallejo made settlements at Petaluma and Santa Rosa. In 1834 Governor Figueroa gave him the title to the Petaluma Rancho. Later he received grants from Alvarado and Micheltorena, making him one of the greatest landowners in California.

Although Sonoma was the last Mission established, from 1823 to

1834 there were 1,315 baptisms and 278 marriages. Population in 1832 was highest: 996. Cattle in 1833 numbered 4,849, horses 1,148, and sheep 7,114. When secularization came in 1834, Father José Jesus Gutiérrez retired, but Father José Lorenzo Quíjas of San Rafael took his place. Under instructions from Governor Figueroa, Vallejo placed Antonio Ortega in charge of the Mission. The major-domo scandalized the community; no woman was spared. To make matters worse, he ordered Indians to disobey Father Quíjas; the missionary remained at San Rafael.

After secularization, Indians demanded land. They were given movable property and told to live where they pleased. Sonoma remained their head town, but they returned to their *rancherías*. Vallejo had charge of their stock. At his own expense he supported the Presidio company to overawe the Russians and discourage foreign colonization.

Governor Echeandia also felt that Russian encroachment must be thwarted. With the co-operation of General Vallejo, in 1834 the Padrés-Bandini-Híjar expedition of 250 Mexican colonists en route from Monterey appeared in ox carts and on horseback at the Strait of Carquinez. Mission San José neophytes piloted them on rafts across the water. At Sonoma they were housed in Mission buildings.

These intelligent teachers, farmers, builders, carpenters, shoemakers, blacksmiths, and saddlers planned to make a settlement on what was later called Mark West Creek. Soon Padrés and Híjar were revealed as planning to seize the Mission property for themselves. They were arrested and exiled. Many of the colonists remained and became influential in California.

Vallejo brought other important families to Sonoma; one was that of his sister-in-law, Doña Josefa Carrillo, who in the 'twenties had eloped from San Diego with Captain Henry Delano Fitch. In 1841 Governor Micheltorena granted Fitch and his wife their eleven-league Sotoyome Ranch. Captain Fitch died in 1849 and was carried back to San Diego to be buried on Presidio Hill. Regal Doña Josefa finished her days at the ranch. The family name is borne by Fitch Mountain, which was on her property. The two-story Fitch adobe still stands facing the Plaza.

Although Vallejo was an intellectual rebel and read books banned by the Church, he added a bell tower to Sonoma Mission in which services were seldom held. He placed the bells therein, taking them from the beam outside the church. He also arched the windows and made them larger.

General Vallejo possessed too much power in the north to live tranquilly. South from Sonoma was another ruler, Sum-yet-ho, or Mighty Arm, an Indian chieftain six feet seven. This chief of the Suisunes had been baptized Francisco Solano, but, a ruler of 40,000 tribesmen, he lacked that saint's humility.

General Vallejo with an army met the chieftain in Suscol Valley to obliterate the Solano menace. Bows and arrows and spears were no match for guns and swords. Defeated, Solano formed an alliance with Vallejo. Frequently he visited the *Comandante's* hacienda, and even learned to speak Spanish. When the General wished to control the government at Monterey, he let it be known that he would appear with Solano and a thousand Indians. This threat brought goose-flesh to the politicians, and Vallejo usually compromised by an escort of thirty or forty Indians.

The General showered Solano with honors, gave him a horse with fancy trappings, a silver watch, and riding boots. The presentation was made at a full dress parade. The Indian chief had a guard of forty-four Suisunes and Napajos under Sergeant Fernandez, all in uniform: short jacket, linen cloak, cap, trousers, blanket, and saddlebag. Solano made a speech asking his followers to obey Vallejo.

The General campaigned with Solano against the Guapos and other hostile tribes in 1836. The next year Solano allied with Captain Salvador Vallejo, brother of the *Comandante*, warred with him against the Yolos. They captured Zampay, but at Solano's request the chief's life was spared.

Solano protected his Sonoma ally from common foes, but he himself fell captive to romance when he saw Princess Helena de Gagarin first European princess to inhabit California. She was the wife of Alexander Rotcheff, Governor of the Russian colony at Fort Ross. Although dwelling among seal hunters, Indians, and Siberians, the Rotcheffs lived a civilized European life at this remote fortress. Like that other Helen for whom a thousand ships were launched, the princess was a disturber of men's hearts. When Solano accompanied General Vallejo as a bodyguard to call upon her, his life was transformed. Many red-bearded Russians at Fort Ross had married Indian women who worked for their husbands in the fields. Why should not he, Chief Mighty Arm, have the princess? Solano lay in wait in a thicket to carry off the devastating Helena.

Comandante Vallejo discovered Solano's intention and saved the princess. The Vallejo family have a chest of silver bestowed upon them in gratitude by Helena Gagarin Rotcheff.

Princess Helena's name lingers in the land. With her husband and a party of friends she climbed Mount St. Helena in June, 1841, and there placed a plaque recording the visit.

Solano's name is also recalled by Solano County. General Vallejo obtained for him a four-league grant of land, Suisun. On June 3, 1934, a bronze statue of Solano twelve feet high was unveiled near Fairfield, California.

In their short, busy eleven years at Sonoma the missionaries cleared a large acreage and harvested 25,000 bushels of grain. But when Governor Pico planned in 1845 to sell the Mission, it was declared without value. Neighboring Moquelumne Indians were given to burning grain fields and killing horses for food.

Occasionally in these days services were held at the Mission by Father Antonio Real, who came from Santa Clara to Sonoma; but he ministered also Mission Santa Clara, St. Joseph's Church of the Pueblo San José, and the Missions San José and Dolores.

On June 14, 1846, a few weeks before American occupation, the colors of Mexico were lowered at Sonoma, and the new Bear flag was run up. Ezekiel Merritt led the Bear party. With him were thirty-two other Americans. Mrs. Abraham Lincoln's nephew, William L. Todd, designed the Bear flag. It was made from a woman's skirt of unbleached Mexican *manta*, five feet long and three wide. At the base was a stripe of red flannel from a man's shirt. A star outlined in ink and filled in with red paint was in the upper left-hand corner. Facing it was a bear. Underneath these emblems were painted with black ink the large roman letters: CALIFORNIA REPUBLIC.

On July 9, 1846, the Bear flag yielded to the red, white and blue of the United States. Lieutenant James Warren Revere of the *Portsmouth*, grandson of Paul Revere, raised the Stars and Stripes. The original Bear flag was burned in the San Francisco fire of 1906. A monument commemorating the Bear Flag Revolution was unveiled on June 14, 1914, in the public square of Sonoma.

When Bishop Alemany came to Monterey in 1850, he asked Father Stanislaus Lebret to preside at Sonoma, but the Mission was almost deserted till the 'sixties, when there came a brief revival. The church was supplied with seats, cushions, carpets, gas lighting, and an orchestra. The end of the Mission as a house of worship came in 1881, when the Bishop sold the buildings and grounds of San Francisco Solano to Solomon Schocken for $3,000.

A modern parish church was erected in which vestments and sacred vessels of the Mission were housed. Fire destroyed the church, but another was built. Of the furnishings of the Mission, only a tabernacle screen remains, loaned by its owner, Mr. A. W. Adler, to the Sonoma Mission Museum. The Bancroft Library at the University of California has the registers.

For thirty years hay was stored in the church, and wine in the cloisters. A picket fence separated the building from the street. Storms weakened a corner of the Mission. The walls were disintegrating when the California Landmarks League, with Congressman Joseph R. Knowland as president, collected through the *San Francisco Examiner*, owned by William Randolph Hearst, who headed the subscription list, the sum of $13,000. With this money the Mission was bought and given to the state, which added $2,000 more for restoration.

The belfry and arched window frames installed by General Vallejo were removed. A tile roof replaced shingles. Restoration was made on the lines of the original structure, after a sketch of the building drawn by Lieutenant Colonel Victor Prudon previous to the Vallejo alterations. The building was opened to the public as a museum in October, 1922. Later the chapel and Fathers' living quarters were restored.

San Francisco Solano is a long, low adobe structure 150 feet wide.

The chapel is 110 feet deep. The church has a vestibule 15 feet square with stairs leading to the choir loft. The side walls join the building in a curve instead of square. Of all Franciscan planting at Sonoma, only a tall cactus remains, twenty feet high, the largest at the California Missions.

The lower floor of the Sonoma barracks is a private musuem of Mr. and Mrs. Walter Murphy, who live on the upper floor. At Lachryma Montis, the house where General Vallejo passed his last years, is another museum, of which Mrs. L. V. Emparan, daughter of the General, is curator for the state of California. Miss Zolita Bates has restored the adobe of *Alcalde* Nash for her residence. Another interesting adobe is the Blue Wing building, the first hotel and tavern north of San Francisco in operation as early as 1844.

General Vallejo bought several bells for Mission Sonoma, one an English *campana* made at Sheffield in 1855. Dr. Platon Vallejo, son of the General, gave it to St. Vincent's School, Vallejo, California. It hangs on a high standard in the school yard of the Dominican Brothers and Sisters. The El Dorado Chapter of the Native Sons of San Francisco owns the small Sheffield bell once belonging to the Mission. A third Sheffield bell, made in 1858, and also presented by Vallejo to the Mission, is now in the little whitewashed church at Nicasio, Marin County.

The large crowned bell of 1829 disappeared in 1881; sold for junk, was the accepted belief. Twenty-five years later members of the Woman's Club at Sonoma found the missing bell at the Sutro Museum in San Francisco. There was no mistaking its crude lettering with unskilled workmanship nor its crown. Triumphantly the women brought the lost *campana* back and hung it before the Mission. There the broken bell seems to proclaim:

> I am one of California's Mission bells—
> Iron, bronze, copper, silver bells
> That have sounded sanctifying words
> Since Christ's centuries began.
> From Spain and Mexico we came
> With the sons of Saint Francis,
> With palms, pomegranates, and the Cross—

California pioneers
Bearing a message for pagan ears.

Mornings we rang the Angelus
To commemorate the Resurrection.
At midday, the Passion.
Evenings the Incarnation.
At San Diego our muffled tone
Tolled for the martyred Jayme.
At Carmelo with a thousand triumphant tongues
We pealed out for Serra and Lasuén.
At San Gabriel all the air was alive
With our swell of glory for the Arcángel.
At San Luis Obispo we rolled out renunciation of a kingdom.

Compassion was in our healing melody
At San Rafael enshadowed by the purple mountain.
Majestic was our *Laudate* for Peyri
At San Luis Rey and Pala.
The plaintive white love of Amatil
We hailed at San Buenaventura.
At joyous Santa Barbara, Queen of Missions,
We caroled our salutation.
Bleak was our reverberation at Soledad
For starving Sarría.
At the blue-lilied *laguna* of Dolores
In thanksgiving we throbbed for Saint Francis
    and Lady Poverty.
At Sonoma in the Valley of the Moon
Our knell was desolate *adiós!*

We are undefeated.
We are immortal
In cadenced names,
In mellow colonnades,
In exalted towers,
In the beauty and daring of the race
That embravens and enriches California.

Appendix

MISSIONS IN THE ORDER OF THEIR FOUNDATION

With Founders and Dates

San Diego de Alcalá, Frs. Serra, Vizcaíno, and Parrón; July 16, 1769.

San Carlos Borromeo (Carmelo), Frs. Serra and Crespi; June 3, 1770.

San Antonio de Padua, Frs. Serra, Piéras, and Sitjar; July 14, 1771.

San Gabriel, Arcángel, Frs. Somera and Cambón; Sept. 8, 1771.

San Luis Obispo de Tolosa, Frs. Serra and Cavaller; Sept. 1, 1772.

San Francisco de Asis (Dolores), Frs. Palóu and Cambón; June 29, 1776.

San Juan Capistrano, Frs. Serra, Mugártegui, and Amúrrio; Nov. 1, 1776.

Santa Clara de Asis, Fr. Tomás de la Peña; Jan. 12, 1777.

San Buenaventura, Frs. Serra and Cambón; March 31, 1782.

Santa Barbara, Frs. Lasuén and Paterna; Dec. 4, 1786.

La Purísima Concepción, Fr. Fermin Francisco Lasuén; Dec. 8, 1787.

Santa Cruz, Fr. Fermin Francisco Lasuén; Aug. 28, 1791.

Soledad, Frs. Lasuén, Diego, and Sitjar; Oct. 9, 1791.

San José, Fr. Fermin Francisco Lasuén; June 11, 1797.

San Juan Bautista, Frs. Lasuén, Catalá, and Martiarena; June 24, 1797.

San Miguel, Arcángel, Frs. Lasuén and Sitjar; July 25, 1797.

San Fernando Rey, Frs. Lasuén and Dumétz; Sept. 8, 1797.

San Luis Rey, Frs. Lasuén, Peyri, and Santiago; June 13, 1798.

Santa Inés, Frs. Tápis, Ciprés, Calzada, and Gutiérrez; Sept. 17, 1804.

San Rafael, Arcángel, Frs. Sarría, Abella, Durán, and Gíl; Dec. 14, 1817.

San Francisco Solano (Sonoma), Fr. José Altimira; July 4, 1823.

LOCATION OF CALIFORNIA MISSIONS

Mission San Diego de Alcalá is seven miles from Fifth and D Streets, San Diego, or six miles from Old Town. It can be reached by automobile.

Mission San Carlos Borromeo, or Carmel, is five miles from Monterey on the Big Sur Road.

Mission San Antonio de Padua is in the southern part of Monterey County, six miles from Jolon or twenty miles from King City. It can be reached by train.

Mission San Gabriel, Arcángel, is located nine miles from the center of Los Angeles.

Mission San Luis Obispo is in the heart of the city of San Luis Obispo.

Mission San Francisco de Asis, or Dolores, is located on Dolores Street at Sixteenth Street, San Francisco. Take Valencia and Howard streetcars; distance, three miles from Third and Market.

Mission San Juan Capistrano is in Orange County, about sixteen miles south of Santa Ana. It is about sixty-three miles from Los Angeles and seventy miles from San Diego via El Camino Real, the state highway.

Mission Santa Clara de Asis is in the city of Santa Clara, forty-two miles south of San Francisco, and four miles from San José.

Mission San Buenaventura is located in the town of Ventura and is sixty-one miles from Los Angeles via El Camino Real.

Mission Santa Barbara is located in the city of Santa Barbara.

Mission La Purísima Concepción is in the Lompoc Valley, four miles north of the city of Lompoc.

Mission Santa Cruz is on Mission Hill in the city of Santa Cruz.

Mission Soledad, the ruins of which alone remain, are to be found in Monterey County about one and a half miles from the town of Soledad.

Mission San José is fifteen miles north of the city of San José and twenty-seven miles south of Oakland on the Oakland Highway.

Mission San Juan Bautista is at San Juan Bautista about forty-two miles south of San José.

Mission San Miguel, Arcángel is located in the extreme northern part of the county of San Luis Obispo. It is nine miles north of Paso Robles and is directly on the state highway, El Camino Real.

San Fernando Rey is twenty-three miles from the Plaza of Los Angeles. The route via El Camino Real is along Sunset Boulevard to Hollywood, thence through Cahuenga Pass to Sherman Way, and then along Camino Real de San Fernando. There are also Pacific Electric cars which stop at the door of the Mission.

Mission San Luis Rey is forty-five miles north of San Diego and four miles inland from Oceanside. It is eighty-five miles from Los Angeles via El Camino Real.

The *Asistencia* of Pala is located at the foot of Palomar Mountain. It is twenty miles inland from Mission San Luis Rey, with which it is connected by Camino Real de Pala. From San Diego it is sixty-five miles.

Mission Santa Inés is thirty-three miles northwest of Santa Barbara and three miles east of Buellton, a station on the main highway, El Camino Real.

Mission San Rafael, Arcángel, is now marked by a Mission bell guidepost in the city of San Rafael. The tablet bears the following inscription: *Erected 1909 by Mount Tamalpais Parlor, N. S. G. W., San Rafael.*

San Francisco Solano, or Sonoma, is in the city of Sonoma thirty miles north from San Francisco.

Index

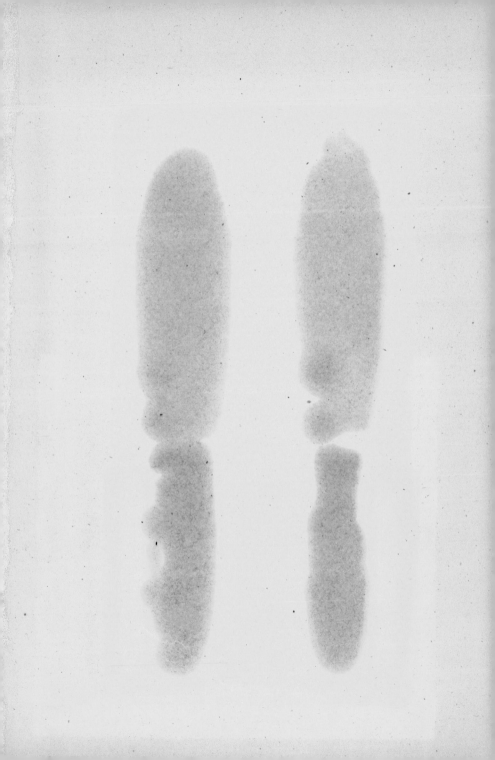